Societal Constructions of Masculinity in Chicanx and Mexican Literature

From Machismo to Feminist Masculinity

Edited by

Bryan Pearce-Gonzales
Shenandoah University
Kathryn Quinn-Sánchez
Georgian Court University

Series in Literary Studies

VERNON PRESS

www.vernonpress.com

In the Americas:
Vernon Press
1000 N West Street, Suite 1200
Wilmington, Delaware, 19801
United States

In the rest of the world:
Vernon Press
C/Sancti Espiritu 17,
Malaga, 29006
Spain

Series in Literary Studies

Library of Congress Control Number: 2020950207

ISBN: 978-1-64889-368-1

Also available: 978-1-64889-046-8 [Hardback]; 978-1-64889-308-7 [PDF, E-Book]

Cover design by Vernon press using elements designed by macrovector / Freepik.

Table of contents

Preface

Vinodh Venkatesh

Virginia Tech

Societal Constructions of Masculinity in Chicanx and Mexican Literature: From Machismo to Feminist Masculinity collects a set of essays that address the production, representation, and mobilization of masculinities amongst Chicanx and Mexican bodies. Parting from the notion that masculinity is socio-culturally dependent and constructed, Kathryn Quinn-Sánchez and Bryan Pearce-Gonzales posit that there is a genetic link between Chicanx and Mexican masculinities. They argue that both bear vestiges from the colonial history of the region and that, even with the establishment of the United States centuries later, the migrations and diasporas of latinidad have ensured that these gender systems and tropes have endured.

This underlying analytic lens is important and central to *Societal Constructions*, thus separating it from previous monographs and anthologies that have tended to sit on only one side of the Southern Border; that is, the book you have in your hands undertakes the original approach of placing Chicanx and Mexican literature in conversation, probing and teasing out their approaches to the representation of masculinities instead of separating both bodies of literature into neat, yet artificial siloes. Across seven content chapters and expertly melding together critical theory, literary analysis, and sociological critique, *Societal Constructions* offers incisive and suggestive analyses of some of the most important literary voices in Mexico and the United States.

In the first chapter, Leigh Johnson examines the representation of domestic violence and how it crafts and perpetuates a specific dynamic of gendered power in works by Américo Paredes, José Antonio Villareal, and Mario Suárez. Johnson skillfully reads these works against the backdrop of the second half of the twentieth century, honing in on the impact of war on the practice of masculinity in public and private spheres. Next, Fernando Hernández Jáuregui studies the poetry of Ricardo Castillo, paying particular attention to voice, style, and aesthetics to highlight how the poet may present a "poetic masculinity" that runs counter to hegemonic and complicit variants. In the subsequent chapter, Alejandro Puga and Patricia Tovar parse through the novels of Juan Villoro, paying particular attention to how Mexican masculinity was reified and deployed from the nation-building efforts of the post-Revolution period to the contemporary neoliberal state. In the fourth chapter, Quinn-Sánchez traces the intergenerational practices of masculinity and gender systems in the works of Cherríe Moraga, Sandra Cisneros and Margarita Tavera Rivera. The author analyzes performances of masculinity and femininity in children and parents, highlighting how the hegemonic variant of the former is often transmitted through male and female bodies in the nuclear family. In the next essay, Pearce-Gonzales follows his co-editor's lead by reading the transmission of masculine hegemony in the works of Dagoberto Gilb and Domingo Martinez. Pearce-Gonzales focuses specifically on the power of patriarchs within the family unit to set the tone of gender expectations and permissibility. Next, Jess Brocklesby tackles the representation of masculinity in the most consumer-friendly medium analyzed in the anthology—the telenovela. Brocklesby specifically addresses gay bodies in these narrative worlds as a point of inflection in decentering the previously unquestioned role of the macho. In the final content chapter, Joshua D. Martin studies borderland masculinities in the work of Benjamín Alire Sáenz. Looking at how masculine bodies negotiate themselves, their homoaffective and sexual relationship, and their spaces in the interstitial terrain of the border.

In sum, *Societal Constructions of Masculinity in Chicanx and Mexican Literature: From Machismo to Feminist Masculinity* is a timely, rigorous, and original piece of scholarship that is of interest to both scholars of Chicanx and Mexican literary and cultural studies. Importantly, the essays that follow enrich the broader field of gender studies by addressing masculinity through multiple national, racial and sexual matrices, thus providing the reader with a more complete understanding of the stakes of gender today.

Introduction

Kathryn Quinn-Sánchez, Ph.D.

Georgian Court University

Bryan Pearce-Gonzales, Ph.D.

Shenandoah University

Our journey begins in Mexico, keeping in mind the historical implications of a society that has assimilated the cultural tenets that the Spaniards imposed upon most of Latin America for three hundred years of colonialism. One aspect of this cultural imposition specifically underscores the role of masculinity within society and how each institution—the Roman Catholic Church and the State—have reinforced the dominance of what present-day society has deemed appropriate masculine behavior. Indeed, the twentieth-century Mexican poet Octavio Paz deemed Mexico a nation that struggles constantly to grapple with what he determined to be their bastard heritage, due to their indigenous mother being raped by a Spaniard. Culturally, economically, and psychologically, Mexican literature has spoken at times in agreement with Paz and other times against his conclusions for almost a century. This volume studies a continuum of texts to analyze how twentieth and twenty-first-century authors have represented the role of masculinity from the post-revolutionary era of Mexico 1959 to 2020 Chicanx authors living and writing in the United States.

The diaspora of a long-lived patriarchy followed the Spaniards to New Spain and what was to become the Americas. With the onslaught of violence during the ten-year revolution that began in 1910, the Mexican diaspora to the United States furthered the reach of masculine hegemony that arrived with Spain and traveled north with Mexicans who live in the USA and self-define as Hispanic, Chicano, Chicanx and/or Mexican-American. Of course, the national relationship deepened due to the economic opportunities that arose during World War II, as the governments of both nations officially allowed each other's citizens to cross the border in order to work. Such a development occurred during World War II; the bracero program allowed Mexican workers to fill the US' needs while the male citizens of the US were fighting the Nazis in Europe in the 1940s. Officially as well as unofficially, this welcoming of Mexican workers into the US aided individuals, those who could earn money in the US and take it back to their families in Mexico, as well as the US companies who could find workers when they desperately needed them. However, the power dynamic was unbalanced as the US found ways to deport the Mexican workers when it no longer deemed their contribution necessary. Yet, it is clear that the US economy still relies on the undocumented workers, as capitalism privileges profits over people. That is to say, pay as little as possible to the workers to allow the company to earn the largest capital gains.

Capitalism and gender in the US have always been intertwined. James W. Messerschmidt grounds the term dominant masculinity or hegemonic masculinity through a lens that corroborates heterosexuality, breadwinning and aggressiveness (75). Furthermore, the emphasis on unequal relationships is key to understanding the social dimension of hegemonic masculinity; these relationships take place between men and women, as well as between men and men. Indeed, masculinity is taught, modeled, and reinforced as we see particularly in the pieces written by the editors of this collection that speak to the role of the Chicanx family in furthering the ideal of masculinity. It has taken more than two decades for masculinity studies to emerge; in 1997 Alfredo Mirandé suggested further research was necessary by feminists to include the concept in their research: "the topic of Chicano/Latino masculinity remains neglected and virtually unexplored both within the so-called new men's studies and feminist scholarship" (118). Since then, scholars from both Mexico and the United States have answered Mirandé's call for deeper dives into masculinity and its relationship with feminism. The editors of this volume choose this time to enter the dialogue to continue the unmasking of masculinity, especially for those who have inherited machista ideals from centuries ago. Our volume continues the work of Jennifer Domino Rudolph and her *Embodying Latino Masculinities: Producing Masculatinidad* (2012) as well as Vinodh Venkatesh's *The Body as Capital: Masculinities in Contemporary Latin American Fiction* (2015). While Rudolph emphasizes Latinx works, and Venkatesh focuses on Latin America, the current text dialogues with Mexican and US Latinx cultural production.

Specifically, this edited collection, titled *Societal Constructions of Masculinity in Chicanx and Mexican Literature: From Machismo to Feminist Masculinity* is to demonstrate the breadth and range of how masculinity is constructed and deconstructed as a challenge or as a reinforcement of patriarchy. Mexicans and Chicanos struggle against the cultural norms to which society dictates they must conform. While the cultural tenet of what is deemed appropriate masculine behavior has changed during the past century, while there is hope that masculinity and feminism can coexist without friction, the path that we have traversed has not been easy. Indeed, the portrayal of new behaviors as masculine is exposed throughout the chapters that analyze Mexican canonical authors to Chicanx writers as well as a chapter on telenovelas.

For the first chapter, Leigh Johnson shines a light onto the undercurrent of domestic violence that takes place in the works by Américo Paredes *(George Washington Gómez* 1990), José Antonio Villarreal *(Pocho* 1959), and Mario Suárez (Short Story "Las comadres" 1969). Incorporated into Johnson's analysis is the role of World War II by implicating the changing gender roles to the war's influence. Not only does the definition of masculinity come into play, but also 'war-masculinity' and how this type of masculinity impacts the heterosexual male's relationship to his wife. Violence, citizenship, and masculinity become intertwined as patriarchy fights (literally and figuratively) to regain the ground it lost to women's agency during WWII.

Next in our continuum, we move to Fernando G. Hernández' undertaking the charge to demonstrate how Ricardo Castillo's *El pobrecito señor* X (1976) subverts the status quo through imagining a new aesthetic based on poetic masculinity. For Castillo, poetry exists as a unique space with its own ethics based on an intersubjective exchange between poet and reader. Castillo's poetics is presented by Hernández as a counterhegemonic discourse and a practice in which social disenchantment becomes enchantment. Within the aesthetic, within the possibilities it provides for a different way of being in the world, the poetic voice finds an anti-hegemonic subjectivity that he designates as poetic masculinity which highlights new forms of social relations and a validation of new definitions of masculinities, especially those historically perceived as macho or hyper-masculine.

Alejandro Puga and Patricia Tovar delve into nationhood in the third chapter via Juan Villoros's representation of Mexican masculinity as a challenge to the morality of how the nation has idealized hegemonic masculinity during and after the 1910 Revolution. By focusing on such a pivotal and defining event, Puga and Tovar show that by pairing the successes and failures of the nation with masculinity, one can see the parallels between the very definition of what it signifies to be a Mexican male adapting and morphing along with the State's identity, from Dictator Díaz' hyper-masculinity to the Neoliberal State's new and therefore awkward masculinity. Through the application of the work of A. Rolando Andrade to Villoro's novels *El disparo de argón* (1991) and *Materia dispuesta* (1997) this "awkward machismo" may eventually become the new norm for a new century.

We see Kathryn Quinn-Sánchez highlight the family and how gender is modeled by the parent(s) and hence, learned by the children in chapter four. When one and not both parents support a particular goal that the child has in mind for his/her future the child understands that s/he most likely will have to disappoint one of the parents. Common to the works Quinn-Sánchez studies is the fact that while some of the young protagonists are successful in gaining access to his/her dream, the path is fraught with dangers that spill over from the individual to the entire family, and in one case to the definition of the nation. Specifically, Cherríe Moraga's play *The Hungry Woman* (2001), Sandra Cisneros' *The House on Mango Street* (1984), and Margarita Tavera Rivera's play *La condición* (1991) focus on how fatherhood has been represented in Chicanx Literature. Attention is drawn to the endurance of hegemonic masculinity which makes the societal change towards feminist masculinity an ongoing enterprise.

For the fifth chapter, Bryan Pearce-Gonzales brings the inheritance of patriarchy to the fore in his analysis of two Chicanx novels that focus on masculine relationships and the difficult path away from hyper-masculine behavior when one's own father refuses to refrain from being ultra-macho even in the event of causing pain to his own family members. Dagoberto Gilb's *The Flowers* (2008) and Domingo Martinez' autobiography *The Boy Kings of Texas* (2012) are presented through Alfredo Mirandé's and R.W. Connell's theoretical perspectives on masculinity within the Chicano family.

In Chapter Six, Jess Brocklesby moves into the realm of the telenovela, as a medium in which directors have begun to slowly challenge hegemonic masculinity in recent decades. As the most-watched television format in Mexico, telenovelas are the disseminators of implicit and explicit messages about diverse identities as represented in these productions. The audience for a telenovela crosses categories of age, sex, race and socio-economic status. By including new forms of masculinity in telenovelas, homosexuality serves as the catalyst for a re-examining and reconfiguring of gender narratives, allowing representations of different types of masculinity to humanize characters, ultimately leading to change and acceptance within Mexican society while providing an unequivocal look into the future of masculinity as it begins to overthrow its historical gender binaries. This chapter posits that post-patriarchy is possible within Mexico, and that Mexico is showing signs of adopting a healthier masculinity as is evidenced through the representation of certain characters within recent telenovelas.

Ultimately in chapter seven, Joshua D. Martin's *On the Border, In the Bar: Approaching Feminist Masculinities through Border Thinking in It All Begins and Ends at the Kentucky Club* (2012) by Benjamin Alire Sáenz, brings us full circle. The protagonists are emphasized through an intersectional lens that highlights the changes in how masculinity is currently being represented in the borderlands. The author challenges hegemonic masculinity by focusing on homosocial and homosexual desire while negotiating racialized antagonisms and generational points of view all with the backdrop of the femicides in Ciudad Juárez.

In conclusion, it is evident that, as Lourdes Torres states:

> Still today, popular culture reinforces static, homogenizing, and pathologizing notions of Latino men. Quite often both in popular culture and the social sciences, the diversity within the Latino population or transitions in Latino cultures and societies are not acknowledged. Instead, images continue to proliferate of macho men and passive women embedded in strict patriarchal families, and of conservative religious people with undemocratic tendencies and stagnant cultures (462).

And yet there are successful attempts at moving towards a feminist masculinity. The path is clear, Messerschmidt draws our attention to the need for counterhegemonic practices that will destabilize gender hegemony by removing the binary of superior versus inferior and its seemingly inherent nature. These unequal gender relations must be drawn into the light over and over until their ability to hide in plain sight is no longer the norm, but an egregious slight against what must become the norm: equality. The inclusion of men into the feminization of our society continues to evolve thankfully, and consequently we are entering an era of wide discussion on what it means to be a Chicanx or Latinx man in the 21st century. This collection of essays challenges patriarchy's authority by demonstrating the ways in which a hegemonic masculinity has been constructed and deconstructed.

Works Cited

Messerschmidt, James W. *Hegemonic Masculinity: Formulation, Reformulation, and Amplification.* Rowman & Littlefield, 2018.

Mirandé, Alfredo. *Hombre y machos: Masculinity and Latino Culture.* Westview Press, 1997.

Torres, Lourdes. "Becoming Joaquin and Mind if I Call You Sir?: Exploring Latino Masculinities." *Biography,* vol. 34, no. 3, 2011, pp. 447-466.

Chapter 1

Women's Work: A Revision of Gender in Américo Paredes, José Antonio Villarreal, and Mario Suárez's Fiction

Leigh Johnson

Marymount University

Américo Paredes, José Antonio Villarreal, and Mario Suárez are responsible for many of the most influential Mexican American literature written before the Chicano movement, and as such, their work is widely studied and considered a valuable depiction of Chicano masculinity and identity. However, their work contains scenes of domestic violence in which the narrator seems to warn women not to tell cultural outsiders about violence while also implicating women by suggesting that they desire the violent expressions of "love." In this sense, these scenes of domestic violence present in canonical narratives blame women as cultural betrayers who explicitly enjoy erotic violence. Moreover, within these scenes we see an undeniable Chicana presence that belies the narrative of male dominance; specifically, we view how the female protagonist picks herself up and continues her life, creating her own agency in the process. Furthermore, the narrators inadvertently undermine male privilege while attempting to justify male dominance over women in their communities, revealing deep anxiety and ambivalence over the changing social and gender roles of men and women within the Mexican American community.

Two climatic scenes of domestic violence come from revered novels, *George Washington Gómez* (1990) by Américo Paredes and *Pocho* (1959) by José Antonio Villarreal. These two novels contain scenes of domestic violence that police the boundaries of women's sexuality but ultimately create space for women to emerge as empowered Chicanas, controlling their own sexuality and futures. Mario Suárez's "Las comadres" first published in 1969, and set just post-WWII, does not idealize the *barrio* but implicates the war in changing roles for men and women. Moreover, the male protagonists of *George Washington Gómez* and *Pocho* are speechless in the face of domestic violence, signaling anxiety about men's place in a new world where women work outside the home and make their own sexual choices. The young men cower as their sisters experience domestic violence; and as their sisters gather strength to envision an independent future away from the oppressive social and patriarchal structures, the young men cry from their anguish that the family is changing from the rule of the father, which further emasculates them. These narratives take place just before, during, and after World War II, which was a particularly tumultuous time for Mexican Americans. The *pachuco* (zoot suiters) beatings in Los Angeles, the assertions of patriotism in New Mexico, and the military as a way for young Mexican American men to "get ahead" all converge with women working outside the home, the legacy of the Mexican Revolution, and the changing economic conditions in the United States. For instance, as Mexican-American women entered the workforce, Richard Griswold del Castillo explains:

> [V]iews of acceptable social independence did differ, ranging from having the freedom to smoke, wear lipstick, wear pants, and date without chaperones to expecting equality in decision making at home and the right to education. Some women commented that their independence during the war prepared them for being widows or divorced women after the war." (66)

As women embraced their freedoms, they sometimes ran afoul of their families, who expected them to adhere to cultural norms of submission and domesticity of the past. In the literary texts, scenes of domestic violence serve to show how anxieties about women's shifting roles cannot be contained within the home; rather women and their abilities permeate into the public realm including the nation.

Furthermore, these particular scenes of domestic violence all rely on war and its threat to masculinity and Mexican American citizenship. For young men, joining the war effort seemed to be a way to assimilate and gain access to the privileges of citizenship in a way that had not been accessible to them throughout Jim Crow segregation, which affected Mexican Americans in all regions, but especially California and Texas. For example, according to Maria Eva Flores, "Division characterized almost every facet of life in Fort Stockton [West Texas], prior to World War II; employment opportunities were limited to low-skilled labor on ranches and farms for men and domestic work for women. *Mexicanos* could enter only the west and north parts of town to work; they worshiped in a segregated church and attended a segregated school" (180). Because of lingering suspicions about Mexican Americans' loyalty to the United States, the young men sought to advance their claims to civil rights via honorable service in the armed forces. While "anti-Mexican attitudes prevailed in Fort Stockton long after the war [...] the world had grown larger [...] the war against racial discrimination still had many battles to fight before they could declare victory" (Flores 196). World War II does mark a turning point in gender equality in the United States, but the lingering resentment of racist institutions that did not change after the war created anxiety in returning Mexican American servicemen, despite loyal service to the United States, who felt that their sacrifices had been in vain.

Paredes's *With His Pistol in His Hand: A Border Ballad and Its Hero (1970)*, the story of Gregorio Cortez and the definition of the *corrido* tradition, made him famous as a theorist of pre-Chicano movement masculinity. Earlier in his career, in *George Washington Gómez*, Paredes inadvertently supports the potential for future Chicana activism. The protagonist Guálinto finds that emergent Chicana feminism creates a nationalist identity that he is too uncomfortable with to embrace.[1] Rather, he becomes a *pocho vendido*, selling out his people for the Anglo war establishment.[2] This text, written between 1936 and 1940, takes place along the Texas/Mexico border. The protagonist, Guálinto, is the youngest child and only boy; his name comes from his mother's desire to give him a "great man's name" and an argument ensues between his father and uncle over the greatness of the gringos (16). In a twist of irony, he is named "Jorge Wachinton" and called Guálinto (17). Later, when he moves away to marry an Anglo woman, he assumes the Anglicized name, George. The family consists of his two sisters, Maruca and Carmen, his mother, and his uncle Feliciano who takes on a paternal role after Guálinto's father is killed by Texas Rangers. As Leif Sorensen notes, the novel's setting is particularly important because "the struggle between Anglo-Texans and Mexico-Texans has become less obvious, because U.S. nationalism has successfully domesticated the border, foreclosing criticism of the imperialist violence that made Mexico-Texans U.S. subjects" (121). Guálinto/George seems to believe that the only way to get ahead is to collude with the US military and marry a white woman. However, his sisters embody a different kind of resistance that stems from their reaction to the mother beating one of the sisters. A gendered analysis of the novel's scene of domestic violence is particularly appropriate for understanding how women become "other" in the text. I argue that in this scene, the protagonist sees his mother and sister as cultural betrayers, but that ultimately the novel assigns genuine cultural treason to Guálinto.

This scene of domestic violence stems ostensibly from efforts to police women's sexual identities while revealing anxieties about social change for women coupled with their internal colonization.[3] In point of illustration, Guálinto comes home to find Carmen crying on the couch. He thinks she's overly emotional, until Maruca and her mother return from the doctor where it has been confirmed that Maruca is pregnant. Guálinto has no idea that pregnancy was even a possibility for Maruca. In this scenario, the mother acts as enforcer, following Maruca into the back room where she begins to beat her with a barrel stave. As Héctor Pérez persuasively argues, the mother "functions [...] as a vessel that conveys problematic patriarchal values and assumptions" (39). This is not sufficient to explain Guálinto's cultural shame and betrayal, a talent Pérez attributes to the mother's actions. Since an unmarried daughter presented to the community an example of lax parenting, the mother must reassert her control over the family. Because the mother sees the family's future success as dependent on Guálinto, she beats Maruca as a way of protecting *his* social status.

Because Guálinto is the prized possession and hope for the family's future, he's been largely shielded from his mother's ire and discipline. As she mostly spoke demurely to him, when she chastises Maruca, Guálinto hears his mother's unlady-like speech as a betrayal of her femininity. The description of her linguistic transgressions makes her a cultural traitor in Guálinto's eyes, even as she enforces cultural codes on Maruca:

> Maruca crouched close to the floor, seeking to protect her belly. And the blows went on, the horrible thudding and cracking, and the two women cursing, panting, grunting, pleading. [...] The animal sounds coming from his sister filled him with a crushing sense of shame. But it was his mother who sickened him the most. He had never heard her curse before. Nor had he ever thought whether or not she knew about such words. (224)

In Guálinto's ears, the women become two animals which leads to a visceral reaction in Guálinto, wherein he wants to "rub desperately at [his mother's] lips, to make them soft and gentle again" (224). Interestingly, Guálinto is not disgusted with Maruca's pregnancy or the beating itself; rather the vision of his mother transformed is what causes him to be ill. This domestic violence, the transformation of women through the capitalist, sexually liberated Anglo influence, causes Guálinto to distance himself from family. In this way, the narrative blames women for Guálinto's transformation into a soldier-spy, husband to an Anglo daughter of a Texas Ranger, and a cultural *vendido*.

The circumstances of Maruca's pregnancy reveal social and historical conditions for young Mexican-American people in South Texas in the 1930s. Employment and educational opportunities frame the social status of Maruca, Carmen, and Guálinto. Vicki Ruiz shows that those women "who challenged or circumvented chaperonage held a full-time job" (63). Because Maruca's employment placed her in a public space without supervision from family members, the mother blames the job for Maruca's pregnancy, which causes her to forbid her second daughter's continued employment. She cannot bear to have Carmen end up in the same social disgrace that Maruca has brought to the family. The national freedoms that have come to women threaten the mother's ability to control her daughters' sexuality, and within that it threatens the status and upward mobility of the family into the middle class. While Carmen does not protest the prohibition, it is a double injustice for her, since she has already given up her education for her brother Guálinto's studies. The actions of her family members have constrained Carmen's choices. Although she has been disempowered in multiple ways, Carmen persists to study on her own and will emerge as a well-balanced Chicana presence. Carmen, by leaving school, furthers her own education, increasing her literacy by reading magazines about far off places and telling these stories to her mother. Carmen also furthers her community by sharing her newly garnered knowledge with other women. As we shall see later, Guálinto's education, which the family assumed would be more beneficial than the girls' educations, ends up being used against the Mexican American community when Guálinto turns spy for the Anglos. The subtext of this detail suggests that women's education is more valuable for the community and should not be neglected.

While Maruca is beaten by the mother, Guálinto simply watches and cowers, he never comes to his sister's defense. He is emasculated by his lack of response, in that he does not step up to restore order and justice in the home; instead, he cedes this power to Carmen. His passive reaction contrasts with Carmen's active mediation; she cleans Maruca up, prepares food, and acts as a "liaison between the different members of the family" because she "seemed less affected by the tense atmosphere than the others" (227). Carmen takes on the role of the head of the family, working to heal the wounds and create a community in which they can thrive. She shores up community building and family ties. However, because the family has achieved middle-class status, when Carmen marries a darker man and has children with him, it complicates Guálinto's feelings about her. Even though she had been his favorite sister, and the sister who was capable of and should have received the education over Guálinto, her marriage is a cultural and class betrayal in his eyes. Carmen's husband works a respectable desk job, and the family has taken in the mother as she ages in order to care for her. However, even though she and her family are attached to the land and will inherit the family farm, Guálinto sees her aspirations as beneath him and his wife. Rudolfo Acuña describes the Mexican American middle class of the 1930s as color conscious and comments: "Aside from "marrying up" by marrying someone lighter or with more economic resources, over time being American became a form of moving up while retaining a Mexican identity, yet adopting many middle-class values of Euroamericans" (258). Because Carmen is content with her mother and children, she creates a viable community for the family, and through these connections she retains land and power. Unlike Guálinto, who has now fully become George, who leaves and returns uninterested in land, she rejects what Olguín calls Paredes's "antithetical citizen"—he who is by virtue of "cruel circular logic [...] that links land ownership to civic legitimacy [...] is the embodiment of underdevelopment that enables the new capitalist empire to thrive" (124). Carmen, not Guálinto, becomes the hero of the people by preserving the link to the land for Mexican Americans in South Texas.

One of the tragedies of the novel is that Carmen must give up her pursuit of formal education because the family cannot afford to educate more than one child. Her persistence in continuing to read and share her knowledge with others reveals education as a site of resistance in the novel, which reflects the historical conditions of the time. Even though the family takes segregation as a fact in the novel, *Tejanos* protested segregated schools. For instance, in 1910, Mexican Americans in San Angelo had protested segregation by "withholding their children from the school census, thus denying state aid to the school district" (Acuña 172). The 1920s brought increased segregation and charges that "Mexican Americans were slow learners" yet, they "scored 70 percent higher on IQ tests administered in Spanish" (193). Desegregation cases mark the League of United Latin American Citizens (LULAC)'s early commitment to civil rights ("History").[4] The classrooms at Guálinto's school enforce segregation and reveal that the classrooms for Mexican Americans, reflecting Richard Steele's description of "Mexican schools" in general, were "a dumping ground for less-competent teachers" (14). However, rather than fight the system that allows this inequality, Guálinto blames his teacher, revealing his impotence in the face of marginalization. Guálinto cannot be true to himself, because his name contains too many contradictions, Anglo, Black (as his father-in-law will vulgarly point out), and Mexican. Roumiana Velikova sees the novel as pointing "to the violence inherent in U.S. history and the frustrated, ultimately self-destructive, tendencies it engenders in the protagonist, who was reared in the corrido tradition of active, often violent, resistance to Anglo domination" (35). Because there is no place in South Texas for Guálinto to release his anger physically against the Anglos, he instead turns his rage and desire for violence toward his family and community.

Guálinto/George's position as a spy, his position working for the US government as a border patrol agent ostensibly keeping Germans and Japanese out of Texas, his participation in politics that raises Anglo candidates above *Tejano* ones, and his starting a family with a woman whose father was a Texas Ranger solidifies his cultural betrayal. Having gone away to move up in the world, he, in effect, has reentered the homeland of his people in order to do them violence. Originally sickened by the physical violence he saw in his home, he brings imperialist violence to the border under the auspices of his successful education. Guálinto/George embraces his new role even as he derides Carmen and her dark-skinned children. In this manner, the narrative betrays the potential that exists for Carmen and the others on the border. As Pérez seeks to resolve Guálinto/George's failure to be a great man among his people, he notes that there:

> is certainly a sense of hopelessness in the novel—at least as far as radical social and political change for the border community—the novel's narrative consciousness does seem to seek out promising characters and potential subplots [...] a core Chicano/a group remained in Jonesville and attempts to cultivate organic roots and empower the community (42).

He is specifically speaking about Guálinto/George's former friends, but I argue that Carmen, as storyteller and mother of dark-skinned children, also foreshadows the hope of a powerful Chicana presence. She is the only family member who is easily and proudly bilingual, and she raises her children to be fluent in Spanish and English, while George maintains that his children will never need to know Spanish. By embracing the land, language, and education of her community, Carmen offers the hope that social and economic justice can become possible through Chicana feminist activism in the borderlands.

The possibility of an emergent Chicana feminism in opposition to an assimilationist *vendido* masculinity appears even more conspicuously in José Antonio Villarreal's *Pocho*. The novel has fallen under heavy criticism for being the first Chicano novel at the start of the Chicano intellectual movement, but, at the same time, *not being Chicano enough*. As Ramón Saldívar explains, "*Pocho* has always been somewhat of an embarrassment to Chicanos [...] seen as assimilationist tendencies, indicating an uncritical acceptance of "melting pot" theories of American immigration" (65). Originally published in 1959, the novel predates the upheaval of the Chicano civil rights movement, but it engages changing social roles for women. However, much of the focus on how *Pocho* falls short is centered on the failure of the protagonist, Richard Rubio, to fulfill his coming of age into a Chicano identity. Much like Guálinto, Richard is the only boy in the family and, when he is born, it seems that his family's lineage will live on and their destiny as great men among their people will commence. Instead, also similar to Guálinto's decision to become a border agent, Richard joins the Navy and plans to remain distant from his family and community long term. Thomas Vallejos notes that the failure of the coming of age ritual in *Pocho* means that "the final outcome of the novel is the undermining of Chicano family and community ties" (6). Other criticism of the novel focuses on its perceived misogyny. Alma Rosa Alvarez comments,

"Because preservation of [manhood and nationalism] in the United States is often done through the subordination of women, the women in [*Pocho*] were depicted as weak, static characters who at best were obstacles, and at worst traitors to a Chicano nationalist movement" (5). Instead of projecting the women as weak, I argue that the scene of domestic violence at the end of the novel undermines male privilege in such a way that the novel actually, albeit inadvertently, affirms *Chicana* family and community ties.

The Zoot Suit Riots and *pachuco* culture of World War II play an important role in the novel, as Richard hangs out with *pachucos*, and his ability to code-switch in *pachuco* slang keeps him out of trouble.[5] Since he speaks like an Anglo and acts like a pachuco, Richard moves smoothly between communities, yet the contradictions he sees within these abilities make him feel like a fraud. Later, Richard joins the army as a rejection of *pachuco* lifestyle. His sister, Luz, also seems to embrace *pachuco* behavior as she, like other *pachucas*, "challenges wartime gender norms by venturing into the public sphere" (Ramírez, "Crimes" 11). The backdrop of emergent *pachuco* culture sheds light on the conflict between Luz and the men in her family.

Two significant scenes of domestic violence occur in the novel as first Richard and later his father, Juan Rubio, attempt to physically impose and police sexual and social mores with regard to Luz. When she and her boyfriend drive up in front of the family's house in her boyfriend's car, Richard goes out to meet them and demands that Luz enter to clean the "filthy" house, thereby revealing that there are social norms that the woman must fulfill. Her boyfriend does not speak Spanish, so he does not understand Richard's dictate. Luz uses this to her advantage to start a fight between her brother and her boyfriend. She tells her boyfriend that Richard is trying to keep them apart; when he asks what Richard wants, she lies, "He don't want me to be out here with you" (Villarreal 147). Her boyfriend threatens Richard by being "big [and] powerful" but when Richard "[takes] a brick from an abandoned incinerator" the boyfriend backs off (147). Luz, quite cleverly, uses her linguistic power to control her circumstances. She is in a position to translate for the non-native speaker, but when she translates, she does so to benefit herself. Her translation keeps Richard away from the house; moreover, it shows how she uses English for her own gain. Luz resists the patriarchal domination of her home life by using her power of language for her own agency.

The novel focuses on how women (especially Richard's mother) have failed to embody the expectation of domestic cleanliness. The rebellion of women and the mess in the home become an allegory for the changing social roles and opportunities for women. Her refusal to keep a clean house foreshadows the scenario in Mario Suárez's "Las comadres," which paints women as responsible for the home and consequently deserving of domestic violence if the home is in squalor. In *Pocho* the domestic disorder reveals tensions over the place of Mexican Americans within the larger social fabric of the United States during World War II. Ramírez posits, "Although many pachucas may have labored on behalf of their families inside and/or outside the home, they also nurtured "a separate culture" distinctive from that of their parents. In doing so, they appeared to privilege individual desires over the family's survival (as well as the nation's survival" ("Crimes" 12). Luz and Consuelo (Richard's mother) threaten the family and community, and as wayward Mexican American women, they threaten the traditional Chicano culture. Domestic violence, then, becomes a tool to keep them in line, and it serves the purposes of the male family members as well as the perceived assimilationist agenda of the Mexican American generation. Becoming a member of the army, Richard aligns with the US soldiers and sailors in the zoot suit riots, enacting domestic violence on Mexican American men as well as women.

The second instance of domestic violence is much more brutal and more telling. Richard comes home from his own sexual dalliance to find his father beating Luz for the suggestion of impropriety – she has arrived home at three in the morning. He accuses her of being a whore, but she tells him, "If I'm a whore, it is having your blood that makes me one!" (165). She references the double standard that turns women into whores for sexual liberation but excuses men's behavior as simply inherent. What makes Richard most angry, however, is her insistence that the father is no longer in control of the home. When Luz attempts to stop her father from shifting the beating to her mother, she accuses Richard of weakness: "Stand there! Just stand there, you weak bastard, and watch this son of a bitch hit your mother!" (166). She flings herself at Juan Rubio, but "very deliberately he hit her in the face with his fist. She did not get up" (166). He hits her in the face to silence her—to silence her challenges to his male privilege and to Richard's masculinity. Because she is knocked out and no one stops to tend to her, she does not see her father begin to destroy the house with an axe, but her presence looms like a shadow over the subsequent events. Furthermore, her name, Luz (Light), is significant here. Juan Rubio's destructive performance of masculinity almost destroys her, yet she picks herself up, signaling that her kind of light (the life force of her family) cannot be so easily extinguished.

Unlike Luz, Richard has no agency of his own, he *cannot* act; he's "transfixed by the grotesque masque that was taking place before his eyes" (166). When Juan Rubio begins to destroy the house, Richard "held on to the kicking legs of his father, and when he was shaken off and they were both on their feet, his father hit him a chopping blow" (167), but he cannot convince his father to stop. Finally, he "jumped on his father's back, only to slip off, and as he fell his head struck the floor, knocking him unconscious" (167). Juan Rubio immediately stops what he's doing, and carries Richard to another room, tends to him, and sobs about his son. Several things are important about this order of events. Richard behaves like a child, grabbing at his father's legs, and in the end Juan Rubio carries him like a baby from the room. Richard cannot become the man of the house, because he is unwilling (or unable) to give up his role as a child. When Richard is knocked unconscious, the family stops to take note. He is delicate and cannot get up on his own. The contrast to the family's reaction when Luz is knocked unconscious moments before is striking. Ultimately, the father and son reconcile and realize that the father must leave the family. Rather than say goodbye to Consuelo, Luz, or the other girls, Juan Rubio says goodbye to the only one who matters, Richard: "They put their arms around each other in the Mexican way. Then Juan Rubio kissed his son on the mouth" (169). Juan Rubio, having lost his place of authority in the family, turns to the one member of the family he thinks is still loyal to him. However, Richard, having recognized his family as strangers to him, has decided to join the Navy.

Meanwhile, "In the other room, Luz finally picked herself up off the floor and disappeared into her room" (169). Her father is leaving for good, and she has no use for him. Furthermore, she does not need assistance to pick herself up, and when she disappears into her room, she waits for the men to leave the house, as she knows they no longer have a place of authority in the home. The Chicana presence might be easily lost in the tearful goodbye between father and son, but Luz, who had been knocked unconscious is able to restore herself. Women's agency and the feminization of Richard have solidified the new order in the Rubio home. Ramírez contends, "Chicanas' silence can be and has been as oppositional, rich, and complex as their male counterparts' speech" ("Saying" 3). Certainly, Luz's silent, unheralded rising is complex and oppositional. She is powerful in her own right and signals the strength and resilience of the family she and her mother have made. Her emergent Chicana identity stems from her refusal to participate in the racist, militarist, and sexist maligning of the *pachuca.* When her father accuses her of loose behavior, she lashes back with a rejection of the double standard around sexuality, "If I am a whore, it is having your blood that makes me one!" (Villarreal 165). Both she and Richard have come home late after being with their respective lovers, but she is the one who is called to account for her actions. Ramírez points out that the male *pachuco* has been revived as a political identity, but the *pachuca* remains "unintelligible to Chicano cultural nationalism" ("Crimes" 24). Because Luz embodies oppositional identities with regard to gender, race, class, and nation, her character must reject charges of cultural betrayal and establish a new domestic order. In *Pocho*, the narrative perspective suggests that Luz operates under her own code, refusing to tell her father where she has been and where she is going. She asserts her independence as a harbinger of Chicana feminism. The beginning of countering patriarchy and machismo is a cornerstone of the Chicana feminist movement. To show that as long as a double standard around gender and sexuality exist, neither men nor women will be liberated is important to the ways that Chicana feminists articulated a place for women's leadership in the movement.

Instead of leadership, Richard withdraws from the community. At the end of the novel he questions his father's commitment to fighting battle after battle for a life that was worthwhile to him, but Richard does not know what his own fight means. In this moment, he realizes "for him there would never be a coming back" (187). In this sense, he may have decided to leave his family and community forever, much like Guálinto does, or he may have recognized the futility of war for advancing the cause of Mexican American civil rights. Either way, Richard gives up. Based on this reading, when Richard joins the Navy and leaves his family home it is not a failure of the Chicano family; rather his actions signal a shift to Chicana feminism. Richard's reliance on the old ways does not suit the time and place that his mother and sisters inhabit. His presence asserts the old equivalence of war and violence with masculinity and power. Yet, as he leaves, it is not so much a literal death wish, as Ramón Saldívar explains, "he welcomes a figural one: the death of the child he was, at the mercy of random historical forces and of determinant social codes" (67). Saldívar's interpretation supports my analysis that Richard's impotence in the family is part of the recognition that, as the favored male child, his very presence continues dominant social codes that are inherently problematic and violent. Indeed, as Olguín suggests, "Mexican American soldiers are both active agents and subjects of a nation that in large part is built upon a war of expansion and conquest against their ancestors, and that subsequently consolidates its status as the premier capitalist imperialist power [...through...] heroics of Mexican American GIs" (110). Therefore, Richard's enlistment and acknowledgement that he will not return to his ethnic community signifies surrender to the capitalist imperialist US power.[6] Women then are left to resist US policy on the home front. The US national body cannot assimilate or accommodate Richard as a Chicano, and possible *pachuco*, so his option is to join the Navy to try to salvage his dignity. It is especially poignant, because none of Richard's friends from the *barrio* can find a peaceful, upwardly mobile place in wartime US. One of his friends is sent to the internment camps, and others join the war effort.

Luz represents a different mode—one that equates power with independence and connections with other women. Consuelo expects Richard to stay and become the "head" of the family (a role he rejects), but Ruiz points out that teenagers "did not always acquiesce in the boundaries set down for them by their elders" as both young women and men rebelled (54). In this case, Luz's public behavior, more than Richard's, sets a new course for the family—metaphorically, she is the light leading them into a Chicanx future, away from rigid social mores of hallowed masculinity. Richard's sisters and mother have emerged as new standard bearers for a Chicana identity—one that threatens the men in the novel. The narrative is deeply anxious about the changing roles of women, and since Richard will not adapt to the new social norms, he exiles himself from this reality into a masculine playground of war. Since he doubts his ability to return, it suggests a reordering of patriarchy within the home and nation. The war did create new roles for men and women of all races, and *Pocho* shows the complexity and ambiguity with which those roles were embraced.

Women's ability to work outside the home and how men responded to their emerging financial independence reflects the changing social mores of World War II and afterward. "Las comadres," a short story by Mario Suárez originally published in *Con Safos* in 1969 seems to blame women for wanting men to take control—physically, financially, and emotionally. A veteran, Suárez took advantage of the GI Bill and began writing in college.[7] Generally suggested to be overwhelmingly beneficial for veterans of color, the GI Bill complicated opportunities for women as they had difficulty taking advantage of it even if they qualified for benefits, while at the same time it purportedly expanded opportunities for men. As Glenn Altschuler and Stuart Blumin point out, even though the bill did not discriminate in and of itself, the "majority of beneficiaries were white—and the legislation did not act affirmatively to overcome Jim Crow institutions and instrumentalities—the GI Bill did not reduce racial disparities in the United States" (129). The GI Bill both "challenged the discriminatory admissions policies of many colleges and universities" and simultaneously revealed how "strategic use of scholarships and grants of financial aid, [...] limited numbers of Catholics and Jews, Mexican Americans [etc.]" (139, 149). Suárez, even though he attended college on the GI Bill, would have experienced these contradictory approaches of discrimination. He may, as James D. Lilley suggests, be writing as "a nostalgic, conservative mode of discourse that mourns the changes that have beset a privileged and traditional communal space" (103). Indeed, he does seem to hold women responsible for negative change in the community. Because "Las comadres" is set during World War II yet written in 1969, the reality of the GI Bill affects the narrative's outlook. While the GI Bill did provide opportunities, an uncritical analysis of it would miss that those moments that look like gains for Mexican Americans in employment and educational opportunities, are actually much more complicated experiences.

Suárez's story opens with two comadres engaged in conversation about domestic abuse.[8] Anastacia often runs to her neighbor Lola's house and cries to

Lola about the beatings her husband inflicts on her. Without really believing that he will change, Lola assures Anastacia that he will transform his behavior, but the reader learns that Lola believes that Anastacia brings the beatings on herself by being such a bad housekeeper. To escape the abuse and to empower herself, Anastacia cashes in some war bonds and leaves her husband, literally moving to the other side of the tracks. However, her daughter gets pregnant by Lola's son who is joining the army, and Anastacia returns to her husband. They live peacefully, and she thinks he doesn't love her anymore, until he beats her and she is satisfied. According to the narrative, Anastacia cannot escape from her violent relationship because the material conditions of her life pull her back—and her daughter will follow the same path.

The narrator presents a strikingly different point of view from the characters. The short story begins with definitions of comadre and compadre— characterizing men as the agents of the relationship and women as joined through their husbands and a love of *mitote*, gossip. In this way, the narrative blames women for their misfortune because they have nothing better to do than to gossip. The narrative blames Anastacia for being a "lousy housekeeper" which causes her husband to beat her (55). Lola suggests that he will change, but she wants to tell Anastacia "to correct her housekeeping habits" (57).[9] The conflict between women exemplifies what Ruiz describes as the "dialectic, often expressed as a conflict between personal liberation or family first" that forms a "theme of Chicana feminist history" (102). Here, Lola discourages Anastacia's desire for personal liberation by suggesting that she conform to the domestic sphere. This conflict intensifies when Anastacia moves out of the *barrio* and becomes the subject of gossip for Lola and her friends. Not until Anastacia comes to believe that her husband only loves her when he beats her, (and, because of this, she continues her bad housekeeping) does she become acceptable to the other women. In fact, they take no notice of her screams, justifying the home space as private and familial.

The specter of war plays a significant role in the narrative and links Anastacia's escape from a violent situation in her home to the cycle of violence Anastacia's daughter will experience. In order to leave the situation, Anastacia cashes in war bonds and moves. No one hears from her, but gossip suggests that "she was now working at the air base and had dyed her hair" (57). Anastacia has benefited to some degree from the war; she is able to use the bonds to remove herself and her daughters from the abusive, violent El Hoyo *barrio*. However, she has also sold out in that she dyes her hair, works for the war machine, rejects gender roles, and, most significantly, betrays her people and denies her old self by saying, "I do not know any Lola López" (57). Because gossip is responsible for word getting out about the betrayal, it is clear that the women in the barrio resent Anastacia's work and social mobility and attempt to rein her in.[10] Anastacia's fictional experience mirrors many women's lived experiences during the war. One woman working at Douglass Aircraft as a riveter during the war "became aware that her financial abilities irritated some of her nonworking women friends since she was "getting ahead"" (Quiñonez 255). Anastacia goes to work in the war industry factories with jobs available to women. Like Richard and Guálinto, she seeks an escape from her community and World War II has created an opportunity for her to leave. Unlike them, she is still bound to her place; she will not go to Washington or travel overseas. Being a woman means that her labor is valuable to the war effort, but her "place" remains at home. Because she does not join the armed forces, she will not be eligible for post-war economic advancement; instead, she will be forced to give up her job so that returning male soldiers and sailors have work.

Anastacia represents both the World War and a more intimate "gender war." By going to work for the defense contractor, she rejects gendered space, yet she cannot escape the parameters of gendered social inequality. The defense industry sees her as a Mexican American version of Rosie the Riveter, and as Ramírez describes this class of women, they were "far from dainty" and "appeared to threaten gender norms" ("Crimes" 17). At a time when "American women were called upon to contribute to the war effort by sacrificing their allegedly innate femininity as they entered the labor force" there was simultaneous pressure for "American women—namely, white American women—[...] to do their part for the war by being pretty and ladylike, for they not only remained at home, they embodied the home front" ("Crimes" 18). Within these contradictory identities, Anastacia seems to reject innate femininity by engaging in work outside the home (and conspicuously refusing to do domestic work at home). Nevertheless, at the end of the story, she returns home and begins to clean, thinking that her domestic actions will regain her husband's love. However, in a cruel twist of fate, Anastacia equates beatings with love, and he only beats her when the house is messy. Yet, as she attempts to conform to a feminine identity, she feels that she has lost his love. If their relationship depends on the squalid home, then the violence can be read as a metaphorical assent to destroying the home front through domestic squalor. In other words, domestic servitude does not lead to love, but keeps the national house in order, which is more valuable to the dominant gender ideology of the US.

The cycle of domestic violence repeats with Anastacia's daughter and Lola's son. As children they expressed their interest in each other by scratching, biting, and kicking, and as adults they marry because of an unplanned pregnancy. Because Tino is going off to war, the pregnancy contrasts Anastacia's Riveter role by suggesting another of the roles for women during the war. Anastacia's daughter's pregnancy signifies that she is a "Victory Girl" ("v-girl") who "pursued sexual relations with servicemen to do their part for the Allied war effort" (Ramírez "Crimes" 14). By being sexually available for a soldier, the daughter embodies women's complicity with the war, and she rebels against her mother's lack of femininity as a worker. The wedding takes place while Tino is on leave; Anastacia's husband gave the daughter his blessing, asking her to be a good wife (58). Anastacia's daughter flaunts her pregnancy, which flies in the face of Ruiz's claim that "autonomy on the part of young women was hard to win in a world where pregnant, unmarried teenagers served as community "examples" of what might happen to you or your daughter if appropriate measures were not taken" (63). Instead of being the "bad," sexually available girl, Anastacia's daughter's sexual transgression is cause for celebration and a return to domesticity. All of these factors point to a continued cycle of domestic violence that blames the woman for her material and physical conditions. In the midst of this pressure, Anastacia realizes that she can never escape. The war machine and the cycle of domestic violence are a part of her life, as they always have been. She must either be a cultural traitor and gender transgressor or a woman, mother, and victim. She cannot reject some elements of femininity without losing her place in the community.

The short story does not idealize the *barrio*, it does not critique the culture of domestic violence, nor does it offer economic mobility and assimilation as a way out. The sacred space of the home, where none of the neighbors will intrude, is a common trope in stories of domestic violence. This narrative goes further though, and makes domestic violence seem erotic, with the final picture of "Anastacia, lying in bed with a pair of black eyes and her hair disheveled" (59). The image of black eyes calls to mind the multiple descriptions of Mexican women's sparkling, flashing, alluring black eyes in popular fiction, but here the description underscores the sexualized construction of violence on Mexican-American women's bodies as abusable and desirable.[11] By blaming women and eroticizing violence against them, this story attempts to relegate Mexican American women to their place within the home and economic structure.

"Las comadres" is a bleak story in its inability to imagine an alternative future for Anastacia, especially in light of her attempts at social and economic mobility. Naomi Quiñonez argues that World War II empowered Mexican American women in unprecedented ways:

> Having experienced greater freedom to make decisions about their lives as autonomous individuals, many Mexican American women gained the skills and confidence to manage and negotiate their personal, social, and economic circumstances. Hence the social agency they acquired during

the war reinforced a sense of independence that held many implications as they entered the postwar period of the 1950s, when the framework for the Chicana feminism of the 1960s would be constructed. (266)

However, this social advancement does not happen for Anastacia and her daughters. The narrative then presents a serious quandary: if working empowered so many Mexican American women, and helped them save money for their daughters to attend college, why does the narrative relegate Anastacia and her daughter to the continued circle of domestic violence? Other critics find this lack of indictment of domestic violence troubling also: "One hopes that Suárez's intentions in "Las Comadres" were to critique the interpersonal relationships fostered by El Hoyo's patriarchal codes, but the text itself offers no alternative or autonomous space for women either within or outside of the community" (Lilley 115). While it is too early for there to be a vast alternative or an autonomous space, I do not agree with Lilley that there is no space left for women; however, they must wrestle agency and space from masculine control through their ability to influence future generations. An alternative reading might suggest that, possibly, with Tino off at war, Anastacia's daughter can make her own mark in the world as an independent woman and single mother. The text cannot support her going to college, but the birth of the "screaming, kicking *chicano*" foreshadows political upheaval in the next generation (58). In this way, the narrative denigrates Anastacia's contribution to her family by suggesting that the possibility for political and social change must come from a male child.

Even though the war itself provided opportunities for women in the workforce and in education, the aftermath of the war created a "patriotic duty" for women to give up those hard-earned places in factories and universities. Servicewomen, beneficiaries of the GI Bill, experienced difficulties in taking advantage of the bill: They did not receive a living allowance for a spouse (like the men did) and the government "had not contemplated providing childcare credits and facilities to student-veterans even though the federal government had made allowances for female workers in defense plants during World War II" (Altschuler and Blumin 123). Furthermore, war widows' average income was 33 dollars a week. Given these conditions, it makes sense that Anastacia's daughter would have had limited opportunity for social mobility after the war. While women's social position had changed, their economic and educational conditions experienced a strong backlash. Perhaps this explains why the hope for the future in this narrative is a "screaming, kicking *chicano*" rather than a Chicana (58). The narrative, written in 1969, ascribes value to the Chicano Movement without recognizing (yet) the contributions Chicanas make via social protest of their own. However, the narrative establishes the possibility for Chicana mother-work in recognizing the impossibility of change without education and economic progress—thereby instilling these values in the next Chicano generation.

These scenes of domestic violence place the blame on women as they define Mexican American women's behavior—impudence, bad housekeeping, and sexual promiscuity—as rationalizations of aggression. Even through violence toward women, the male protagonists cannot halt the changing social mores that World War II have brought. Consequently, Chicanas have emerged, picked themselves up, and have claimed their own agency. Domestic violence in these narratives signals that the patriarchal model of the family cannot hold under looming social pressures. National changes in women's economic and educational conditions are reflected in domestic environments. Even as men writing about domestic violence blamed women for the social conditions surrounding that violence, they inadvertently created a space for female characters to metaphorically pick themselves up, and in the process gain power and agency from their own actions. The implications of this space are endless because even in texts that seem to be misogynistic, women prevail, not through some innate femininity but through cleverness, or sheer will. Indeed, these fictional portrayals of gendered identity during a period of upheaval for the nation and for its citizens enable, albeit unwittingly, critical feminist (re)readings of the texts, pointing to the early stages of what today has become Chicana feminism.

Notes

[1] Chicana feminism is well documented. See Norma Alarcón's "Chicana Feminism: In the Tracks of "The" Native Woman" for a good overview of the founding and history.

[2] A *pocho vendido* is both an Americanized Mexican and a sellout to the American government and its hegemonic culture. As Spencer Herrera explains, "Pochos have been defined as vendidos, inferior, and cultureless. By losing their entire cultural inheritance they have become an extreme form of Mexican, to which Paz warns we can all arrive, a particularly dangerous fate for those Mexicans who become Americanized while living in the United States" (32).

[3] See Ramón Gutiérrez's excellent history of the term in "Internal Colonialism: An American Theory of Race," which explains, "Internal colonialism was a modern capitalist practice of oppression and exploitation of racial and ethnic minorities within the borders of the state characterized by relationships of domination, oppression, and exploitation" (289).

[4] Still in operation, LULAC was one of the first and most influential organizations working for Mexican American civil rights. See https://lulac.org/about/history/.

[5] The Zoot Suit Riots took place in Los Angeles in June 1943, when military and civilians attacked young men wearing zoot suits (a fashion popular among jazz musicians), took their clothes and destroyed them (Acuña). The Pachuco is the spectral lead character in Luis Valdez's play *Zoot Suit*, and he leads Henry through his coming of age in the Zoot Suit Riot and Sleepy Lagoon trial (Ramírez "Saying Nothin'").

[6] And if he does come back, as a member of the Navy specifically, he will be torn with the zoot suit riots that pitted Mexican American young people against the sailors in Los Angeles port.

[7] According to Susan Mettler, "Following World War II, the "Servicemen's Readjustment Act of 1944" – better known as the G.I. Bill – helped returning veterans earn college degrees, train for vocations, support young families, and purchase homes, farms and businesses. Beneficiaries also become more engaged citizens. Compared to veterans who did not use education and training benefits, recipients reported involvements in 50 percent more civic associations and became significantly more politically active. Some joined the Civil Rights movement to expand citizenship for future generations." Suárez certainly became more politically active through his writing.

[8] "Literally translated, comadre and compadre mean co-parent, co-mother, or co-father. Comadres and compadres can refer to the relationship between parents and godparents of a child, to a close friend or confidant, or to a genre of folk tales that relay stories of gossips and braggarts" (Johnson 344).

[9] This woman blaming excuse appears also in *Pocho* when Richard justifies violence against his mother and sisters as a result of their slovenly housekeeping. This "reason" for domestic violence overtly blames women for problems within the home. As part of the domestic sphere, a messy house becomes a symbol for squalor in the nation. Men, and other women, punish women for "allowing" their homes to get out of order.

[10] The impulse to control Anastacia could also reflect allegorically on Chicana feminists as the piece is published in *Con Safos* in 1969 as Chicana feminists were becoming more vocal. As a closing for a letter, *Con Safos* means "with respect" and protects the words from meaning something unintended. Because it is the venue for this story, *Con Safos* allegorically protects Suárez's words from Chicana feminists' deconstruction and charges of misogyny.

[11] Many references, especially in pulp fiction, exist, but see *Empire and the Literature of Sensation* edited by Jesse Alemán and Shelley Streeby for several examples.

Works Cited

Acuña, Rodolfo. *Occupied America: A History of Chicanos*. 4th ed., Longman, 2000.

Alarcón, Norma. "Chicana Feminism: In the Tracks of "The" Native Woman." *Cultural Studies*, vol. 4, no. 3, 1990, pp. 248-256.

Altschuler, Glenn C., and Stuart M. Blumin. *The GI Bill: A New Deal for Veterans*. Oxford UP, 2009.

Alvarez, Alma Rosa. *Liberation Theology in Chicana/o Literature*. Routledge, 2007.

Flores, Maria Eva. "What a Difference a War Makes!" *Mexican Americans & World War II*, edited by Maggie Rivas-Rodriguez, University of Texas Press, 2005, pp. 177-200.

Griswold del Castillo, Richard. "The War and Changing Identities: Personal Transformations." *World War II and Mexican American Civil Rights*, edited by Richard Griswold del Castillo, U of Texas P, 2008, pp. 49-73.

Gutiérrez, Ramón A. "Internal Colonialism: An American Theory of Race." *Du Bois Review*, vol. 1, no. 2, 2004, pp. 281-95.

Herrera, Spencer. "The Pocho Palimpsest in Early 20th Century Chicano Literature from Daniel Venegas to Américo Paredes." *Confluencia,* vol. 26, no. 1, 2010, pp. 21-33.

"History." *lulac.org,* https://lulac.org/about/history/. Accessed 30 March 2021.

Johnson, Leigh. "Comadre/Compadre." *Celebrating Latino Folklore: An Encyclopedia of Cultural Traditions,* edited by María Herrera-Sobek, ABC-CLIO, 2012, pp. 344-345.

Lilley, James D. ""The Short Way of Saying Mexicano:" Patrolling the Borders of Mario Suárez's Fiction," *MELUS,* vol. 26, no.3, 2001, pp. 100-18.

Mettler, Suzanne. "How the G.I. Bill Built the Middle Class and Enhanced Democracy." scholars.org/sites/scholars/files/ssn_key_findings_mettler_on_g i_bill.pdf. Accessed 30 March 2021.

Olguín, B.V. "Barrios of the World Unite!: Regionalism, Transnationalism, and Internationalism in Tejano War Poetry from the Mexican Revolution to World War II." *Left of the Color Line: Race, Radicalism, and Twentieth-Century Literature,* edited by Bill V. Mullen and James Smethurst, U of North Carolina P, 2003, pp. 120-34.

Paredes, Américo. *George Washington Gómez.* Arte Público Press, 1990.

——. *With His Pistol in His Hand: A Border Ballad and Its Hero.* University of Texas Press, 1970.

Pérez, Héctor. "Voicing Resistance on the Border: A Reading of Américo Paredes's *George Washington Gómez,*" *MELUS,* vol. 23, no.1, 1998, pp. 27-48.

Quiñonez, Naomi. "Rosita the Riveter: Welding Tradition with Wartime Transformations." *Mexican Americans and World War II,* edited by Maggie Rivas-Rodriguez, U Texas P, 2005, pp. 245-67.

Ramírez, Catherine S. "Crimes of Fashion: The Pachuca and Chicana Style Politics." *Meridians: Feminism, Race, Transnationalism,* vol. 2, no.2, 2002, pp. 1-35.

——. "Saying "Nothin':" Pachucas and the Language of Resistance." *Frontiers: A Journal of Women Studies,* vol. 27, no. 3, 2006, pp. 1-33.

Ruiz, Vicki. *From Out of the Shadows: Mexican Women in Twentieth-Century America.* Oxford UP, 1998.

Saldívar, Ramón. *Chicano Narrative: The Dialectics of Difference.* U of Wisconsin P, 1990.

Sorensen, Leif. "The Anti-*corrido* of *George Washington Gómez:* A Narrative of Emergent Subject Formation." *American Literature: A Journal of Literary History, Criticism, and Bibliography,* vol. 80, no.1, 2008, pp. 111-40.

Steele, Richard. "Mexican Americans in 1940: Perceptions and Conditions." *World War II and Mexican American Civil Rights,* edited by Richard Griswold del Castillo, U of Texas P, 2008, pp. 7-18.

Suárez, Mario. "Las comadres." *Chicano Sketches.* U of Arizona P, 2004, pp. 55-59.

Vallejos, Thomas. "Ritual Process and the Family in the Chicano Novel." *MELUS,* vol. 10, no. 4, 1983, pp. 5-16.

Velikova, Roumiana. "Américo Paredes' *George Washington Gómez* and U.S. Patriotic Mythology." *Recovering the U.S. Hispanic Literary Heritage Volume*

V, edited by Kenya Dworkin y Méndez and Agnes Lugo-Ortiz, Arte Público, 2006, pp. 35-54.

Villarreal, José Antonio. *Pocho*. Anchor, 1959.

Chapter 2

Poetic Masculinity:
Poetry as Counterhegemonic Subjectivity
in Ricardo Castillo

Fernando Hernández Jáuregui

Cal State University

When Ricardo Castillo's (born in Guadalajara, Mexico in 1954) first poetry book *El pobrecito señor X (Poor Little Mr. X)* was published in 1976, it caused such a stir that it was, according to famed Mexican literary critic Evodio Escalante:

> ...as if some barbaric boulder had been thrown onto the dinner table. The bewildered dinner guests having to scramble away to grumble about their soiled suits or to praise the sudden appearance of this 'noble savage' who was returning an anti-academic furor to poetry, a critical and completely anti-Culturan causticity, a bitter and liberating vulgarity that was opening new paths for the poetry of our country" (quoted in Dávila, 390).

Culteranismo refers to an aesthetic movement during the Baroque period in Spain. It takes its name from the term *culto*, which means learned or cultured. It is characterized by an ornate, opaque style that emphasized highly intricate syntax, neologisms and high-brow terminology, often to describe everyday objects or mundane occurrences. Its main proponent was the Spanish poet, Luis de Góngora.

Castillo's fame—if we can talk about fame in reference to a poet—is still largely due to that first poetry book and its self-deprecating, colloquial, even vulgar, language that was, or is still, a major departure from the aesthetics of the well-wrought verse and the universal outlook of most Mexican poetry. However, circumscribing the value of Castillo's poetry to its initial reception—to its novelty—is a major disservice to it as it forecloses other interpretative possibilities. In the same vein, the fact that the protagonist, the poetic subject of Castillo's first book (and most of his subsequent books) is a teenager, or very young adult, lends itself to the poetry being misread as simply juvenile and as inherently limited in its literary capital. However, it would be reductive to ascribe the life struggles of the protagonist solely to his age, to see it simply as a transitory state to be overcome in the natural progression of his life and the process of maturity. More than an organic developmental stage, it represents a rejection of the status quo, one that will ultimately be an affirmation of an alternative way of being. As such, it represents an ethics and a paradigm that are averse to the prevailing sociocultural structures—notably, hegemonic masculinity. The young man perceives that society wants to turn him into a vacuous consumer-citizen and a *cabrón*—a macho whose self-worth is contingent upon the sexual conquering of women and his violent imposition on other men.

The poetic subject in Castillo goes beyond this dichotomy by presenting poetry as a third space with its own outlook, ethics and sociality. Poetry is presented as a performative experience of authentic self-affirmation and a place for constructing social relations based not on economic transactions or violent imposition but on a deeper intersubjective exchange. Poetic activity is presented as a counterhegemonic practice in which social disenchantment becomes a poetic enchantment. Within the realm of the aesthetic, within the possibilities it provides for a different way of being in the world, the poetic voice finds an anti-hegemonic subjectivity we might designate as *poetic masculinity*. While *poetic masculinity* is not a panacea, it represents the possibility to constitute new forms of social relations and a validation of a non-macho or non-alpha male masculinity.

In the first part of this essay, "Guadalajara, Guadalajara...The Most Mexican Soul," I establish the context and salient characteristics of the hegemonic masculinity that is thrust upon the poetic subject. In "Mama Lupe and Papa Guille," I focus on the poetic subject's parents as key figures in the process of identity formation. At the same time, I point to instances in which the poetic subject struggles to resist the subjection process that would render him an alienated consumer of Modernity and national stereotypes, and a reproducer of macho violence.[1] The refusal to conform ostensibly renders X, the poetic subject, a *pendejo* (a loser), but he is able to conform a space of authentic self-affirmation through poetry, which I examine in "Non-Alpha Male Lyricism." In the section, "Defeat as Ethics; Song as Triumph," I explain how his status as a loser constitutes an ethical stand and how poetry allows for a positive project that counters the void left by his rejection of societal norms and expectations. Finally, in the last section, "Heterosexual Desire and Feminist Criticism," I analyze poems that mark the limits of *poetic masculinity*, while looking more closely at X's gender identity and the representation of women in Castillo's poetry.

Guadalajara, Guadalajara...The Most Mexican Soul

The first poem of *Pobrecito* is a quasi-confession in which he quickly sketches out his home life. [2]

> I was born in Guadalajara.
> My first parents were Mama Lupe and Papa Guille.
> I grew up like a clover,
> like a nickel, like a tortilla.
> I grew up with reality contradicted by my gut,
> with corniness in the dressing room of love.
> Mom would cry within the corners of the house
> her rage amidst darkness, a groping violence afloat.
> My dad dying as he stares into my eyes,
> dying in the slow-motion of the passing years,
> demanding more from life.
> And then grandfather's blindness, my brothers,
> the sexual neglect of my female cousins,
> the neighborhood in shadows, and me,
> always looking, always so melodramatic.
> I've never been good for nothing.
> I've done nothing but keep time as it ticks down to annihilation.
> As someone once told me: I'm Fucking Worthless. (19)

The poem, titled "Autogol" ("Own Goal"), which in soccer parlance is a goal scored against one's own team, establishes several important themes that will continue throughout *Pobrecito* and an important part of Castillo's work, particularly the poetic voice as disenfranchised—socially, sexually and culturally. He stands looking at his family and seems to be little more than a witness to his own sad life without the necessary agency for self-determination. His self-image is an internalization of his familial and societal surroundings, and the discourses which try to mold him into a particular type of individual. The system of values imposed on the speaker is easily deduced from the poem: emotions and sexuality are repressed, they should remain unspoken; stoicism should prevail—thus emotions happen *within the corners of the house, amidst darkness,* gropingly and within the silent stare of the father. The acknowledgment of emotional life will cause one to be designated as *melodramatic*—it is not difficult to imagine that the poetic voice is deemed by family, and even friends, as such, precisely because he expresses the unsaid, because he sees the intra and interpersonal tensions and acknowledges them. The life depicted in the poem is one of individual isolation, of closed-off, private suffering and suppressed communication. Yet, it is noteworthy that the dramas and events of his family members are not represented in the poem; the reasons behind their lives of frustration are not depicted, the anecdotal is left out, remaining unexpressed. This anti-expressive element establishes one of the anchors in what will be a fundamental dichotomy in Castillo's poetry: repression vs. expression. As we will see, the poetic subject generally moves from (emotional-sexual) repression to (poetic) expression.

In another poem that has become iconic within Mexican poetry, "El que no es cabrón no hombre" ("If You're Not a *Cabrón* You're Not a Man"), it is even more evident how societal discourses imposed upon the poetic subject are simultaneously internalized and rejected by him. The fact that the title is in quotation marks is important because it signals that those words, and the ideological viewpoint it espouses, do not belong to the speaker. The term *cabrón* requires some explanation as it has multiple meanings. Generally, the definitions associated with *cabrón* are negative—both in Spain and Latin America. The Real Academia Española—the institution that attempts to govern the correct use of Spanish and manages the official Spanish dictionary—defines *cabrón* as a person who is "bothersome or plays bad tricks," as a man "who suffers the infidelity of his wife, and especially if he consents to it", "a person of ill character," and even as the devil himself, but the term is also defined as "an experienced and astute person" ("cabrón"). The most productive way of understanding the term *cabrón*, however, is by reviewing what Octavio Paz wrote about another word that he saw as a fundamental to Mexican identity—though in reality, we can say that what he is really describing is male Mexican identity or masculinity. In any case, Paz describes the verb *chingar* as "to do violence to another." He goes on to say:

> In Mexico the word [*chingar*] has innumerable meanings. It is a magical word: a change of tone, a change of inflection, is enough to change its meaning...But in this plurality of meanings the ultimate meaning always contains the idea of aggression, whether it is the simple act of molesting, pricking or censuring, or the violent act of wounding or killing. The verb denotes violence, an emergence from oneself to penetrate another by force. It also means to injure, to lacerate, to violate—bodies, souls, objects — and to destroy. [3] (76-77)

While the sociological validity and anthropological soundness of Paz's observations have been questioned, his book is undeniably still a point of reference when reflecting on Mexican identity.[4] More importantly, for our analysis, Paz's essay makes visible the subtext of Castillo's poetry—specifically, the discursive axes of Mexican imaginary at play in Castillo's use of the figure of the *cabrón*. We can understand the *cabrón* as the one who wields the action of *chingar*, the one who possesses the bodies of women and vanquishes, humiliates, male adversaries. The poem we've just referenced begins with a statement "If You're Not a *Cabrón* You're Not a Man" and ends with the following acknowledgement, "[I'm] such a *pendejo*, such a long way from being a *cabrón*."[5] The *pendejo* is the figure of the one who is duped, he is "dumb," "stupid,",a "coward," "pusillanimous," as the Real Academia Española defines the term ("pendejo"). In contrast to the *chingón*, the *pendejo*, also present in this poem as the poetic voice's assumed identity, represents the opposite pole within the spectrum of Mexican masculinity. He would be the dummy, the fool who is less of a man and whose lesser manhood is evidenced in his capitulation to the superior *chingón*. These are the two models of masculinity offered up by the poetic voice's surroundings. Again, Paz's contrasting of the *chingón* with the *chingón's* victim is insightful.[6]

> The person who suffers this action [of *chingar*] is passive, inert and open, in contrast to the active, aggressive and closed person who inflicts it. The *chingón* is the macho, the male; he rips open the *chingada*, the female, who is pure passivity, defenseless against the exterior world. The relationship between them is violent, and it is determined by the cynical power of the first and the impotence of the second. The idea of violence rules darkly over all the meanings of the word, and the dialectic of the "closed" and the "open" thus fulfills itself with an almost ferocious precision. (77)

Paz argues that a key component of Mexicanness can be traced to the historical figure of La Malinche, an indigenous woman who was used by the Spanish conquistador Hernán Cortés as an interpreter and who played a vital role in the defeat of the Mexicas, or Aztecs, as they are better known. Doña Marina, as she was referred to in Spanish, became the lover, and ostensibly, the wife of Cortés. She is seen as a traitor in Mexico but paradoxically also as a woman who was violently taken, like the land and possessions of the ancient Mexicans, by Cortés. The offspring of La Malinche and Cortés are symbolically, if not historically, the first mestizos and first Mexicans. But just as important, Mexicans would be the byproduct of rape—not of a loving symbiosis or synthesis but of sexual violence. According to Paz, this violent history is ingrained in Mexicans, who are also conflicted by the quasi-prostitute status of their symbolic mother who paradoxically gave herself willingly/was forcibly taken for the sexual benefit of the invader. La Malinche is the original *la chingada*, the fucked one—and here we have the most apt translation of *chingar* meaning to fuck, to screw and to screw over. Again, Paz:

The word has sexual connotations but it is not a synonym for the sexual act: one may *chingar* a woman without actually possessing her. And when it does allude to the sexual act, violation or deception gives it a particular shading. The man who commits it never does so with the consent of the *chingada. Chingar*, then, is to do violence to another. The verb is masculine, active, cruel: it stings, wounds, gashes, stains.[7] (77)

While Paz's characterization of the passive and impotent person who suffers the act of *chingar* undoubtedly refers to women—*las chingadas*, the ones who are fucked are women—it nevertheless functions as an accurate description of the poetic voice. The notion of *chingar*, of taking advantage, of screwing over the other, permeates all of society including male-male relations. The poetic subject, X, is continually in a subordinate position, unable to take control of his life or to materialize his desires. He states: "luck...has finally sent me off to go fuck myself"[8] (25). The city he lives in is presented as a hostile place that "doesn't lend a hand, doesn't open its legs, it kicks / like toy players in a foosball game"[9] (25). The urban space, which might otherwise present an opportunity for social interaction, ends up being a dead-end, another closed-off space that intensifies the isolation of his family life. This is seen in subsequent works such as *La Oruga* (*The Larva*, 1978), in which he reiterates the antagonistic relationship with the city: "what you are looking for is not in the city / because she only wants your blood and your energy for its nourishment / and waste"[10] (51). The city does not provide any viable alternatives to alpha male masculinity because it is the product of its vacuous fantasies of modernity: "what did they achieve what did they gain by planting their stupid / dreams / among heavy machinery"[11] (49). The possibility of fulfillment by stepping away from the domain of the familial is foreclosed by the emergence of the city as a space of repression and exploitation, "and who determines where your body should be with its vitality / or its sorrows...there is no possibility where the combustion of diesel / searches out the sky"[12] (49). X's experience in the city only serves to confirm his doubts about the possibility of fulfillment within societal expectations:

> and of course you're going to doubt about having anything other than
> garbage in your head
> garbage that image the city demands from you in exchange for who
> knows what."[13] (50)

The city is the manifestation of political power players and businessmen who think their desks are "worth more than a square / meter of desert", and whom X rejects stating, "I detest your golden pens and fat fingers / that do the signing"[14] (51).

Although in some verses taken from *Pobrecito*, the city is presented as female, it is not so unequivocally, as at various other times its characterization is that of the male *chingón*—so much so, that even in its tranquility it is aggressive: "The evening calmness of six o'clock hits me in the ribs / with six tolls of the bell in all its might. / This tranquility is a baton at the ready for any task"[15] (25). Serenity, usually a synonym of peace and security, is here presented as a threat, as an always available violence. This makes sense if we see it through the lens of the antagonisms that animate Castillo's poetics: the institutional vs the individual, repression vs expression, societal/cultural mores versus vital energy/sexuality, and the dichotomy presented by Paz of the closed/male vs the open/female: "The idea of violence rules darkly over all the meanings of the word [*chingar*], and the dialectic of the 'closed' and the 'open' thus fulfills itself with an almost ferocious precision" (21), writes Paz. The poetic voice makes himself vulnerable by opening-up, by acknowledging an affective and emotional dimension not usually made public. His lamentations and his poems are evidence of that realm. Castillo's poetry thus constitutes a challenge to the macho or alpha-male model of masculinity prevalent in the Mexican imaginary. His behavior undermines the hegemonic masculinity of Mexico by aligning himself with the open and the vulnerable, with the expressive, with the non-violent and even impotent—socially, culturally, economically, and romantically.

Almost the entire book of *Pobrecito* constitutes the reconstruction of the matrix of discourses that would have X be an unthinking, emotionally repressed womanizer and a passive consumer of mundane goods and nationalist culture. The opening poem is already a salvo against the most folkloric of national imaginaries when he qualifies his being born in Guadalajara as "an own goal"—a mistake, a self-inflicted wound. The poem reads like a confession because for X being from Mexico's second-largest city is shameful. Evidently, there is nothing objectively wrong with being from Guadalajara—or any other place—but it is not hard to understand where he is coming from. Guadalajara is the capital of the state of Jalisco, birthplace to two of Mexico's most iconic goods: mariachis and tequila. These goods are part of a national imaginary that includes brave men on horseback, *charros*, and a recalcitrant, belligerent attitude reflected in countless *ranchera* songs and the saying "Jalisco never loses...and when it does it takes by force." The city is continually described as *colonial*, a reference to a period of Mexican and Latin American history that comprises the arrival of the Spanish up to the independence movements of the second decade of the nineteenth Century, but it is also a euphemism for white/European. Like most of the western and northern parts of Mexico, there are no major remnants of indigenous cities in Jalisco and the version of national pride associated with Guadalajara is clearly mestizo and not pre-Colombian. The very name of the city is a transplantation of the name of a city in Spain and not of indigenous Mexican origin. The term *colonial* also implies provincialism, fervent Catholicism, and a general ideological and political conservatism, and even backwardness. During the first half of the twentieth Century, after the Mexican Revolution, there was another major military campaign between absolutist government secularists and pro-Catholic militants, called the Cristero War or *La Cristiada*—as labeled by French historian Jean Meyer. The pro-church forces were centered in the state of Jalisco, and Catholicism continues today to have an important stronghold over the entire region. These focal points are always contrasted with Mexico City, which represents the modern urban center; cosmopolitan, progressive and forward-thinking. All this makes Guadalajara not just a concrete place but a paradigm of Mexican national culture and life.[16] Thus "Guadalajara" can also be understood as a chronotope associated with a particularly conservative, folkloric, and provincial way of life. These are the sociocultural referents that X is born into and it is those that he is responding to and rejecting when he characterizes his autobiographical sketch as an "own goal." X is aware of the value system implicit in the designation "to be from Guadalajara;" it is that same system that labels him as being "worth shit."

Mama Lupe and Papa Guille

The transmission of sociocultural values begins at home with one of the pillars of ideological formation: the Family. In the poem "My Mother and the Vegetables" the poetic voice tells us that his mother and the vegetables:

> gives advice about love to my sister
> and about the art and vocation of wasting away life, and a certain way
> of making her understand that whatever happens she should never ever
> open her eyes, nor her smile, to the unknown.[17] (27)

This is a devastatingly simple way of showing how the acrid attitude of self-limitation and defeatism is perpetuated from one generation to the next. The mother tells her daughter to be afraid of the unknown, to say "no" to new experiences, to reject life while preparing lunch or dinner. "As if corny sentimentality," continues the voice, "were more important than those moments / in which the testicles swell just from the desire to live"[18] (27). The poem begins with the verse "My mother in the kitchen." with period at the end; it is not qualified nor subordinated, as such, it is a general statement that speaks to her perpetual condition as the traditional mother. "My mother in the kitchen."; a statement easy to imagine that the poetic subject has made or thought countless times and an image, a condition, that the mother transmits metonymically and discursively to her daughter through their daily domestic tasks. "The maternal connotation of the domestic space ... configures the place of the feminine as an environment of crushing burden that turns the subject into the object of others' actions, which the subject suffers with passive resignation ... The house is the space of the mother's hurt and rage, and it is through her that the family's legacy is transmitted" (Stellini 7). In another poem, the speaker asks: "What's the use of so much good advice like mom used to do?"[19] (23). It is a poem that illustrates the forces of socialization and subjection that operate in and through mundane acts, and that the poetic subject finds himself trying to ward off. The fact that the poem is concentrated on the two females of the house is significant because it counters the notion that the poetry book is about a self-centered teenager who is oblivious to others. It also generalizes what X is going through, establishing the tribulations he describes as something having to do with the social order and not as something of psychic origin. It is quite surprising just how explicitly the poetry book represents the discourses that try to inhere and compromise X's subjectivity. Even "Guadalajara," which I had earlier represented as a paradigm and a chronotope, may be said to encapsulate or synthesize a series of conservative discourses on what it means to be Mexican, to be a good Catholic, to be a man, to be a woman. It is a symbol of a traditionalist outlook and sociocultural conservatism that transcend the vicissitudes of the poetic subject. As Cristina Stellini writes, in one of the few essays dedicated to Castillo's work, "In the gallery of pictures belonging to his familial and social past—the home, the barrio, the city—which intermix with the I of the sentence, the contours of his individual identity become blurred and confused with the place where the vicissitudes of a collective story are told" (6). The references to "neighbors," specific spaces of Guadalajara, his neighborhood, and recognizable figures within the urban landscape, such as the ice-cream man and the seller of jicamas, reinforce the notion that his story is imbued within a specific spatial-temporal context and within a matrix of social discourses.

It is, nevertheless, the domestic space that constitutes the main generator and replicator of discourses. In "El Vecinito" ("The Little Neighbor"), X states: "yesterday my dad looked at me in terror / yesterday my mom spoke to me about God and of the respect that I owe to / myself"[20] (29). It would not be surprising to think that what his mother tells him is similar to what she tells his sister, but for him it is about him *choosing* not to debase himself—through masturbation, womanizing, drug use—while for his sister is about not being *duped* into debasing herself—being tricked into sex, drug use or love, through the oratory of men. There is a clearly defined system of family values and a corresponding discourse that prioritizes tranquility—stability, safety, and stoicism. In the second poem of *Pobrecito*, X says:

in my family
we all take things in stride:
'Dad and mom have died already.'
'My socks have holes in them.'
'I ate a fly.'
'Everything is so expensive.'
'We're going to die now.'[21] (20)

In another poem X states:

My father loves us,
my mother loves us
because we've been able to be a united family, lovers
of tranquility.[22] (32)

In both poems, the family's official discourse and outlook is put in tension with the speaker's liveliness and desire for something else. In the first, he explicitly contradicts the ethics of tranquility espoused by his family, "I think it'd be good to be less civil / and start a great big scandal"[23] (20). And in the second poem, X states:

But right now it's ten at night,
now that as usual no one has nothing to do
I propose closing the doors and windows
and opening the gas valve.[24] (32)

A third poem, aptly titled "Christmas Card" (a space where families represent themselves as impeccably happy, united, and fulfilled), breaks the nihilism of the previous verses by giving us a glimpse of what X would affirm in place of his family's sedated way of being, when he urges:

To have someone throw over a cliff their infamous coin of a face,
...and put love on stage...
To have someone live, to have someone die at night
...is like making Santa Claus fart
like breaking the balance and prosperity of the New Year for
the pretty families.[25] (33)

There is an opposition between the superficiality of customs, traditions, the image of a perfect family life, and the will to live and to love. As can be anticipated from the verse urging for someone to "place love on stage," love and the desire for the other are at the core of X's preoccupations, of what he is working out, (re)configuring or renouncing. However, the primary impulse is not to construct but to reject; X has only a vague idea of what he seeks and his energy is directed towards criticizing and repudiating what society continues to instill in him, principally through his family. A major element in what is rejected centers on the figure of the father and the paradigm of Mexican masculinity that he embodies.

As would be expected in a tale that depicts the landscape of a young person's world still centered around his domestic life, the figure of the father occupies an important place. In this case, the father is a drunk who is both uncommunicative and a whirlwind of alcoholic song and rage. X identifies him as "Señor Guillermo, Cabrón" in the poem that has him as the central figure, aptly titled "Papa Guille", and in a very symbolic way describes his song as being "that of the drunk cock that gives jolts and gives life"[26] (21). Having the *verga* (cock)—a colloquial, and to some vulgar, way of saying penis—as the characteristic element of his father's song points to the notion of a hyper-masculine identity that is a performance staged for the outside—X's father deploys his impassioned song when inebriated in different bars of the city. The difference in the way of addressing him, "Papá Guille" versus "Señor Guillermo," point to two distinct incarnations or versions of his father. The first way of addressing him is much more familiar and loving, while the second is formal and cold, clearly associated with hierarchical systems of interactions. The "Señor Guillermo" is both ceremonial and bureaucratic, and points to the image of the father as authority—not as deriving from organic respect but as imposed power. Evidently, this along with the presence of the phallus (*verga*/cock), makes a Lacanian reading almost obligatory. However, as might have been already sensed from my framing of *Pobrecito* in terms of discourses related to the subjection process, I am partial to a more poststructuralist approach because it is a tool more attuned to Castillo's poetics. The emotional tribulations of X and his father are psychological processes that are always already invested in the social.[27] In the case of his father's neurosis (X calls him "the Impeccable Rider of Neurosis"[28]) it is derived from a social lack and driven by societal norms and expectations. His *phallus song* is a song of pain—one that originates in "love and loneliness that would gallop around him within a parallel / circumference." He "understood," X says of his father, "that there was no other vocation in the world / than that of being a demon"[29] (21). Being a demon becomes a vocation—a calling and a job—a recognizable role, a partially socially-sanctioned outlet for his unmet emotional needs. The fact that being a demon is classified as a vocation underscores its structural character and social viability—a vocation being the intersection of personal drives and aptitudes, and collective roles and needs. Although neurosis was eliminated in 1980 from the *Diagnostic and Statistical Manual of Mental Disorders*, contrasting it with psychosis underscores the importance of its social aspect, as in the person experiencing neurosis still maintains a link to reality, in contrast with psychosis in which there is a break with reality.

X's father is a tragic figure and a tyrant, but he is also pathetic: a caricature of the macho Mexican male, the *charro cantor* or singing cowboy who drinks and sings about failed love and life's injustices. X describes how his father would run into the street naked, darting cars and slinging crap at them and how, in the end, he ends up saying "I'm terminal" before dying at a bar named *The Revolution*[30] (22). The bar's name and the scatological nature of the father's neurosis accentuate the difference between the idealized male figure of the war hero and the sadly absurd image of his drunken father. His death in *The Revolution* parodies the national hero of contemporary Mexico whose identity and imaginary are rooted in that military conflict. The Mexican Revolution is the most important event in contemporary Mexican history and is foundational to Mexican identity, political discourse, national imaginary and visual arts. Its importance is reflected in the visual representation that artists such as muralist Diego Rivera made of it. Its protagonists, such as Emiliano Zapata, Pancho Villa and Francisco I. Madero, are icons still admired by the Mexican people. The epic quality of the Mexican Revolution contrasts with the drunken idleness and mundaneness of the space of the father's last hours. The father is not the all-seeing, all-powerful Law that imposes its will but a caricature of hegemonic masculinity of modern Mexico. In his degraded, alienated state, X's father is more a byproduct of toxic masculinity, the recipient of its harmful effects, the incarnate future of what awaits X if he were to follow his father's and his family's path.

The toxicity of this closed-off, affectively repressed masculinity is articulated in a well-known Latin-American poem by the Uruguayan poet Alfonsina Storni, "Peso ancestral." In it the poetic subject is told by an unknown interlocutor, "my father did not cry /...my grandfather did not cry" and then the poetic voice states, "in saying this a tear sprouted from you / and fell into my mouth; more venom / I have never drunk in a glass so small"[31] (Storni). The repression of affection in males becomes an intergenerational sadness that then becomes venom for the woman who opens up to the repressed and, ultimately, depressed male. This stoic depression in males transforms into violence against females. In the case of X's family, there is no physical violence that we witness but the same dynamic of male depression is apparent as well as family dysfunction. The "groping violence afloat" associated with X's mother in "Own Goal" and his dad's throwing of crap speak to an underlying volatility that permeates every member of the family.

Non-Alpha Male Lyricism

The discourses that penetrate and regulate the family, posit X as a failed male, a *pendejo*, unable to find any economic, social or sexual agency. The poetic voice meekly assumes this imposed moniker almost as a symptom of his inability to formulate an effective counterargument to that of the *cabrón* vs *pendejo* dichotomy. The reluctant acceptance by X of his status as a *pendejo* belies his search for something more. It is not until he assumes the identity of a poet that he is able to gain any sort of foothold in self-determination and posit poetry as a counterhegemonic discourse. In "The Poet of the Plaza," the poetic voice assumes an ethical-political stance in announcing that he is a conscientious poet and that, as such, he must make his poetry a publicly available resource. In reality, it's not *his* poetry that he wishes to put to use for his fellow city-dwellers, but his ability to write, to do poetry. This is significant because X does not assume the position of authorial/authoritative voice but rather that of a subordinate transcriber. What he values is not his voice (his point of view and subjectivity), but the capacity that allows for a saying, an expression, and a communication. The image of the poet, sitting with a tiny desk in the public plaza, recalls the image of professional scribes that can sometimes still be found in Mexico and other Latin American countries, who type letters and various documents for those who do not have the means to write for themselves. The poet, then, is closer to this mundane worker of words than to the image of the poet as a seer or a lightning rod for divine inspiration. Within the poetry of Castillo, the image of the poet as a sensitive soul who masterfully shares his affective world or wisely turns mundane images and events into insightful perspective, is upended through humor and self-deprecation. Just as *Pobrecito* subverted the solemnity of Mexican poetry, it undermines the lyric as founded on a universal poetic subject, of a subject capable of expressing a universalizing outlook. Stellini summarizes this as "the demystification of the character of the poet" (2). This is realized so well in Castillo, that his poetry, after its initial attraction as a novelty of youthful rebellion, has been mostly ignored, dismissed as the lamentations of an overgrown teenager. As the poet and critic from Guadalajara, Luis Vicente de Aguinaga states, "it's a fact that such a reputation as an angry young man ended up tarnishing the correct reading of that book [*Pobrecito*] and that of those that came after" (de Aguinaga). While de Aguinaga does not say what that "correct reading" is, it is clear that for certain critics, *Pobrecito* lacks literary capital because its poetic subject is embodied and contingent and, as such, lacks the credibility of the universal subject. Castillo's and X's loci of enunciation are outside the domain of power—they are to a large degree, and to a significant majority, not worth listening to. This constitutes another step away from the adoption or acceptance of the masculine as the knowing and speaking subject par excellence.

It is from this locus of enunciation that X, as a poet in the diegesis of the poem, decides to install himself in the plaza sitting before a desk ready to write poems for his fellow city dwellers. He tells us that he has had only one client whom he hopes to have helped to "find a better solution than suicide"[32] (30). The man tells him, "mister poet, write a poem about a sad *pendejo.*" "His bitterness made me make faces," he says, and then X, as a poet, writes: "'there are no sad people who are *pendejos*' / and we left to get drunk"[33] (30). With this simple and brief statement, the poetic voice disarticulates the binomial structure *sadness/pendejo*, in which emotions such as sadness are equated with weakness and unmanliness. In doing so, the feelings of unbelonging, inadequacy and isolation are validated and serve as the foundational elements in a new type of community. The fact that two men decide to get drunk in the face of emotional turmoil is far from revolutionary, and plays into the commonplace image of men repressing their emotions through alcohol. It also parallels the emotionally charged excursions of X's father into the local bars as a ubiquitous but destructive way of coping with his overwhelming loneliness and alienation. It is also true, however, that the connection the men make is one based on emotional empathy that puts the affective at the forefront—an approach wholly absent in the interpersonal interactions of the people that surround the poetic voice. The interaction between these men contrasts greatly with the logic of violence that underpins the relational approach crystallized in the notion of *chingar*. The fact that the (only) person who requests a poem is suicidal underscores the notion that poetry is an appropriate space for confronting issues such as mental illness and psychological strife—not so much as an individual activity that keeps the personal personal, but as a space where the personal becomes collective. The lyric becomes a public space for the revealing of the afflicted self, subverting and going beyond the notion of lyricism as merely or purely an expression of the subjective.

The possibility of a sociality based on personal traumas and fears—of the emotional and affective world we live in private—is a radical departure from the discourses present in the society of Castillo's poetry. The homosocial bonding it represents is also significant when we recall the development of this trope in Mexican literature. In *Mexican Masculinities*, Robert McKee Irwin makes the argument that in nineteenth-century Mexican literature, male homosocial bonding was the key to the formation of a national imaginary community, as opposed to the heterosexual romances proper to the national literatures of other Latin American countries, according to the thesis presented by Doris Sommer in *Foundational Fictions*. By the middle of the twentieth century, however, McKee Irwin argues, homosexuality had entered the national conscience of Mexico as a sexual practice inherent to certain individuals, and as a category with which to group those who participated in those sexual acts. The paradox is that while homosexual sex was taken as a sign of categorical, or even ontological, difference, homosexual men could influence ("pervert") their heterosexual counterparts into participating in this essentializing practice. Homosocial activities, previously praised as edifying for the elemental role they played in the formation of a national community, were now seen with suspicion as they carried the risk of being nothing more than a front for homosexual activities. This so-called *homosexual panic* derived from the scandal that happened after police raided a party of only men, of which about half were dressed in women's clothing. This historical event is posited as the entrance of homosexuality into the national consciousness of Mexico. Since then, McKee Irwin argues, relations between men had to be represented in literature as overtly antagonistic as proof of their non-homosexual nature. A man had to be violent in relation to another and so, in general, within Mexican literature there comes to be an absence of solidarity, friendship, love, and loyalty among men. McKee Irwin's description of the evolution of masculinity in Mexico and its literature dovetails with Paz's characterization of relations among men in Mexico as necessarily violent. What McKee Irwin's study also does well is to historicize Paz's assertions on Mexican identity and masculinity, presenting these concepts as shifting, contingent, and non-essential.

In any case, the fact that two men in Castillo's poem bond over their respective emotional vulnerabilities—their non-macho sensibilities and affective milieu—is significant in that it goes against the status quo of male relations within the literature and national imaginary of Mexico, as described, respectively, by McKee Irwin and Paz. It constitutes an opening for a different way of being in the world and of conceptualizing masculinity and male-to-male relations. The community of the two men does not expand nor develop into a stable structure as it is limited to just one poem. However, its negation of sadness as being equivalent to being a *pendejo*—"there are no sad people who are *pendejos*"—is a vindication of male feelings and a disavowal of the non-macho male as simply a *pendejo*. It subverts the rigidity of hegemonic masculinity that would disqualify any non-macho male as a *pendejo*, creating a space to imagine a different type of masculinity.

Defeat as Ethics; Song as Triumph

While *pendejo* is no longer completely accepted by X as an apt description of himself as a sensitive young man that doesn't conform to the image of masculinity that is expected of him, a key aspect of him can still be labeled as defeatist. From the opening poem in which he consents to the judgement that "I'm worth shit" to his lamentations of not being able to find a space in which "to be okay;" in Castillo's performance works in collaboration with the musician Gerardo Enciso, X is constantly presented as displaced, a person estranged from his surroundings, unable to comply with others' expectations or to fulfill his own desires for companionship, well-being and love. His inadequacy materializes in the image of the larva (which is the title of his second poetry book, *La Oruga*), a non-human species in a transitory state. It is noteworthy that the third and fourth poetry books by Castillo also have titles that include non-human species: *Cienpiés tan ciego* (*Centipede so blind*) (1989) and *Nicolás, el camaleón* (*Nicholas, the chameleon*) (1989). The title, *The Larva/La oruga*, does not literally correlate with the figure of the poetic subject as it is once again a young man, this time angry at the vacuity of his being and his surroundings. The book begins with him descending a bus, talking in second person— presumably to himself—about walking the city without a "fixed destiny / because you have to ask yourself two or three questions / that you can't even define" (49). The book ends with a very different scene than the urban ones that are ubiquitous in *Pobrecito* and in the first part of *La Oruga*—it is constituted by a dystopian landscape with "Chaos having blown down the ruins of man"[34] (66). In *La Oruga*, the tone of disempowerment continues and the repressive nature of society (its need to form consumers and compliant citizens) is evident to the poetic subject who laments:

> what's the use of walking and walking
> trying to gain strength and health
> if they say you won't get anywhere
> if you don't participate if you don't collaborate
> in the urban and fatal achievements of growing like a bladder
> like a toad bursting into a citizen that peruses
> the sales on a given Sunday."[35] (50)

The dystopian reality at the end of *La Oruga* continues in *Nicolás, el camaleón*, retaking the urban and contemporary context of most of Castillo's poetry. The poetry book tells the tale of Nicolás/Nicholas, a young man who has become addicted to heroin. At first instance, it is a scathing condemnation of a young man for his apparently inherent flaws:

> The final drop has fallen, Nicholas,
> you're now the witness that accuses you,
> not the ship that wrecked, but the one unworthy
>   of ever knowing the sea;
> the sea was for you nothing more than a personal torment,

a life sentence that you never considered just.
But the sentence, Nicholas,
was chosen by you when you were nothing more than a small
    sphere of living substance;
ill-fated the moment the egg allowed you in
ill-fated the moment you made it to paradise, when everything
    was already taken,
the only thing left for you was an egocentric brain, an insecure
    heart,
a badly used body that you've never made your own.
Who told you to have a nervous system, to make your residence
    in a stomach that churns and travels,
poisoned by memories and absurd desires.
And don't, don't talk to me about love, about good intentions,
those were just the worms that made your cadaver
    seem alive. [36] (32)

Thus, the pessimism of *Pobrecito*, his calling for ending it all by opening the gas valve, crystallizes in Nicholas' nihilism and total alienation. Throughout Castillo's work we find this defeatist tone—a mixture of cynicism, hopelessness and grief. To a large degree this anguish is the characteristic element of what is Castillo's most important work, *Es la calle, honda...*, along with *Pobrecito*—a performative collaboration with Gerardo Enciso. In that work, which was released as a CD in 1992[37], we can hear Castillo's voice lament and singsong verses such as "cemetery within the haze is my life without a path, a steep incline of a street that leads to nowhere...a cruel stabbing to the back of God[38] ... I see my life like a disarray that is not worthy of cleaning up", "subtract my illusions from the sea, today only the desert is capable of moving me a bit, so big and so alone, like some remote image of myself"[39] (Enciso). Immediately, after those opening verses Enciso sings, "I make songs to survive, I don't know how to do anything but sing, I have a rock n' roll band and the truth is I'm doing really bad because I don't have a thing, I don't have a love or anything" (n/p).[40]

The performance runs about an hour without much of a break in the self-deprecating darkness. By this point, many listeners of the CD, and many readers of Castillo, may have already given up on the work deeming it too repetitive and gloomy without the possibility for a diverse and rich gamut of readings. However, there are two aspects that add depth and complexity to Castillo's work that make it have a lasting impact beyond an adolescent identification with its emo-like qualities. The first is the reading of its defeatism as the adoption of an ethical stance; X, and the rest of Castillo's poetic subjects, reject the internalization of a system of values that degrades and exploits them by attempting to turn them in vacuous consumers and stunted individuals emotionally-subservient to heteronormative patterns of family life and gender identity. Initially, X is left without a positive (in philosophical terms) counter-project so he can only posit it as an absence and a general inconformity with the world that surrounds him. The position is dangerous as it leaves the subject in a state of perpetual precarity, without alternative discourses and models to facilitate his rejection of the hegemonic. One of the dangers becomes a reality in the form of Nicholas' drug addiction. His life might be seen as a waste, or a product of an illness, or of a lack of discipline and self-respect, but should actually be considered in opposition to the value system it contradicts. X, Nicholas and the other poetic subjects of Castillo are losers, but their loss is an ethical one; they are the antiheroes of the macro-narratives of progress and modernity, and the ultra-conservative value system of contemporary Mexico. They represent, following Ana María Amar Sánchez, the "antihero loser." As Amar Sánchez states, "[t]he figure of the ethical, antiheroic loser has a double aspect: *defeat* for him is the realm of his *ethical* triumph" [original emphasis]. She continues, "[t]hose that assume the path of the defeated as the only possible ethical conduct, persist in their rejection of the present of the winners, and they triumph over oblivion by not allowing themselves to be included in the world of those who vanquished"[41] (218). Amar Sánchez is writing about Latin-American narratives of the second half of the twentieth Century, in the specific context of post-dictatorial South America, but also of other countries where politically and culturally conservative forces were in place and where Neoliberalism was taking form as the hegemonic economic ideology. In her readings, Amar Sánchez finds that certain novels posit withdrawal as the only possible counterforce to these repressive contexts—a withdrawal that is synonymous with the rejection of being coopted by the parties in power. In contrast, to this acceptance of defeat, Amar Sánchez posits the figure of the "disenchanted loser" who does not accept his defeat and who searches out those in power in an effort to live within the umbrella of the winners, to curry their favor or even share in their power. But this, of course, can only be done by compromising their political and ideological convictions. Lacking an ideological north, they see themselves lost:

> The feeling of disappointment and the attitude of having to adjust to the present—thoroughly rejected by the antihero losers—causes a constant flight, the uprooting of these characters. So, life after diverse political defeats, the fall of utopias, in the context of the mutation of ways of thinking and of living, leads to new ways of dealing with defeat. This is how the protagonists of these novels [the ones analyzed by Amar Sánchez], at the antipodes of resistance, give themselves up to disillusionment and cynicism.[42] (221)

In the case of the poetic subjects of Castillo, we see both disillusionment and an ethical acceptance of defeat. His disillusion does not originate in a betrayal of his politics and his fight for justice, but in the state of the world. Castillo's poetic subjects never had a political ideology to lose because they do not ever represent a political or ideological discourse as their own; their resistance is organic and not guided by any utopian telos. The speaker in *Es la calle, honda...* states: "I leave it all, what isn't possible to abandon, what is impossible to flee from, I don't care about the balancing wire, charge someone else with the fear of the void, today I escape from me" [43] (Enciso). He accepts uprootedness as a condition of his rejection of a system that would have him be nothing more than a dupe: "someone wants you to be a grimace, a mirror of yourself: cold, castrated, and stupid"[44] (Enciso). The poetic subject's lack of a political ideology, of a discourse that articulates his stance does not diminish the validity and power of his ethics because his rejection of the structures of hegemonic power was never based on a political discourse or ideology. His errancy, his displacedness is something to be suffered by him for his radical inconformity, but it also serves as an opening to another way of being in the world. It represents a freedom to innovate, to create, and love. Twenty-five years after its release, *Es la calle, honda...* still holds up because of Castillo's ability to craft captivating verses rooted in a beauty constructed through precision, sensuality, and daring. The poetic subject of *Pobrecito* is continually longing for sexual fulfillment, and it is found by subsequent poetic subjects in Castillo's work. That sense of joyful fulfillment is transferred to the writing or, maybe more accurately, it is materialized, made present in the words. Though the poetry and music of *Es la calle, honda...* is dark, even gloomy, it produces a deep sense of joy because it is masterfully articulated. This goes beyond the skillful representation of that reality; Castillo's poetry is an experience of language. It is not surprising, then, that Castillo would collaborate with a musician, Enciso, and that the readings of his poetry are much more in line with spoken word and artistic performances than the readings of poets that write poetry to be read in silence. Poetry, then, is a place of living language, in contrast to the castrated language of his mother's trite advice and the conservative discourses that frame him as a *pendejo*, as an individual that is worth shit. Castillo's poetry is a lamentation, an expression of alienation, of emotional and psychological discomfort, but, in its precision and love of expression, it is also a poetry that incarnates the sensual and the beautiful.

A few years ago, while talking to a friend about Castillo, he recommended I read José Sbarra (born in Buenos Aires in 1950, died in 1996). Sbarra was a rebellious, anti-social *poète maudit* who contracted HIV and died from AIDS in 1996. For a generation of poets in Buenos Aires he was an important role model and still exerts a strong influence. As a gay drug user at home in the gritty streets of Robert Arlt's old haunts, he was the epitome of rebelliousness and anarchic freedom. The Argentinian's poetry is direct, colloquial, and adolescent like Castillo's—not only in the sense that it is a young voice but one that hurts, that is shunned and alienated from his surroundings. However, reading his poetry also revealed a nebulous difference with Castillo; Sbarra's poetry seems more desperate, downcast, and defeated. For example, the very first lines of Sbarra's first poetry book—from my perspective, somewhat ironically titled *Obsesión de vivir* (*Obsession for Life*)—read:

> This sadness that reaches us with the evening is
> common currency, come from far (maybe from
> our childhood) to remind us we are the chosen
> for whom the hour of pain was reserved.[45] (7)

Just a few lines down, we come upon a question, which helps us understand the difference between Sbarra's and Castillo's poetic stance:

> Is there a place for the solitary, for those who
> did not compose symphonies, who did not
> make our sadness burst into colors?[46] (7)

If Sbarra (or his poetic voice) feels he has been unable or unwilling to make his sadness explode into colors, it is exactly what his Mexican counterpart does. Making sadness burst into colors is an insightful description of Castillo's poetics and the relationship that the feelings of grief and inadequacy have to the beauty of his poetry. Castillo's and Sbarra's poetry ostensibly deal with the same topics and subject matter, and similarly use colloquial language, but the difference is that Castillo's personal and social disenchantment becomes an enchantment of the aesthetic. "Make our sadness burst into colors:" sadness explodes into a sensorial experience, an embodied reality that is, itself, marked by pleasure, one that is jouissance. Poetry is the anti-discourse, as such, poetry is jouissance in language. The poetic voice in Castillo metaphorically composes symphonies; it sings and indulges in the experience of the word. In this sense, his performances with Enciso seem almost predestined, since it is there that angst is materialized into spoken word, rhythm, and song. Castillo and Enciso created a second performance project involving poetry, music and dance in 1998, *Borrados*. Significantly, the performance pieces, *Borrados* and *Es la calle, honda...*, are comprised in large part by existing poems already published by Castillo.[47] That continuity reinforces the notion that performativity, orality, register, and timbre are fundamental to Castillo's poetics (particularly after *Pobrecito*) and not limited to his performance work. Castillo's delivery is deliberate and rhythmic, he accentuates certain sounds, repeats vowels, words, and verses. It is significant that one of his earliest poetry books is titled

Concierto en vivo, (*Live in Concert*) (1981), because it represents an early manifestation of Castillo's interest in the intersection of poetry and music. Castillo himself pushed back on the notion that he emphasized the narrative aspect in his poetry, clarifying to de Aguinaga that he was more concerned with *how* to tell a story than the story itself and that the sound of that telling was a fundamental part of his poetics:

> I think that in all the poetry books mentioned beforehand there is an intention, not without failings, to homogenize song and story. However, I think that what was truly important and determined the writing of this or that poetry book...had to do, from the beginning, more with the taste for verses and the poem than any previous will to structure a given narrative. Everything was deduced from the rhythm of the verse, from the music. I think poems and poetry books are made starting from the verse, and, above all, *from* their particles. Before the seeking of any narrativity, I first looked to make a poetry that was a rhythmic and sonic entity. Putting aside the design of verses in visual terms, I think I always associated—when writing—the poem with the oral experience. It seems to me that I have always written verses paying special attention to what sounds within them. (de Aguinaga)

This preoccupation with sound can be seen as culminating in *Il re lámpago* (2009) Castillo's latest poetry book, in which words disintegrate into sounds and allomorphs suggesting solmization, defined by dictionary.com as "the act, process, or system of using certain syllables, especially sol fa syllables, to represent the tones of the scale" ("solmization"):

No sé si re   no sé si la

Sí sé si sí   do   sol   fa   mi   pa
                                    sión (Il Re Lámpago 26)

Large segments of the poetry book follow this pattern and parallel the fifth and final section of Vicente Huidobro's quintessential avant-garde poetry book, *Altazor* (1931). Huidobro's book is a classic but the last section has divided readers, who interpret it as either the disintegration of language—as its failure—and, thus, the failure of poetry, or its elevation into music and song, the ultimate transcendence of language's utilitarian dimension. Castillo's latest poetry has divided readers in much the same way with at least one critic reading it as the logical exhaustion of the Mexican poet's project rooted in existential angst. Enrique Gallegos sees a fundamental lack in Castillo's latest poetry, "...*Il Re Lámpago* corroborates the poetic dearth that

Ricardo Castillo is going through, because a poet marked by such an existential sense can assume such a formal posture only with great difficulty" (26). We can like or not like Castillo's more experimental poetry, but we have to recognize that it is congruent with his overall vision and with the process that his poetic subjects have gone through in search for an alternative way of being and thinking. Castillo's poetic subjects find fulfillment in expression itself, that is, the aesthetic act; language becomes an aesthetic performance, as does sex. They are both activities liberated from the utilitarian constraints of capitalist consumption and production. What they produce, what they do is pleasure, as fulfillment and plenitude.

More importantly they constitute a propositional (positive) stance that counters the void created by the refusal to incorporate societal norms and expectations. Poetry is posited in opposition to a society that is always postulated as repressive. And although there is a constant lamentation by X and most of the other poetic subjects, there is also, right from *Pobrecito*, a will to live and to resist the imposition of a degraded self: "It's not that I think death is your worst enemy / But I want you living / But I want you risking"[48] (45). What his family and society have taught him goes against life: "life has little to do with the family album"[49] (31). He sees everything projected onto him from those spaces as a falsity, a treason against life. What is offered by society are platitudes and sterile conventions: "Making mountains out of molehills is a lie / What you know about yourself is a lie"[50] (43). The individual is in a constant struggle to be true to himself and to be fulfilled; a process that involves undoing the lie that is the subjected self. It is in poetry where this realization happens and where this is materialized.

Heterosexual Desire and Feminist Criticism

The arguments I have been making all move toward the premise that Castillo's poetry represents a movement against the imposition of the discourses and practices that make up hegemonic masculinity; that poetry is represented in Castillo as fundamental to the refusal of hegemonic masculinity and as a point of departure for another more inclusive masculinity. Yet, there are issues that problematize this reading. In his essay, "Un poeta sin pelos en la lengua", Arturo Dávila writes: "there's a lot of issues that one can bring up when talking about Castillo's first book. I don't know if a female reader would agree with the analysis we've tried to make of his poetry. It articulates a juvenile, masculine voice, it can even be branded as *machista*"[51] (394). Speaking specifically of one of the most cited poems in that book, "Las nalgas" ("The Ass"), he says, or rather admits: "[m]aybe Postcolonial Feminism is right. This poem can be considered sexist. It objectifies women. Reducing women to a pair of buttocks. Additionally, the word 'also' implies that only in that can they be equal to men...The poet is a voyeur. He masturbates with the female body enjoying himself while looking at her butt...He turns a young girl into a piece of meat"[52] (395). Dávila's condemnation makes it practically impossible for any reader with any reservation whatsoever about participating in and promoting misogyny of any sort, not to disown the poem. We can agree with the assessment that this poem (and others) objectify women but there are two interrelated problems with Dávila's assessment. The first is that it is too simplistic in that it reduces his complimentary reading of Castillo and a postcolonial feminist one to mutually exclusive opposites. The second is that he believes the criticism afforded by a feminist reading can be set side, tabled and ultimately ignored in constructing his own reading. It is also problematic to think that only a female reader or a feminist would have problems with the objectification of women and to think that pointing out sexist images or attitudes constitutes the extent of feminist criticism. Recognizing the insightful possibilities of a feminist approach, in this section I take a closer look at the poems that problematize my general thesis and I examine X's conceptualization of love, sex, his relationship with women, and their development in the poetry books that I have referenced.

The poem that Dávila rightly believes would draw the ire of feminists is the following:

Women also have their butt divided in two.
But it's undeniable that the ass of a woman
is incomparably better than a man's,
it has more life, more joy, it's pure imagination;
it's more important than the sun and god together,
it's a basic good that doesn't affect inflation,
a birthday cake on your birthday,
a blessing from nature,
the origin of poetry and of scandal.[53] (34)

I have been constructing micro-arguments to support the notion that X's teenage angst is much more than that, that it is significant and meaningful because it derives, to an important degree, from his reluctance and ultimate refusal to be a subject (in)formed by hegemonic masculinity—the *cabrón*. However, the male gaze projected in certain poems by Castillo prompts us to ask if the arguments for a reading of Castillo's poetry as developing a counterhegemonic masculinity should be discarded, or if it can somehow be maintained without ignoring the poems' implications. If X reproduces the male gaze upon the objectivized female body, can X's alternative to hegemonic masculinity have any validity beyond it not being its most macho incarnation? Can we truly credit Castillo's poetry as being counterhegemonic when there are poems that clearly objectify women? How do we establish the line that demarcates what we as readers find acceptable and what we find reprehensible? If we posit that these poems are exceptions to the rule, or contradictions within X's outlook, or points of contention in his struggle against hegemonic masculinity, or that they are eventually overcome in subsequent poetry books (as I will postulate that they are), do we end up justifying them or whitewashing their sexism? Their presence, though, also helps us interrogate the limits of a feminist or non-hegemonic masculinity. To ask, for example, whether it's even possible for male heterosexual desire to exist divorced from the male gaze? And, if so, what would that look like? Finally, could we accept that X, in subsequent poetic subjects, is able to construct a counterhegemonic masculinity that completely expunges the objectification of women of earlier poems? The answer is more complex than an outright dismissal of Castillo's poetry as misogynistic would suggest.

We could look at the poem "Lili Doll and Ledy," which contains the verses: "Oh!, false face of a whore in the social section, / Oh! damn bitch, / one day I'm going to undress you" [54] (*El pobrecito* 35), and think, there it is: plain sexism, down to the title that paints a young woman as an inanimate object, nothing more than a plaything for the male observer. This is true, but it is also true that there are aspects which complicate such a closed reading. For one, the female subject has a name, something shared by only X's parents. This gives her a clearly defined identity, while also placing her in the realm of the adults, those firmly within the patriarchal system, which X identifies with falsity, vacuity and the repression of life. It is unsurprising then, that the woman reproduces the empty gestures and rituals of high society and confuses life with "things of lawyers and businessmen"[55] (35). Her values are exactly what X opposes, what he sees as the domestication of life's vital energy by death through conformity, quotidian tedium, and a profit-driven society. Considering X's lack of agency, his promise to undress her one day seems like a toothless threat, a sketchy goal that will not come to fruition. But it also underscores a desire for the young woman to lose her pompousness, to drop her mask—it is significant that he does not reproach her being a whore but a fake one. His issue is not that she is, or might be, a whore but that she is not one truly or is not truly herself. He also equates her to the superficial reality he lives in: "but you, like reality, think yourself so decent"[56] (35). It seems he would be satisfied with her being a whore. What that is, if it is in direct relation to him or a true untroubled expression of her agency as a sexual being, is ambiguous enough to be difficult to define. But considering that being a whore is opposed to the disingenuous decency of her upper-class values, it must represent a positive manifestation of life. The trouble here is not that he wants that for her (that he wants to share being undressed of the imposed superficiality of society), but that his reading of her in the newspaper is that of a whore. At any rate, the poem represents a socioeconomic preoccupation as much as it does a sexual one: the first verse reads, "I wait for you like I wait for payday" (35). When he takes her as the incarnation of reality, whose hips he wants to "plow with my yoke," we can read her as a symbol of life itself—again problematic in that it objectifies her by turning her into a mere metaphor in his imaginary[57] (35). She becomes the old metaphor of the American continent as a woman waiting to be put to use, to be plowed and made to produce. He invokes an image of rural life, one that involves a quasi-feudal contact with the earth and that has a strong current within the discourse of the Mexican Revolution and the demand for agrarian reform, as in the slogan *"Tierra y libertad"* ("Land and Liberty"). We know that X is an adolescent, not only biologically but in terms of economic and social capital, cut-off from the spoils of the Mexican Revolution and of the modernizing discourses that promise economic prosperity. The fact that the poetic subject waits for her like he "waits for payday" belies his externality to the system that seeks to entrap him in an alienated existence. Unwittingly, X conflates money with the object of his desire that would presumably allow him happiness, pleasure, and fulfillment. It may simply be that for X (and for us) there is no outside the system, no pre-discursive unity of self, and that any movement toward fulfillment is entangled by, and with, the discourses and practices that subject us. That X is unable to fully remove himself from what he opposes, what wills itself to degrade him, is more telling than any categorical dismissal of him as sexist.

When X says: "the women are good and cold like ice-cream cones, / they don't want to go to bed with one" (25), it is possible to foresee that in a future, when he is not lacking economic, social, cultural capital and agency, he might use his newfound agency to take women as his objects. But this reading is hard to sustain when we see that overall his identity is that of the non-*cabrón* and that, rather than making this lack of sexual prowess with women a fatal tragedy that might lead to violence, he laughs it off in a self-deprecating way:

> [T]hey don't even dare to stick
> their hand through the...Oh,
> oh desolation (this is dumbass laugh)
> And what a fucking ruse
> what a moment to be worth shit
> such a *pendejo*, such a long way from being a *cabrón*.[58] (25)

X's male suffering is subverted by the parody he makes of it. He seems unable to keep himself from laughing at his own pain and, in doing so, disavows the macho suffering that, like in Storni's poem, turns male tears into poison for females. In the end, the agency he lacks (and his unwillingness or inability to be a *cabrón*) is contrasted by the ability of the women to refuse him. While they have some agency, women are involved in the same struggle for an authentic self—X's female cousins are labeled as being sexually repressed and his sister is subjected to the same repressive discourses in the guise of self-care and self-dignity during her mother's kitchen talks.

The point of re-reading these specific poems is not to defend them or to construct a vision of them that makes them less offensive but to analyze them more deeply, while getting away from a strict binary system of valuation in favor of one that allows for more nuanced readings. In this vein, a feminist perspective gives us nodal points of analysis that go beyond pointing out obviously sexist images. The basic notion of three waves of feminism already points to its diversity, which is erased in Dávila's reference to a general feminist criticism. One of the more interesting poems in this regard is "*Testiculario*" ("Testiculary"):

> Today I could say that my heart hurts with sadness.
> But it would be false
> and I'd prefer not to involve the heart with falsities.
> The truth is that I am sad.
> Withered like a forget-me-not
>
> ....
> The truth is that I have a needle-pain in each pupil,
> that sadness doesn't hurt me in my heart
> but in my testicles.
> I'm not ashamed to say that that is where my soul resides.[59] (26)

The poem places, paradoxically, what is ostensibly the metaphysical basis of the self in wholly materialist terms. The canonical division in Western thought of mind and body (Cartesian dualism) is subverted. Not only does X manifest this but he also presents the origin of his emotional self within the maleness of his body. His experience is completely embodied and inscribed by this status as a male—a movement which is repeated in another poem when speaks of "putting love on stage...with a very sexed soul"[60] (33). The poetic subject is a wholly sexual being—within the realm of the particular and without the pretense of a male universal subject. But, of course, it also prompts us to ask what (else) is a "sexed soul?" If we look at most of the instances in which X expresses desire, he links it with love (and vice-versa). Love and sex are synonymous; X asks, "But how can we sleep / knowing sex is the supreme love in life?"[61] (36). Love is, evidently, not a familial one, not one geared to reproducing that institution. Because of this, it is much freer and liberating. In the same poem I am quoting, the poetic subject speaks with a certainty that is unusual for him: "I have in my body / the clearest idea of what love is"[62] (36). The fact that it is through his body and not his mind—a realm influenced, if not contaminated by the moralizing discourses of his surroundings—that lets him know what love is, is significant because it is what allows him to place love in the realm of the subversive, along with those things that contain the vital energy that society and quotidian existence turn into the dead forms of customs and so-called decency. Here someone like Judith Butler may intervene to say that there is no *natural* correlation between body and desire, that any assumption that X's male body equals a desire for women is already a social construct that naturalizes heterosexuality, and that there is no recourse to a pre-discursive body. Ironically, the first poem referenced in this section, "The Ass," allows for a reading more in line with Butler, in that the male and the female bodies are presented as equivalent in their capacity to be objects of desire. The male and female bodies are presented not as different, with distinctly unique body parts but as commensurable —there is no mention of female breasts and vagina in contrast to the penis. This is not to say that the poem is a beacon of feminist or queer thought, but that it does offer a more complicated outlook than that afforded to it by a cursory reading that summarily dismisses it as sexist. We might even say that there are homosexual overtones in X's comparison of men's and women's butts, along with a subtle subtext of anal intercourse. Using the female butt as the focal point of the male gaze is a known trope within the poetic tradition, but it also allows for a butlerian reading of sex as a construct, with the penis and vagina as arbitrary elements from which to fabricate a categorical difference among humans. While Dávila claims the gaze in the poem is that of a voyeur, it is too abstract for me to agree with his assessment. What X is doing is not seeing (much less masturbating) but remembering and thinking; though charged with desire, his gaze is more philosophical than phenomenological in that he is at a loss as to why one object holds such a powerful, visceral attraction for him while the other doesn't. In a way, X's awe in the face of his sexual impulses towards women's bodies is due to an implicit recognition that there is nothing inherently *natural* about the directionality of his desire. Even though he immediately states that, while there is no difference between a man's butt and a woman's, a woman's is "incomparably better than a man's," that valuation, while absolute in X's mind, is also undeniably arbitrary. What is arbitrary, then, is X's heterosexuality and, as such, it is non-compulsory. This does not mean that X's sexuality is subjective nor is this an iteration of the myopic argument that homosexuality is a choice. On the contrary, what is implied is that heterosexuality and homosexuality are equally *natural* and ontologically valid.

One salient feature of X's discourse on sex and women is that there is never a physical description of the woman he desires (either of her body or face, as in traditional love poems) and, when he speaks of his own sexed body (X as a male body), he does not reference his penis but his testicles. This penis-less male sexuality or non-phallic male sexuality constitutes a type of aporia within poetic tropes, and for thinking of male sexuality and masculinity. Even when X does talk of the sexual act (in a singular poem in *Pobrecito*), it is not centered on penetrating the woman's body with his penis: "I would rather have / your legs as a scarf," he confesses, "and burrow that hill of clouds / covered by your transparent panties"[63] (36). What X is describing more closely resembles oral sex—a ubiquitous enough act but one that has traditionally been frowned upon from a macho point of view, at least externally, and one that goes against the mores of the *cabrón* because, on the contrary, instead of implying dominance over the woman, it puts her desires and pleasure at the forefront. At the same time, we see in another poem that love and sex are not simply libertine expressions of a self-centered individual, but that they imply a responsibility: "To kiss a woman /...entails a responsibility," affirms X[64] (39).

It is not until *Cienpies, tan ciego*, and more overtly in *Nicolás*, that we see any sort of fulfillment of X's desires for companionship, happiness and sex. There is no doubt that in *Cienpies*, and *Nicolás*, the poetic subject's partner is not just an instrument for achieving sexual pleasure or even some spiritual plenitude, but an equal participant in that act of wellness and vitality. For the first time, his interlocutor is not himself but an actual other to whom he confesses: "I tend to be happy, I'm not sure if unjustifiably so"[65] (13). There are also instances in which the language becomes more indulgent, sensorial and sensual:

> Nighttime on the inside, your back.
> The venom that does not kill
> but undeniably distills with the thirst
> of who discerns lightning
> without the need for rain.
> Today, I dream myself in your clothes
> and know without signs the devout path,
> the touch of light on your back,
> or the silk that be or the light I am.[66] (16)

There is a slowness that the poem's language demands and its moments of soft alliteration combine to give it a sensual quality; it is a sensorial and sensual experience in itself, and not merely its representation. The speaker transcends his physical existence and becomes light. There is a tension between absence and presence, between effects and cause—knowledge without signs, lightning without rain, venom that does not kill. And here, we can also see that the butt, present in the poem we began this section with, re-emerges as the lover's back, as a living object, of touch, of intimacy and familiarity. I say object but the speaker's care with his words and with his lover's body, speaks to a respect and admiration that belie any notions of possession or violence. As *ass* transforms linguistically into *back* (from one poem to another), and it also suggests the back of God that had appeared previously as being stabbed. That stab to the back of God was a representation of the poetic subject's disarticulated, uprooted, anguished life. Now, the lover's almost metaphysical presence, her back restored and sublime, represents a life that is whole, substantial and full of well-being.

In *Nicolás*, we see another breakdown of the poetic subject's self-contained identity. It begins with the appearance of a *we*—the poetic subject and his lover: "Our eyes," he says, "a well." He continues: "we close our eyes.../ and in the kiss become vertigo and oblivion... / ...We burn"[67] (71). The sexual act becomes transcendent: "through our bodies, like the iguana's, / flows not blood, but Time"[68] (72). The poetic voice sees his lover squarely and he becomes her: "I look into your white eyes, magical, / and I bleed like you with the moon, / I bleed for you, to be like you and know you"[69] (73). This is no longer X of the male gaze, of alienation, and sadness. The moment of sexual fulfillment is not a *chingar*, not a taking or a using of the other but a communal well-being. The poetic voice does not just identify with his lover and her menstruating body, he transforms and loses what is generally taken as the basis of identity—his gender. He becomes female, saying: "I am the woman who sees, / the one who hears" (73). It is the woman who now occupies the locus of enunciation and is the speaking, knowing subject. We might have qualms about the verses that follow veering into an idealized image of the women (the self?): "I am the woman who sees, without seeing.../...I am the unity" (73), but it is undeniable that these verses represent a sexual relationship based on the mutual fulfillment of both individuals and that the male poetic subject is completely emotionally invested in the female other's desire, pleasure, and well-being. [70]

Conclusion

The poetic subjects in Ricardo Castillo's poetry and performance pieces struggle with the processes of subjection whose goal is to produce nationalistic citizens and unthinking consumers. X's inconformity contains a good deal of adolescent angst but it is also rooted in a deeper, more significant refusal of the societal impositions centered, to great extent, on the violent alpha-male masculinity of the *cabrón*. X refuses to perform the performative acts of hegemonic masculinity while struggling to recognize an alternative model of non-macho masculinity. He begins to find an opposition to the conservatism and repression of the family and society he was born into in the practice of poetry. The lyric in Castillo is an experience of language as authenticity and fulfillment—eventually as a parallel complement to love and sex. It affords him the possibility of subverting the repression of expression that contributes to male depression and potential violence. As a space that is available to the non-*cabrón* male and one that legitimizes him, it constitutes what we can term a *poetic masculinity*. The argument is not necessarily that X is an ideologically progressive character/poetic subject, that he is the instantiation of a feminist ideal, or that the intention of Castillo is to create a feminist poetry, but rather that we, as readers of *Pobrecito*, are witnesses to the struggles of rejecting hegemonic masculinity and the attempt to construct a counterhegemonic one. To a large degree X is able to do just that, despite the early instances in which the male gaze is reproduced. We might be skeptical that X, and his various incarnations of poetic subjects, is able to completely disentangle himself from the discourses and practices that subject him. But as Butler has said:

> "[t]he critical task for feminism is not to establish a point of view outside of constructed identities...[t]he critical task is, rather, to locate, strategies of subversive repetition, enabled by those constructions, to affirm the local possibilities of intervention through participating in precisely those practices of repetition that constitute identity and, therefore, present the immanent possibility of contesting them." (147)

This is a far as the task can go, this is as far as Castillo's poor little subjects can take it.

Notes

[1] I use the term as Judith Butler succinctly defines: "'Subjection' signifies the process of becoming subordinated by power as well as the process of becoming a subject" (*Psychic* 2).
[2] Beginning here and continuing throughout this essay I will be offering my own translations and including the original Spanish quotes in the End Notes.
Nací en Guadalajara. / Mis primeros padres fueron Mamá Lupe y Papá Guille.
Crecí como un trébol de jardín, / como moneda de cinco centavos, como tortilla.
Crecí con la realidad desmentida en los riñones, / con cursilerías en el camarote del amor.
Mi mamá lloraba en los resquicios / con el encabronamiento a oscuras, con la violencia a tientas.
Mi papá se moría mirándome a los ojos, / muriéndose en la cámara lenta de los años, exigiéndole a la vida. / Y luego la ceguez de mi abuelo, los hermanos,
el desamparo sexual de mis primas, / el barrio en sombras y luego yo,
tan mirón, tan melodramático. / Jamás he servido para nada.
No he hecho sino cronometrar el aniquilamiento. // Como alguien me lo dijo alguna vez: Valgo Madre. (19)

3 The Spanish original reads, "En México los significados de la palabra son innumerables. Es una voz mágica. Basta un cambio de tono, una inflexión apenas, para que el sentido varíe...Pero la pluralidad de significaciones no impide que la idea de agresión —en todos sus grados, desde el simple de incomodar, picar, zaherir, hasta el de violar, desgarrar y matar— se presente siempre como significado último. El verbo denota violencia, salir de sí mismo y penetrar por la fuerza en otro. Y también, herir, rasgar, violar —cuerpos, almas, objetos—, destruir" (99-100).

4 As Victor M. Macías-González and Anne Rubenstein state, "The view of Mexican masculinity and national character proposed by Octavio Paz first began to be challenged at precisely the moment when it seemed most widely accepted, both by intellectuals and as popularized in mass media. From the perspectives of feminist, gay and lesbian, and postcolonialist studies, three basic critiques emerged. First, critics observed that the image of the Mexican macho was just that—an image. It did not reflect most people's daily lives, or their self-perceptions. Second, they pointed out that collapsing the categories of *Mexican* and *male* disenfranchised women. Third, they noted that this model assumed that the macho always behaved heterosexually, but... while the *ideal* of Mexican masculinity proposed by Paz might be straight, many Mexican men were not" (14).

5 "Si seré pendejo, si me faltará muchísimo para cabrón."

6 The Spanish original is "[l]o chingado es lo pasivo, lo inerte y abierto, por oposición a lo que chinga, que es activo, agresivo y cerrado. El chingón es el macho, el que abre. La chingada, la hembra, la pasividad, pura, inerme ante el exterior. La relación entre ambos es violenta, determinada por el poder cínico del primero y la impotencia de la otra. La idea de violación rige oscuramente todos los significados. La dialéctica de 'lo cerrado' y 'lo abierto' se cumple así con precisión casi feroz" (100).

7 The Spanish original is, "[l]a voz está teñida de sexualidad, pero no es sinónimo del acto sexual; se puede chingar a una mujer sin poseerla. Y cuando se alude al acto sexual, la violación o el engaño le prestan un matiz particular. El que chinga jamás lo hace con el consentimiento de la chingada. En suma, chingar es hacer violencia sobre otro. Es un verbo masculino, activo, cruel: pica, hiere, desgarra, mancha" (100).

8 "La suerte...acabó de mandarme a chingar a mi madre" (25).

9 "...no da la mano, no abre las piernas, tira patadas / como monito de futbolito" (25).

10 "...lo que buscas no está en la ciudad / porque ella solo quiere tu sangre y tu energía para su sostenimiento / y desperdicio" (51).

11 "Qué lograron para qué sacaron con plantar sus estúpidas / ilusiones / entre máquinas constructoras" (49).

12 "Y luego quién determina dónde debe estar tu cuerpo con sus bríos / o sus penas...//...no puede haber posibilidad donde existe la combustión del diesel [sic] / buscando el cielo..." (49).

13 "...a huevo que dudas de tener algo que no sea basura / en la cabeza / basura esa imagen que e pide la ciudad no sé realmente a cambio / de qué" (50).

14 "...vale más que un metro / cuadrado de desierto". "...aborrezco sus plumas dorados y sus gordos dedos / formadores" (51).

15 "La tranquilidad de las seis de la tarde me pega en las costillas seis / campanazos en todo lo alto. / Esta tranquilidad es una macana lista para cualquier mandado" (25).

[16] Mary-Lee Mulholland writes about Guadalajara in this vein in "Mariachis Machos and Charros Gays: Masculinities in Guadalajara," which is her article in *Masculinity and Sexuality in Modern Mexico* (Macías-González and Rubenstein), where she explores the city's role in forming the national ideal of masculinity and its apparently paradoxical characterization as Mexico's gayest city.

[17] "…da consejos a mi hermana sobre el amor, / sobre las artes y los oficios de desperdiciar la vida, y cierta manera / de hacerla entender que pase lo que pase jamás deberá abrir / los ojos, ni la sonrisa, a lo desconocido" (27).

[18] "como si el sentimentalismo chato / fuera más importante que aquellos momentos / en los que se hinchan los testículos de las puras ganas de vivir" (27).

[19] "¿Para qué tantos buenos consejos como lo hacía mamá?" (23).

[20] "…ayer mi papá me miró con terror, / ayer mi mamá me habló de Dios y del respeto que me debo a mí / mismo" (29).

[21] "En mi familia / todos tomamos las cosas con calma: / 'Papá y mama ya murieron.' / 'Mis calcetines están rotos.' / 'Me he tragado una mosca.' / 'Todo está más caro.' / 'Ya todos vamos a morir.'" (20).

[22] "Mi padre nos quiere, / mi madre nos ama / porque hemos logrado ser una familia unida, amante / de la tranquilidad" (32).

[23] "Creo que sería bueno ser menos educados / y amar un grandioso escándalo" (20).

[24] "Pero ahora son las diez de la noche, / ahora que como de costumbre nadie tiene nada que hacer / propongo cerrar las puertas y ventanas / y abrir la llave del gas" (32).

[25] "…que alguien tire al barranco la ínfima monedita de su rostro, /…y ponga el amor en la tarima /…Que alguien viva, que alguien muera de noche, /…es como sacarle un pedo a Santa Claus / como para romper el equilibrio y la prosperidad del año nuevo de las familias bonitas" (33).

[26] "…su canto era el de la verga borracha que daba tumbos y daba vida" (21).

[27] Here I follow Deleuze and Guattari: "To say that the father is first in relation to the child really amounts to saying that the investment of desire is in the first instance the investment of a social field into which the father and the child are plunged, simultaneously immersed" (275).

[28] "el Impecable Jinete de la Neurosis."

[29] "…el amor y la soledad le galopaban en una circunferencia / paralela". "…no había en el mundo otra vocación / que la de ser demonio" (21).

[30] "estoy desahuciado" (22).

[31] "…no lloró mi padre /… no lloró mi abuelo… // Así diciendo te brotó una lágrima / y me calló en la boca…más veneno / yo no he bebido nunca en otro vaso así pequeño."

[32] "….ojalá haya ayudado / a encontrar una solución mejor que el suicidio" (30).

[33] "'señor poeta, haga un poema de un triste pendejo'. / su amargura me hizo hacer gestos. /…'no hay tristes que sean pendejos' / y nos fuimos a emborrachar" (30).

[34] "y Caos resopló en las ruinas del hombre" (66).

[35] "de qué se trata eso de caminar y caminar / si te dicen que no vas que no irás a ningún lado / si no participas si no colaboras / en las citadinas y funestas consagraciones de crecer como vejiga / como sapo hasta reventar en un ciudadano que mira los cartones / de las ofertas un domingo" (50).

36 "Cayó la gota que faltaba, Nicolás / ahora eres el testigo que te acusa, / no el barco que se hunde, sino el que fue incapaz / de conocer el mar; / del mar sólo hiciste un infierno, / una condena perpetua que nunca creíste merecer. / Pero la condena, Nicolás, / tú mismo la elegiste cuando no eras más que una pequeña / esfera de sustancia viva; / en mala hora te dio cabida el huevo, / en mala hora llegaste al paraíso, ya todo tenía dueño, / solamente te tocó un cerebro vanidoso, un corazón / inseguro / un cuerpo mal usado que nunca has hecho tuyo. / Quién to mando tener sistema nervioso, tener domicilio / en un estómago que rota y se traslada, / intoxicado de recuerdos y deseos absurdos. / No, no me hables de amor, de buenos sentimientos, / ésos nada más eran los gusanos que hacían sentir / tu cadáver vivo" (32).

37 The CD has long been out of stock and is not readily available, but the audio can be found online. I accessed a version on YouTube: youtube.com/watch?v=hsJm_AxXEfk.

38 "cementerio en la bruma es mi vida sin ruta, una calle empanada, que no lleva a nada...una cruel puñalada en la espalda de Dios" (Enciso).

39 "Veo mi vida como un desorden que no vale pena ordenar", "réstenle mis ilusiones al mar, hoy solo el desierto es capaz de conmoverme un poco, tan grande y sin nadie, como una remota imagen de mí mismo" (Enciso).

40 "Yo hago canciones para sobrevivir, no sé hacer otra cosa que cantar, tengo una banda de rock y la verdad me va muy mal, y es que no tengo nada, no tengo amor ni tengo nada...".

41 "La figura del perdedor ético, antiheroico, tiene un doble aspecto: la derrota para él la dimensión de su triunfo ético. Aquellos que asumen el camino de los perdedores como única conducta ética posible, persisten en el rechazo al presente de los triunfadores y triunfan sobre el olvido gracias a su resistencia a dejarse incluir en ese mundo de los ganadores" (218).

42 "El sentimiento de desencanto y la actitud de adaptación al presente—tan rechazados por los antihéroes perdedores—provocan la constante *fuga*, el desarraigo de estos personajes. Es decir, la vida después de diversas derrotas políticas, de la caída de las utopías, en medio de la mutación de los modos de pensar y vivir, lleva a nuevas formas de sobrellevar la pérdida. Es así que los protagonistas de estas novelas, en las antípodas de la resistencia, se entregarán a la desilusión o al cinismo" (221).

43 "Lo dejo todo, lo que no es posible abandonar, de lo que no es posible huir, no me importa el alambre del equilibrio, encarguen a otro el miedo al abismo...hoy escapo de mí."

44 "alguien quiere que seas una mueca, espejo de ti mismo, frío, castrado y estúpido."

45 "Esta tristeza que nos llega con la tarde ya es moneda / corriente, viene desde lejos (quizás desde nuestra / infancia) a recordarnos que somos los elegidos para / quienes fue reservado el dolor de las horas.

46 "¿Habrá un sitio para los solitarios, para los que / no compusimos sinfonías, para los que no supimos / hacer estallar en colores nuestra tristeza?" (7).

47 An important part of the performance comes from the poetry book *Borrar los nombres*. There are several videos online that show parts of the performances.

48 "No es que piense que la muerte sea tu peor enemigo / pero te quiero vivo / te quiero arriesgando" (45).

49 "...la vida poco tiene que ver con el álbum familiar" (31).

50 "Es mentira que los ahogados se mueran en un vaso de agua / Es mentira lo que tú crees de ti" (43).

51 "Se pueden poner muchos bemoles a ese primer libro de Castillo. Ignoro si una lectora coincidiría con el análisis que intentamos dar a su poesía. Articula una voz masculina, juvenil. Incluso se le puede tildar de machista" (394).

52 "Acaso tenga razón el feminismo poscolonial. Este poema puede ser considerado sexista. Objetiviza a la mujer. Se le reduce a un par de glúteos. Además, la palabra 'también' implica que sólo en eso se puede igualar al hombre…El poeta es un *voyeur*. Se masturba con el cuerpo de la mujer, deleitándose al mirar su trasero…Convierte a una muchacha en un pedazo de carne" (395). Dávila goes on to write "[a]nd all this masculine mental onanism is disguised as 'poetry'. What a slime ball!". The Spanish reads, "[y] todo este onanismo mental masculino se disfraza de 'poesía.' ¡Qué pelado!" (395). He adds a footnote to say that he is following the criticism of an outraged female student who attacked Castillo's poetry and this poem in particular with all her rancor, and that it helped him see a possible feminist critique he had not perceived. He closes the footnote by noting: "[o]f course, she received a good grade for her work." The presentation of the student's perspective seems to be a satire of feminist critique, and his assurance that she received a high mark for her essay comes off as a bit condescending—and certainly unnecessary. All this is to say that Dávila's inclusion of the feminist perspective appears to be an acknowledgement of its cultural (and possibly political) force but one that lacks a true conviction in its potential for analyzing Castillo's poetry. The entire footnote in Spanish reads, "[s]igo aquí una crítica del poema que recibí, alguna vez, de una indignada estudiante que arremetió, con todo su rencor, contra *el pobrecito* Ricardo Castillo en un ensayo de clase. En especial, contra este poema. Me abrió los ojos a una posible crítica feminista, que yo no había percibido. Por supuesto, obtuvo una alta calificación por su trabajo" (395).

53 "El hombre también tiene dividido el trasero en dos. / Pero es indudable que las nalgas de una mujer / son incomparablemente mejores que las de un hombre, / tienen más vida, más alegría, son pura imaginación; / son más importantes que el sol y Dios juntos, / son artículo de primera necesidad que no afecta la inflación, / un pastel de cumpleaños en tu cumpleaños, / una bendición de la naturaleza, el origen de la poesía y del escándalo" (34).

54 "¡Ay!, falsa cara de puta en la sección de sociales, / ¡ay! Hija de la chingada, / un día te voy a desnudar" (35).

55 "te crees que la vida son cosas de abogados y empresarios" (35).

56 "…tú, como la realidad, te crees muy decente" (35).

57 "Te espero como se espera el día de pago, … anhelo surcar con mi yunta."

58 "…las mujeres están buenas y frías como sorbetes / no quieren acostarse con uno, no se atreven siquiera a meter la mano / por la…Oh, / oh desolación (esta risa es de pendejo). / Y qué pinche embuste, / qué momento de estar chingando a mi madre. / Si seré pendejo, si me faltará mucho para ser cabrón" (25).

59 "Hoy podría decir que me duele el corazón de tristeza. / Pero sería falso / y prefiero no involucrar al corazón en falsedades. / La verdad es que sí estoy triste. / Marchito como un nomeolvides. /…La verdad es que tengo un dolor de aguja en cada pupila, / que la tristeza no me duele en el corazón / sino en los testículos. / No me apena decir que es allí donde radica mi alma" (26).

60 "y ponga el amor en la tarima /…con el alma muy sexuada" (33).

61 "¿Pero cómo dormir / sabiendo que el sexo es el máximo amor en la vida?" (36).

62 "Tengo en el cuerpo / la idea más clara de lo que es el amor" (36).

[63] "Yo más bien quiero / tener tus piernas por bufanda / y horadar ese montecito de nubes / que cubren, transparentes, tus pantaletas" (36).

[64] "Besar una mujer /...entraña una responsabilidad" (39).

[65] "Suelo ser feliz, no sé si injustificadamente" (13).

[66] "Noche por dentro, tu espalda. / El veneno que no mata / pero innegable destila en la sed / de quien adivina relámpagos / sin necesidad de llover. / Hoy en tu ropa me sueño / y conozco sin aviso el devoto camino, / el tacto de la luz en tu espalda, o la seda ser o esa luz que soy" (16).

[67] "Son nuestros ojos un pozo ... Cerramos los ojos.../ y en el beso modelamos el vértigo y el olvido" (71).

[68] "nuestros cuerpos, como a la iguana, / en vez de sangre, les corre el Tiempo" (72).

[69] "Te veo los ojos blancos, magiosa, [sic] / y sangro como tú con la luna, / sangro por ti, para ser como tú y conocerte" (73).

[70] "Yo soy la mujer que mira sin mirar, /...yo soy la unidad" (73).

Works Cited

Amar Sánchez, Ana María. "Utopía y derrota. Política y ética en la narrativa latinoamericana del fin de milenio." *América: Cahiers du CRICCAL*, no. 39, 2010.

Butler, Judith. *Gender Trouble and the Subversion of Identity*. Routledge, 1990.

—. *Psychic Life of Power: Theories in Subjection*. Stanford University Press, 1993.

"cabrón". dle.rae.es. Diccionario de la lengua española: Edición del Tricentenario, 2020, 24 April 2021.

Castillo, Ricardo. *Il re lámpago*. Publisher not known, 2009.

—. *Borrar los nombres*. Toque de Poesía, 1993.

—. *Ciempiés tan ciego. Nicolás, el camaleón*. Ediciones Toledo, 1989.

—. *Concierto en vivo*. Universidad Michoacana, 1982.

—. *El pobrecito señor X. La Oruga*. Fondo de Cultura Económica, 1994.

Connell, R.W. *Masculinities*. 2nd ed., University of California Press, 2005.

Dávila, Arturo. "Un poeta sin pelos en la lengua." *Historia crítica de la poesía mexicana II*, edited by Rogelio Guedea, Fondo de la Cultura Económica, 2015, pp. 388-410.

de Aguinaga, Luis Vicente. "Avanzar al sesgo: entrevista con Ricardo Castillo." *Periódico de Poesía*, archivopdp.unam.mx/index.php/entrevistas/1324-029-entrevistas entrevista-con-ricardo-castillo. Accessed May 2010.

Deleuze, Gilles, and Félix Guattari. *Anti-Oedipus: Capitalism and Schizophrenia*. Penguin Books, 2009.

Enciso, Gerardo and Castillo, Ricardo. *Es la calle, honda*. Universidad de Guadalajara, 1992.

—. *Borrados*. Directed by Gustavo Dominguez. Universidad de Guadalajara, 1998.

—. *Borrados*. La Casa Suspendida, Guadalajara, 8 September 2011.

—. *Es la calle, honda....* La Casa Suspendida, Guadalajara, 9 September 2011.

Gallegos, Enrique. *Poesía mayor de Guadalajara: Anotaciones poéticas y críticas.* Secretaría de Cultura, Gobierno del estado de Jalisco, 2007.

Macías-González, Víctor M., and Anne Rubenstein, editors. *Masculinity and Sexuality in Modern Mexico.* University of New Mexico Press, 2012.

McKee Irwin, Robert. *Mexican Masculinities.* University of Minnesota Press, 2003.

Paz, Octavio. *El laberinto de la soledad.* 1950. Penguin, 1997.

"pendejo". dle.rae.es. Diccionario de la lengua española: Edición del Tricentenario, 2020, 24 April 2021.

Sbarra, José. *Obsesión de vivir. Los pterodáctilos. Informe sobre moscú. Del mal amor.* Michaux Editorial, date of publication not given.

Stellini, Cristina. "La mirada sesgada: El Pobrecito Señor X de Ricardo Castillo." *Docplayer.es,* docplayer.es/75882378-La-mirada-sesgada-el-pobrecito-senor-x-de-ricardo-castillo.html. Accessed 2018.

Storni, Alfonsina. "Peso ancestral." *Irremediablemente.* Ediciones Torremozas, 2005, p. 35.

Chapter 3

What a Man Ought To Be: Villoro's Awkward Macho in a Neoliberal Mexico

Carmen Patricia Tovar

Oberlin College

Alejandro Puga

DePauw University

It is unquestionable that gender systems in Latin America, and specifically in Mexico, are deeply biased and unequal. However, as Sherry Ortner has noted, "[t]he secondary status of woman in society is one of the true universals, a pan-cultural fact" (21). Thus, gender inequality is a world phenomenon that, in part, can be traced back to ancient philosophical writings and has continued for centuries. Lucía Guerra posits that most societies organize reality based on a traditional binary system of good and bad, superior and inferior, order and chaos, the sacred and the profane, masculine and feminine, and so on. Indeed, Ortner's own formulation is set in a culture versus nature divide. In universal and binary perceptions of gender, men experience several advantages that contradict suppositions of reciprocity or equality. Assumptions of women's physical, mental and emotional limitations allow men to establish societal value systems that exclude or limit women's participation and generally bind women to domestic space and domesticated spaces in the public sphere where they must confirm their primary roles as wives, mothers and homemakers, regardless of their pursuits beyond the home. In Latin American (and particularly Mexican) cultural studies, the consecration of this fundamental role is known as *marianismo*, that is, an emulation of the ever-sacrificing Virgin Mary.

In explaining *marianismo* as the counter-effect of *machismo*, Evelyn Stevens proposes that Latin American women help perpetuate this systemic self-oppression when they excuse and forgive men's impossible expectations on women to be the ethical, moral and religious compass of a household while men act on their lowest, most primal instincts. In more contemporary discussions regarding the agency of women in domestic and public spheres, Stevens's foundational essay on *marianismo* is questionable because it suggests that women generally benefit from their oppression as they are acknowledged as saints for their patient endurance and maintenance of the home, an argument which Elhers (1991) refutes in her ethnography of Guatemalan women in the informal sector. What is more applicable from Steven's essay is the paradox in which women are considered to possess inferior bodies and minds but are expected to be "semidivine" in their nurturing and forgiving behaviors (Stevens 91). Meanwhile, men deemed honorable and virile maintain spaces and practices where they misbehave and dishonor their spouses and family.

In contemporary Mexican narrative, constructions of masculinity vis-à-vis *marianismo* are brought to bear in accounts of interpersonal and familial upbringings, which often generate an analogy of the nation in that exercise. In large part, this parallelism is facilitated by the iconic presence of *grandes hombres* (larger-than-life revolutionary generals, presidents who think of themselves as "fathers" of the nation, perspicacious technocrats, and so on) who write a master script for paternity and manliness, and endorse *machismo* in both visceral and institutional forms. We are referring specifically to the Party of the Mexican Revolution (PRM), which was rebranded as the *Partido Revolucionario Institucional* (PRI) in 1946 by the presidential candidate Miguel Alemán Valdés. Alemán Valdés's presidency marks the institutionalization (the "I" in PRI) of revolutionary ideals as he was the first President, after the armed Revolution, who entered office as a university graduate. With the endorsement of high-ranking party operatives, he steered politics toward a new Porfirian system.[1] Accordingly, for the President, all aspects of modern life in Mexico (be they political, workforce, economic, cultural, or infrastructural) began with him and received his final endorsement. In establishing an institutionalized way of life, Alemán created a social hierarchy conditioned by the same *pan o palo* (compensation or retribution) policies of the Porfirian era. Consequently, a neo-Porfirian administration, with all of its patriarchal trappings, emerges under the guise of Revolutionary politics. Alemán Valdés rose as the new model for a father figure of the nation—a refinement of the rough-and-tumble revolutionary general—and, as such, his aspect was emulated by men of the professional class in the many different circles of societal life from the mid 1940s and on.

In Mexican prose narrative, José Emilio Pacheco's *Las batallas en el desierto* (1981) extends the dynamics of the home to the broader sphere of the city as an allegory of the ascendant PRI. Pacheco's novel speaks to the permeability of masculine constructs in both the public and private spheres, and it suggests the inevitability of the *pater familias* as both a social reality and a metaphor of state power, regardless of how dysfunctional or anachronistic it may become. Pacheco's contemporaries all take their turn at exploring overstated, contradictory, or broken fatherhoods and the difficult filial relationships they generate. The seemingly endless portability of the father-of-the-house/father-of-the-nation image reaches its apex in the mid-1980s, as Mexico City slips into an economic crisis due to inflation, and gives way to the crisis of the megalopolis after the 1985 earthquake. Moving forward, narrators of the city must interrogate constructs of the nation (and by association, constructs of masculinity) for their relevance as much as for their continuity. New iterations of well-known *cronistas* such as José Joaquín Blanco, Carlos Monsiváis, and Elena Poniatowska cease to ask whether the national image is oppressive or corrupt, and begin to ask whether there is any nation at all behind the façade of masculine power.[2] Novelists such as José Agustín, María Luisa Puga and Luis Zapata challenge the supposed absolutism of gender roles within the simulacrum of national identity. Sociologists such as Roger Bartra mirror a narrative experiment that questions the continuity of masculine power by challenging the resilience of national identity construction. The contemporary author Juan Villoro emerges from this identity shift as he novelizes a post-national condition in which he presents vulnerable and corrosive men whose virility is in a clear state of decline, even as they persist in dominating families, communities, businesses, and social memory. In brief, the privilege of associating personal memory with constructs of the nation, however nostalgic or melancholic that exercise may seem, becomes a farcical proposition in Villoro's novels.

Critical reception casts Villoro (1956) as a ubiquitous literary figure, with a diverse bibliography of narrative, journalistic essay, memoir, and media presence. He is cited as an author of post-national narratives (as in the novels discussed here) including an update of the *crónica*. He belongs to a generation of writers who are less interested in the well-trodden discussion of national identity and *lo mexicano*, and who avoid the mandate to incorporate Mexican folkloric allusions in their literary production. As Carrillo-Arciniega explains, after the essentialist explorations of Paz, Fuentes and Rulfo, post-nationalist authors seek to explore alterity and fragmentation in the human experience (56). Hence, Villoro highlights the socio-political and cultural realities of Mexico and writes about ordeals and tribulations of the Mexican people and vestiges of *lo mexicano* in a framework of global capitalism. If his predecessors began to argue that the artifice of national identity problematically imports U.S. economic influence, the co-opting of the national simulacrum to global markets is the baseline condition in Villoro's works. Consequently, the institutionalized father figure is already a compromised figure in Villoro's novelistic landscape, in which from the outset fathers are corrupt and broken role models for the impressionable yet critically-minded narrator-protagonist.

Be that as it may, the North American Free Trade Agreement (NAFTA), with its open markets and cross-border brandings, brings the question of Mexicanness back into novelistic discourse; authors emphasize national anxiety, or, in Liesbeth François's paraphrasing of Saskia Sassen, the focus is on "denationalization," that is, "la inserción de lo local y lo nacional en un marco global que provoca nuevas espacialidades" (74), and a resulting discord between projections of the national and the global in a common space. As an expression of these complexities, Villoro's first novel, *El disparo de argón*, published the same year the NAFTA talks initiated (1991), takes place in fictional Colonia San Lorenzo in the 1970s and serves as a metonymic Mexico City. In it, Villoro questions how cosmopolitan Mexico can be when it preserves traditional societal norms and gender roles that speak to a largely colonial order. With this fundamental contradiction in mind, Villoro imagines a state-of-the-art eye clinic with ambitions of world recognition, built in a working-class neighborhood. The monolithic edifice represents the promise of a trickle-down economics, but it fails in that endeavor due to well-trodden systems of corruption on the one hand, and a lack of vision and experience in the global market among those same corrupt administrators on the other. The literal and figurative blindness of the clinic's founder, Dr. Suárez, speaks to this vulnerability.

While this first novel in Villoro's "Mexico City diptych" (Ruisánchez Serra 90) confronts the more contemporary issue of Mexico in a context of globalization, his second novel, *Materia dispuesta*, looks back at the process of constructing a national identity by means of an institutionalized masculinity, and seeks to describe a process of denationalization by tracking the rise and fall of Jesús Guardiola, a would-be architectural paragon whose attempts to speak to a postrevolutionary national order through grandiose projects that are diminished by the managerial and environmental realities of the Mexican megalopolis. That Villoro sets the novel between two major Mexico City earthquakes (1957 and 1985) speaks to a periodization in which the "Mexican Miracle," marked by the first earthquake, gives way to an economic crisis and the advent of free trade practices marked by the second. In this sense, *Materia dispuesta* (1997) serves as a socio-economic prequel to *El disparo de argón* (1991). What is most notable to us is that in both frameworks of denationalization, Villoro problematizes Mexican masculinity by pairing moral with corporal, corporate, and structural decrepitude.

Villoro's critical reception has not paid close attention to an emerging and vital line of inquiry concerning his representations of masculinity and gender dynamics which still demonstrate some surprising adherence to the institutionalized macho. In the expansive 2001 critical anthology, *Materias dispuestas*, a single chapter by Tamara Williams deals centrally with issues of masculinity and the nation in Villoro's writing. Williams focuses on *Materia dispuesta*, but she foregrounds and describes crises of masculinity that are important for our reading of both *Materia dispuesta* and *El disparo de argón*, namely that in both novels, an array of masculinities informs the difficult transition from revolution, to post-revolutionary nation, and finally to neoliberal state. We discuss these multiple versions of the macho below to argue that Villoro's narrative challenges monolithic forms of patriarchy, perhaps unwittingly, by introducing an "awkward" macho. This is not the typical patriarch who either prevails or is toppled by popular contestation and changing times. Rather, Villoro's awkward macho adapts to ideological shifts, always uncomfortably, and by caricaturing various constructs of masculinity.

The macho archetypes

Machismo, as A. Rolando Andrade problematizes it, operates typically as a catchall phrase to describe masculine actions and attitudes that might (or not) be appreciated by the general population. For this reason, in his essay "*Machismo: A Universal Malady*," Andrade aims to provide a more nuanced view of the macho by identifying four explicit and implicit archetypes that, true to the binary tendencies of *machismo* and *marianismo*, embody positive and negative connotations. Favorable traits embrace patriarchal traditions, which emphasize nobility, chivalry, physical strength, courage, and self-confidence. The less favorable side manifests as impulsivity, aggressivity, hyper-virility, and a general sense of superiority. It is within this wide range of characterizations that Andrade concludes: "*Machismo* is the masculine force which to one degree or another drives all male behavior" (33).

Though Andrade presents examples from Japan, India, the U.S., and Europe to demonstrate the globality of *machismo*, his categories present an evolution of masculinity derived from five hundred years of Latin American colonial and post-colonial history, beginning with the 'conqueror' macho, who takes possession of what he perceives to be duly his by means of opportunistic territoriality. The contemporary heir of the free-range conqueror still demonstrates superiority in violent, public displays. The "playboy" macho emerges around the time of the sexual revolution of the 1960s, as this category refers to *Playboy* magazine and its philosophy of a sophisticated consumer whose discriminating tastes are facilitated by ample means and fashion sense. The "playboy" macho considers women as acquisitions that exist in his service as a housewife or a whore, according to the binaries of *marianismo*. His exuberant masculinity is available for public display and consumption.

In contrast to these more recognizable versions, a "masked" macho is less pretentious, but he conceals an insistent masculine superiority. He is a "lonely hunter who goes about life trying to prove his ability to survive by using cunning, shrewdness, keenness, and subterfuge" (Andrade 37). He is the quiet man who cultivates subtle intentions toward dominance. He can be a revolutionary, or a social disruptor in Robin Hood fashion. In that case, he is adored by his community because he lives simply to confront unjust powers. On the other hand, he can be Machiavellian in his subterfuge of women and public opinion. The "masked" macho becomes petty and vindictive if his dominant core is under threat or exposed.

Andrade's final category is the more evolved "authentic" macho; a simple man who does not necessarily act from an inferiority complex. He allows himself a range of emotions, which make him a balanced human being. He brings harmony to his family and is willing to face any obstacle to keep the peace in his community. In Mexico, the "authentic" macho would be called a *caballero*, or an *hombre de bien*. Andrade imagines this idealized type as a *pater familias* who establishes domestic and neighborly stability, without considering that this social expectation is still a form of gender domination because it requires a male figure to act as the center of order.

More of an ideal than an embodiment, this final category is rarely available to Villoro's protagonists as a model of masculinity, although Villoro does present failing versions of it. In reality, Villoro's protagonists fail to sustain any version of *machismo*, but they do attempt to assume one macho identity or another, with uncomfortable and slipshod outcomes. For that reason, we propose a category of "awkward" *machismo* wherein an anachronistic "conqueror," "playboy," or "masked" macho is pressured by institutional forces to become an "authentic" macho while toxic masculinity prevails around him. We see the awkward macho as a manifestation of the unavoidable transition from a male-privileged patriarchy to a neoliberal state in which women experience only limited access to economic opportunities in the form of employment, credit, property, financial independence, and some provisions to protect them from structurally patriarchal tribulations like sexual harassment and gender discrimination. Our discussion of *El disparo de Argon* will include a portrayal of this limited access.

Challenging the macho model

In *Materia dispuesta* and *El disparo de argón*, Villoro updates the more predictable familial dynamics of Pacheco's *Las batallas en el desierto*, and reflects less romantically and much less nostalgically on the past, particularly during a period in which masculinity, like the revolution itself, is undergoing a process of institutionalization. Pacheco's story takes place in 1948, at the end of World War II and in the middle of the prosperous Mexican Miracle period, while Villoro's first two novels take place between the two earthquakes (1957 and 1985) that shook the city to its core and revealed its unstable infrastructure. If *Las batallas* is at least in part a nostalgic recollection of modernity at its height, *Materia* is a narration of hardship and discontent. Where in Pacheco's novel we never see "El Señor", the patriarch who oversees the *casa chica* that is the site of Carlos's coming of age,[3] Villoro's novel provides a front-row seat to men whose preening and manipulative behavior is consecrated by the national *mythos*. In fact, *Materia* opens with Mauricio Guardiola's memory of witnessing his father's sexual encounter with a mistress, a dalliance that could not be interrupted, not even by the 6.1 magnitude earthquake that shook the apartment. As in *Las batallas*, Mauricio's family resides in the middle-class Colonia Roma, until they were displaced to Terminal Progreso by the 1957 earthquake, and consists of Mauricio's father (Jesús) who represents the socio-economic patriarchy, a mother (Cristina) who embodies the religious provincial mind, and an older brother (Carlos) who acts according to the aggressive hyper-masculine model.

Going beyond the nuclear family configuration, Tamara Williams identifies a counterpoint between the old school, rugged *machismo* embodied by the revolutionary fighter (Jesús's older brother, Roberto), and the slicker, more refined post-revolutionary player (Jesús). The eventual defrocking of what Andrade would deem the "conqueror" and "playboy" macho archetypes (Roberto confesses to a life of alcoholic fantasies and Jesús sees his fortune and body wither away) describes an aftermath of nationalistic masculinity that Villoro's predecessors only began to suggest. Villoro directs his attention centrally to the progeny of these fallen machos and what options are available to them in the neoliberal paradigm. Throughout the novel, the reader uncomfortably accompanies Mauricio as he escorts his father during quick visits, false errands, car rides and meltdowns involving Jesus's mistresses. Jesus's multiple lovers, who coincide with his advancement into professional life, attest to a sexual prowess that positions him as a model "playboy" macho for his youngest son. His string of love affairs signals his consumerist approach to masculinity. For him, as for the "playboy" machos of the 1960s, "[g]irls are play things, and once enjoyed will have to be set aside and replaced with another new and fresh" (Andrade 36). Villoro describes Jesús and a young Mauricio, who has been grotesquely converted into his father's sidekick and a witness to his escapades, coming home in a celebratory mood after a new love conquest. It is at this juncture that we see the duality of the social expectations that dictate a muted relationship between husband and wife who, in *marianista* fashion, performs stoically as the homemaker and the mother of his children while Jesús assumes his responsibility as the breadwinner with benefits. Employment, according to public health researcher Ellen Hardy, is an essential component to a man's identity and self-respect. Therefore, a professional career is most desirable not only for the income and status it provides in the public sphere but also because the man is respected and admired by his wife and children at home. Conversely, as a licensed architect who works as an accountant supplementing his earnings with the questionable sale of surplus merchandise from the warehouse that employs him, Jesús constantly seeks to affirm his masculinity through consecutive sexual encounters. His behavior aligns with that of traditional machos who avert situations in which they perceive themselves at a social disadvantage. When it is unavoidable, as in the case of holding a menial office job in order to subsist, the macho will find outlets to prove his superiority. The most direct expression of masculinity is domination and penetration of a partner, and through the sexual act the macho restores his fragile ego.[4] Adhering to the social expectations of his class status, Jesús will protect his wife, as she is a decent woman, from his sexual desires and fantasies. Accordingly, when he is at home, he takes on the role of the traditional *pater familias*, but he becomes a "conqueror" macho when he is on the hunt for his next coital encounter. As an analogy of a shifting national discourse, Jesús's unfulfilled professional title alludes to the fading authority of a post-revolutionary state, while his improvised financial tactics indicate the emerging deregulated practices of neoliberalism. The coping mechanism of his sexual escapades demonstrates that Jesús is only willing to compromise his official status as long as he can maintain the cultural privileges afforded to the macho.

Jesús Guardiola's professional trajectory matches his sexual domination. At first, his *machismo* manifests as exaggerated sexual prowess with which he overcomes his feelings of professional inferiority by overachieving in the arena of sexual partners. However, once he legitimizes himself as an architect, the quick rendezvous at cheap motels no longer satisfy him, and he adds a *casa chica* to his *casa grande*, thus expanding his sexual horizons from beyond the confines of the *pater familias*. His increased fame and accompanying dalliances, legitimized in the eyes of his powerful associates, speak to the role of professional worth in Mexican masculinity.

Despite the novel's exploration of masculinity in crisis, its women continue to follow traditional gender roles and Villoro depicts them within a "decent" or "sexually easy" binary. To begin with, the wife and mother of the story, Cristina Ferrán, epitomizes a *mujer marianista* as described by Evelyn Stevens. Born in the countryside with a strict religious education, Cristina understands, accepts, and performs the stereotype of the ideal woman who, among other characteristics, embodies moral superiority and spiritual strength: "This spiritual strength engenders abnegation, that is, an infinite capacity for humility and sacrifice. No self-denial is too great…, no limit can be divined to her vast store of patience with the men of her world" (Stevens 9).

Indeed, Cristina is the quiet hand that maintains the house where she serves her husband and two sons. Mauricio, her youngest son, comes to despise her religious values and her resigned stoicism. One day, he decides to provoke her by telling her about her husband's numerous infidelities. In turn, she calmly discloses that she knew about his betrayals all along, thus demonstrating, to the shock of her son, her fortitude and her conditioned understanding of available gender roles. Like many of the women in Villoro's narratives, Cristina accepts without question these behaviors because: "men must be humored, for, after all, everyone knows that they are *como niños* (like little boys) whose intemperance, foolishness, and obstinacy must be forgiven because 'they can't help the way they are'" (Stevens 9). Thus, ideal women never hold men accountable for their trespasses but rather endure them impassively.

In opposition to the devoted suffering wife, Roger Bartra has identified the archetype of the "Chingadalupe," a woman who enjoys sex but who can also be virginal and comforting (*La jaula* 183). This is what Rita Terreros embodies via her backstory, a common one in Mexican narrative fiction and the lore of popular culture where a regional beauty pageant contestant is spotted by a patriarch who offers her the opportunity to see the world, in this case as a flight attendant. Rita is charming and savvy, and she is cosmopolitan and polished enough to be the mistress of various highly ranked politicians and technocrats, including Jesús Guardiola. An early novelized version of the Chingadalupe figure, who is aptly named Mariana, can be found in Pacheco's *Batallas*. However, where Mariana takes on an idealized form in Carlos's memory, Rita is far less idealized in Villoro's novel, as the reader is privy to both her public flair and her private meltdowns.

In sharp contrast, Clarita Rendón represents an antithetical presence to Cristina's abject domesticity and Rita's materialistic ambitions. Not only does she not subscribe to expected models of femininity, Clarita is a vestige of the "universalist" intellectual faction which stood in opposition to the post-revolutionary intelligentsia that helped construct *lo mexicano*, and which paved the way for exponents like Jesús Guardiola (Pérez Daniel 212-213). Moreover, her independence and intelligence defy both hegemonic masculinity and nationalistic discourse. As expected, a self-sufficient woman such as Clarita is not desirable in the macho-sphere, and so she is described as an idiosyncratic old maid who lives alone surrounded by her books. Clarita is a cautionary tale with different messages for both genders: on the one hand, she embodies the assumption that raising a family and personal intellectual growth are irreconcilable in a patriarchal society; on the other hand, her self-sufficiency and intellectual independence speaks to changing options for women in a transitional neoliberal state, options which men will have to learn how to accept if the nation is to be advanced by their progeny.

As with Jesus Guardiola's "playboy" *machismo*, young Mauricio is the direct witness to the various constructs of the feminine that submit to or confront him. Consequently, he develops eccentric perceptions and expectations of women, but there still remains an unmanageable idealization that hearkens to *marianismo*, especially when he muses: "[m]i idea de la belleza femenina tenía que ver con el sufrimiento" (23). This idea of equating feminine beauty to suffering is clear when the reader learns that his first childhood crush is his neighbor, Verónica, who is hit by a car. While she remains at home in a coma for many months, Mauricio daydreams of their non-existent relationship. When she awakens, having fully recovered from the accident, Mauricio is disappointed, admitting: "[y]o quería una loca, una beata profética, una visionaria muy dañada, una gritona incontenible o una pálida dispuesta a nuevos sufrimientos, a soportar sin pasmo los filos, las agujas, nuestra mala sangre" (145). Around the same time, Mauricio develops an admiration for men's bodies, specifically that of the neighborhood rubber vulcanizer whose robust physique resembles those of comic strip superheroes. As Héctor Domínguez-Ruvalcaba points out, within a masculine hegemony there is an irrational connection between heroism and homosexuality. However, through these contradictory predilections, Mauricio exhibits an important shift in going against the beauty standard set by his father's taste in women while his homoerotic desires introduce a reconfiguration of the (younger) national subject who is resisting heterosexual macho archetypes. Accordingly, to forgo macho sexual attitudes is to refuse patriarchal rationalizations of dominance: "Questioning desire foregrounds the problem of the symbolic order of the nation" (Domínguez-Ruvalcaba 99). In other words, challenging masculinity undermines national identity.

Mauricio's variable masculinity and awkward *machismo* is clearly displayed during his relationship with Regina, an "older woman" who, at fourteen years old, is two years older than our pubescent Mauricio. Unlike the idealized Mariana in *Las batallas*, who is depicted as beautiful, mature, and worldly, Regina is working class, bulky, and uncouth. She represents not the desire for an American style of domestic life (as depicted in *Las batallas*), but an experience grounded in the socio-economic profile of most working-class Mexicans. With Regina, Mauricio will experience a sexually dissident encounter because, unlike his father, his intimacy is not for control and possession of a woman's body, but rather a means for a sensorial exploration. In retrospect, he understands this experience as a developmental step in a path to a fully realized masculinity: "Regina me lamía, me dejaba tocar sus trofeos, ... pero nunca la vi como novia. En realidad ni siquiera la vi como mujer; costaba trabajo ubicarla entre las personas, su tibieza era buena de modo fronterizo, que no se agotaba en sí mismo, era una mediación hacia otra cosa..." (112). While it would appear that Mauricio uses Regina as practice towards a more acceptable feminine conquest, Regina's physical and sexual agency speaks to a shift in the macho paradigm. Further, Mauricio develops a pattern of siding with a woman who is at a situational or sentimental disadvantage.[5] His description of Regina indicates that he perceives her as marginal, even liminal, but he likes her precisely because of that: "Para mí era fea, y me gustaba. La sabía grande, simple, enrojecida, extraordinaria" (120). Mauricio's candid descriptions of Regina and her body are meant to be discomforting to his *status quo* of masculinity, as she does not fulfill a standard of beauty that has been modeled for him.

As Tamara Williams has noted, the final episode of the novel reveals Mauricio as a foil to the broken-down masculinities of Jesús and his brother. For Williams, Mauricio's participation in the rescue brigades of the 1985 earthquake distances him from the self-interested *machismo* of his elders. But his idyllic emergence from the rubble of the 1985 earthquake, walking hand-in-hand with Verónica, who, we recall, was preserved in childhood purity by her coma, suggests a final reconciliation with heteronormative masculinity that will somehow survive the disruptions of a neoliberal Mexico. True to a canonical post-revolutionary formula, Mauricio emerges from the crises of political, social and gender identity a fully realized macho, even after a lengthy reflection on the limitations and variations of masculinity in his awkward upbringing.

The awkward macho

In *El disparo de argón*, Villoro presents an isolated Mexico City *colonia* over which looms a monolithic eye clinic. As an imagined community, colonia San Lorenzo serves less as a microcosm of the post-revolutionary state than it does as a portent for the neoliberal state to come. At the beginning of the narrative, Doctor Fernando Balmes questions what makes him stay in San Lorenzo despite its filthiness, chaos, pollution and poverty. He credits his endurance to his upbringing as the son of a history teacher whose favorite lessons were of lost revolutionary battles: "Desde que tengo uso de razón he oído discursos sobre los valientes que le sonríen a la metralla y se desbarrancan gustosos en cañadas" (*Disparo* 14). He concludes that Mexicans, namely Mexican men, have a propensity to endure hard beatings and painful annoyances so that they can boast about them later. However, that type of defiant masculinity does not resonate with a grown Balmes who, at 36 years of age, finds himself stuck (in San Lorenzo, at work, with no serious relationship, and no prospects), and so he begins to narrate his life in search of clarity.

Just as the structures of family, home, and neighborhood infiltrate the professional sphere of the clinic, so does Balmes's professional trajectory become confused with his position in a stagnating patriarchy. At first glance, the clinic, as a metonym of the patriarchal State, gives the impression of order. However, the announcement of an opening for a new Chief of the Retina Department prompts all the male doctors to compete against each other for the new vacant position, even Balmes, who declares at the outset that he is not interested: "No hay jefe de Retina y hasta los que no tenemos mayor interés en el puesto hemos caído en una rabiosa competencia" (17). Considering that the clinic epitomizes the political system in Mexico at a moment of transition, this fight for a directorship is important for the future of the clinic and for the sustainability of patriarchal values. In a discussion of capitalism and masculinity, Harry Brod suggests that the shift in the economic model that transitions from power resting in individual (largely male) hands to those of institutions carried great implications for the male role, specifically culminating in a dilemma between: "public male power and the feelings of men's private powerlessness" (14). While power is still a masculine prerogative, it rests within the institution, not within a single agent. Thus, in the search for a new Retina Chief, the doctors vie for status and influence as a legitimate form of masculinity granted by the hospital's leadership.

Balmes, who exhibits the characteristics of an aloof, "masked" macho, is not ambitiously interested in the new job. However, as he is perceived to be an ethical, hard worker with roots in the community, he is pressured by everyone inside and outside the clinic to bid for the new leadership position. This promotion would literally move him up one floor where the founder, doctor Antonio Suarez, as well as other departmental chiefs, have their offices. The new position would require him to bring order to his department and, eventually, to the clinic. He has the potential to be Andrade's "authentic" macho, for he personifies the simple, decent man who could become a *pater familias* and establish balance inside the clinic and out to the community. However, although he has the full endorsement of his colleagues, his family, and his community, he refuses that (im)position.

As he takes stock of the clinic's situation, Balmes describes a vertical hierarchy that will have him perform an assertive masculine persona to reorganize his department as needed. The ground floor is the threshold between the clinic and the outside world. Some people come in to get a doctor's appointment, and others, in an analogy of the informal sector, come to set up shop to fulfill the necessities of those in the waiting room. Doctor Iniestra manages all the activities of the first floor related to the clinic and to the informal businesses that operate there. The people of San Lázaro find him very charming and amicable. Balmes regards him as vulgar, petty, and corrupt, someone who would require delicate negotiation if he is promoted to the fourth floor. On the second floor, we find the only female doctor in the clinic, Sara Martínez Gluck, who was Balmes's classmate at the university. She is a token of the open educational and professional opportunities afforded to women as the Mexican State is transitioning into a globalized economy. Even though she is a frequently cited researcher, she is confined to a small office because, unlike her male counterparts, she is not a surgeon, that is, she is not a risk-taking agent of medical care. Despite the fact that she is as competent as her colleagues and seems to be more invested in the future of the clinic than the aloof Balmes, the organization of the clinic limits her sphere of influence and leadership. Her second-floor office comes to represent the glass ceiling that will prevent her from being promoted and reaching top positions in the upper-level floors. Other women working at the hospital have even fewer opportunities for professional advancement. They are all the secretaries and nurses that will always only perform at those capacities.

Meanwhile, Balmes, who is being invited to step up into power, deflects the attention directed at him toward the other three surgeons whose offices, like his, are on the third floor. Doctor Briones is a functional alcoholic who jovially dispenses false hopes to his patients when diagnosing their illnesses. Doctor Ferrán is the opposite; he projects an intense, dry personality and is brutally honest with his patients. His zeal for his vocation pushes his body to the verge of a collapse. As embodiments of the transition from the post-revolutionary to the neo-liberal state, Briones and Ferrán are older doctors who are assumed to be close to retirement. Lánder Ugartechea is Balmes's peer, though his profile suggests he is the fulfillment of Balmes's unrealized potential. Where Balmes is a well-liked but unremarkable local exponent, Lánder is of Basque descent and has completed a post-doc in Boston. He has an athletic physique, is energetic, competitive and impulsive, and makes rash decisions and statements in the face of Balmes's reserve. Lánder is an assertive hustler whose favorite pastime, according to Balmes, is to resent and confront his opponents from a superior moral stance: "No hay situación que goce más que la de un médico a punto de corromperse, y si se trata de un amigo, mejor, pues lo toma como una afrenta personal. En sus ojos no había nada como 'sálvate que aún es hora' sino una invitación al fango, a ser otro enemigo meritorio" (52). Although Lánder is an ally and friend, he would not miss the opportunity to be the moral compass and to righteously reproach Balmes for his shortcomings. Balmes's brash self-assuredness speaks to the "conqueror"' macho, while his anti-establishment pretenses and individualism position him as a "masked" macho in the face of institutional decay.

Given the various defects of the candidates involved, it is easy to understand why Balmes is the favorite for the chief position in the eyes of the higher administration. However, as much as he wants to be on the same floor as his professional father, Dr. Suarez (who is successful, wealthy, famous and mysteriously elusive), Balmes fears stepping into the path of Doctor Ugalde, the executive director. Ugalde was a practicing surgeon whose time is now consumed by his administrative responsibilities, and therefore he represents the full institutionalization of the post-revolutionary order. As a director, Ugalde sees himself in a position of power running the clinic by himself in Suarez's absence. His bureaucratic positionality comes easy to Ugalde because, on the one hand, he is the highest-ranking staff member and, on the other, his sick body gives him an excuse to walk away from conflict to take care of himself. The other chiefs on the fourth floor are as old and probably as sick as Ugalde. Seeing the decrepit bodies of older "masked" machos corrupted by administrative bloat, Balmes: "pensó en las ventajas y calamidades del cuarto piso" (85). After much resistance and several rounds of self-doubt, Balmes decides to accept the position but it had already gone to a new recruit. Perez Daniel identifies this anticlimactic end as Villoro's trademark *narrativa de la derrota*, a term he borrows from Ana María Amar Sanchez (205), which speaks to the failing of the nationalistic patriarchal project that began to crumble after the Tlatelolco massacre of 1968.

As much as Balmes seems to embody the most evolved forms of *machismo* in the taxonomy set forth by Andrade, there is another side to him that speaks to his unresolved insecurities and deviation from standards of beauty that befit an "authentic" macho. Like Mauricio from *Materia dispuesta*, Balmes has an older childhood friend, Carolina, whose games contributed to his personality and the way he perceives his masculinity. Rather than a friend, Balmes felt like a vassal following Carolina's orders and getting into trouble for her pranks. He describes her as a terrible goddess who made him feel good when she mistreated him. In an embodiment of a pre-pubescent macho, she would dunk his head in water, cover him in dirt, make him spit on her hands to make mud grenades, make grass juice with her urine and then make him drink it. But she would also lay naked hiding amidst her garden ferns, and ask him to look at her. From this childhood memory, we are led to believe that he associates dirt, foul smells, and atypical behavior with pleasure, and disgust with sexual excitement.

This childhood foundation informs Balmes's account of his sexual partner, whom he refers to with a single initial, *F*. Balmes admits that what he finds most exciting about her is that she surrenders herself to him without words or expectation of a future together, a behavior that he admits: "me producen una excitación física que creí que ya no viviría" (47). He also finds her cheap underwear endearing and he takes pleasure in sensing the different body odors she emanates from spending time in the countryside on journalistic assignments. "¿Por qué las sensaciones más arrebatadas están al borde del asco?" he muses (47). Disgust and excitement seem to go hand in hand for

Balmes, and they are certainly more important to him than his lovers' professional worth.

Balmes directs a similar line of commentary toward Mónica, the new eye clinic employee. He describes her as shapely and anorexic, with a faint mustache and unibrow, stained teeth (as a result of too many antibiotics as a child), sour breath, and a sulfur smell from her nervous habit of burning matches. In his own aloofness, Balmes is intrigued by her distant manner. She is an introvert for whom living seems to take great effort, although it also seems to be a pleasurable suffering. In this sense, she comes close to embodying Mauricio's idealized love interest, Verónica, in *Materia dispuesta*. Mónica is an idealized but likewise marginal figure who dwells in a sustained fatalism about the limited and obstacle-ridden socioeconomic advancement that is available to her in an institutionalized patriarchy. For most of the narrative, Balmes suspects Ugalde hired her to spy on everyone in the clinic. He doubts her allegiance to him even at the end of the novel, when he decides to follow her out of the confines of the neighborhood, acting not out of love, but out of an adventurous desire for the possibility of further unfortunate experiences with her.

While Balmes's predilections speak to a deviation from the macho's ideal of feminine beauty, and to a willingness to confess and display vulnerability to the women in his life, his account sustains a unilateral attraction to the female body in its physicality. As a physician, Balmes applies the rhetoric of diagnosis to his personal relationships, and benefits from a morbid gaze facilitated by the demands of his profession. In this way, he is able to enjoy F as an anonymous body, and he finds Mónica's malaise and poor health arousing. Through his awkwardness, Balmes strips his love interests of their personality and engages them as defective bodies to be diagnosed and potentially healed.

It is through his professional conduct that Balmes more clearly displays the persistence of *machismo*. For example, in his disparaging regard of his secretary, Conchita, Balmes exercises a more identifiable masculine superiority through the derisive critique of what he perceives to be workplace seduction: "Nunca entenderé el alma de Conchita; pasa horas frente al espejo hasta quedar como un fogoso ángel de la noche y exige trato de beata. ... No era difícil ponerse del lado de los ciclistas (que le tocaron la nalga); además, en mis tiempos de recadero yo también tuve mi cuota de nalgas tocadas a velocidad" (59). In this scene, Balmes empathizes with the group of men who just groped his secretary. In line with patriarchal coding, he declares incredulously that Conchita makes a great effort to dress provocatively while expecting everyone to respect her. Moreover, he admits to having slapped women's buttocks when the opportunity was available to him, as if it were a rite of passage in the pursuit of his current position at the hospital. In spite of any vulnerability that he might have confessed in his account of his love interests, Balmes's workplace behavior renders him an operative of institutional patriarchy.

Awkward *machismo* as an expression of neoliberalism[6]

Dr. Antonio Suarez, the founder of the clinic, is absent until the novel's final chapters when he reveals that, at 75 years old, he is going blind and in need of Balmes's surgical skill, which Balmes provides in the novel's culminating moments. An exploration of patriarchal supremacy that in a post-revolutionary novel would play out more formulaically is complicated here by Balmes's social awkwardness, and by the destabilization of the clinic. Along with the open market in the lobby, the clinic positions Balmes in a telling analogy of a NAFTA to come, through the intrigue of an eye-trafficking business conducted between Iniestra and an undefined group of California businessmen described as *los tejanos*. Where in *Materia dispuesta* Villoro laboriously and painfully describes the demise of a national and institutional patriarchy, in *El disparo* his characters sift through the ruins of a precarious intersection of nation, fatherhood, and community. It is not that national patriarchy has been eradicated by this exercise, but rather that participation in it is available through multiple and unpredictable points of entry.

Likewise, Mexico in the 1990s displays "síntomas de una extinción crítica del sistema político autoritario" that manifest "como crisis del nacionalismo, exigencia de democracia y búsqueda de nuevas formas de identidad" (Bartra, *La sangre* 16). The interrogation of the political structure opens the question of national identity and allows for a flow of masculine role models in the 80s and 90s. A reading of masculinity in Villoro's first two novels, as analogies of the difficult transition from a post-revolutionary to a neoliberal state, initially suggests that the personal and situational awkwardness of the narrator-protagonists speaks to a counter-hegemonic position; that is, that the institutional masculinity of the PRI will not correspond to the neoliberal concessions required by NAFTA. However, and as Villoro's protagonists readily demonstrate, Mexican masculinity prevails in this new iteration by allowing for an experimentation not with gender roles but with alternative forms of gender domination. An updating of Andrade's taxonomy might describe the awkward macho as one who recognizes the challenges of masculine constructs, but who ultimately subscribes to the idea of masculine superiority. Rather than hide this concession behind a façade of social justice as the "masked" macho does, the awkward macho distorts expectations of masculinity, femininity and sexuality just enough to adapt to a neoliberal Mexico. That *Materia dispuesta* follows *El disparo* as a concessional prequel to a questionable masculinity speaks to this dilemma. Villoro's protagonists in subsequent novels, such as *El testigo* (2004) and *Arrecife* (2012), continue to play with masculine identity, but, in their deepest personal reflections and recollections, they belie a recognizable deference to what a man ought to be, even as the institutionalization of a national patriarchy stumbles its way into a new century.

Notes

[1] Porfirian and *Porfiriato* refer to General Porfirio Díaz, who was the President of Mexico from 1876-1910, with a four-year interregnum in 1880-1884. The motto of his presidency was "Order and Progress." "Progress" came under the guise of connectivity and magnificent architectural accomplishments. During the *Porfiriato* a great railway system was built and miles of telegraph wires were installed throughout Mexico for commercial and political reasons. In the capital, Díaz commissioned many beautiful buildings, which earned the city the moniker "City of Palaces." However, "order" came at the cost of violence, repression, and the violation of human rights within a totalitarian dictatorship. Thus, "progress" was for the aristocrats, the elite, and foreign investors, while "order" was imposed on the rest of the population estimated to be illiterate and living in poverty. Under such conditions, Porfirio Díaz considered himself the stern but nurturing Father of his poor and unlearned Mexican children. The Mexican Revolution (1910-1921) intended to abolish the two-tier system. However, President Alemán Valdés (1946-1952) established a new iteration of the Porfirian system.

[2] The term *crónica* refers to the hybrid form of journalism and literary essay, popularized in the nineteenth century by *costumbrista* authors, especially Francisco Zarco (1829-1869), and refined in the post-revolutionary twentieth century to bear witness to Mexico City's modernization. Authors such as those mentioned (Blanco, Monsiváis, Poniatwoska) developed a street-level regard of the city inspired by Salvador Novo's *Nueva grandeza mexicana* (1946). However, those *cronistas* departed from Novo's encomiastic register and practiced a critical exploration of the nation's contradictions, ironies, and injustices as demonstrated by a rapidly transforming urban landscape. Villoro's own *crónica* takes a cue from the new *cronistas'* fascination with dynamic but fragmented prose stylings and anecdotal meanderings. However, his *El vertigo horizontal* (2018), a laudatory celebration of the metro system as the central protagonist in contemporary Mexico City, interestingly returns to Novo's encomiastic regard.

[3] *Casa grande* indicates the official legitimate home of a man, his wife and children. *Casa chica* refers to that man's second household set up for his second family: his mistress and the children they might have together. It was a widespread practice among the Mexican political class of the nineteenth and twentieth century, and as such it was emulated by all men who could minimally afford to maintain two households. The practice was deemed "not illegal" in 2011, to protect the rights of the second woman to demand benefits based on years of cohabitation.

[4] In "The Sons of La Malinche," Octavio Paz alludes to the fragile male ego when he explains that Mexican men need to constantly affirm themselves as *machos chingones* in front of others: "The verb denotes violence, an emergence from oneself to penetrate another by force" (76). In this way, any insecurity or vulnerability perceived by a man can be overcome by the domination and penetration of a passive feminine Other. The act reestablishes manliness as a result of imposing oneself on others, even other men, in a quest of recognition as the biggest *chingón*. The social sciences have also looked into sexual dominance as a strategy for ego restoration. In her study, Ellen Hardy notes that

masculinity has come to be understood as an expression of sexualized virility in which the optimum size and performance of the sexual organ becomes proof of a healthy masculinity: "Las conquistas amorosas, la erección del pene, la penetración, y las proezas sexuales son símbolos de autoafirmación de la virilidad" (81). Hence, to be the active partner in a sexual act becomes the most direct expression of masculine dominance and identity.

[5] This pattern is clearer during his childhood years. For example, Jesús would give his lovers teddy bears as gifts. Mauricio who saw the many teddy bears would feel sad for the young women who got a smaller or lesser quality gift. Once Jesús started dating Rita, Mauricio would side with Rita whenever there was an argument. Later, Mauricio finds out Rita has another man and wishes his father would repudiate her and kick her out. When Jesús does exactly that, Mauricio intercedes on Rita's behalf and asks his father to give her a second chance. Jesús doesn't change his mind, and Mauricio laments having tattled on Rita. He also comes to his mother's defense when Jesús is about to divorce her.

[6] In broad terms, neoliberalism is understood as an economic model in favor of free markets and free international trade, and in opposition to existing government regulation. This plays out in late twentieth century Mexican history with the gradual cessation of post-revolutionary oversight of property, goods, and culture to global, and especially U.S., interventions. While Miguel Alemán Valdés takes concrete steps towards establishing a neoliberal state via concessions to U.S. investment, it is the *sexenio* (six-year term) of President Carlos Salinas de Gortari and the advent NAFTA that truly consecrate an endorsement of free market practices in advancement of Mexican elite classes and at the whim of global investors and corporations.

Works Cited

Andrade, A. Rolando. "*Machismo*: A Universal Malady." *The Journal of American Culture*, vol. 15, no. 4, 1992, pp. 33-41.

Bartra, Roger. *La jaula de la melancolía: identidad y metamorfosis del mexicano*. Grijalbo, 1987.

——. *La sangre y la tinta: Ensayos sobre la condición postmexicana*. Océano, 2013.

Brod, Harry, editor. *The Making of Masculinities: The New Man's Studies*. Allen and Unwin, 1987.

Carrillo-Arciniega, Raúl. "Identidades de resistencia y el simulacro de ser mexicano en *Los culpables* de Juan Villoro." *Chasqui*, vol. 42, no.1, 2013, pp. 54-63.

Domínguez-Ruvalcaba, Héctor. *Modernity and the Nation in Mexican Representations of Masculinity: From Sensuality to Bloodshed*. Palgrave Macmillan, 2007.

Elhers, Tracy. "Debunking Marianismo: Economic Vulnerability and Survival Strategies among Guatemalan Wives." *Ethnology* vol. 30, no.1, 1991, pp. 1-16.

François, Liesbeth. "Una isla urbana en el mar transnacional: *El disparo de argón*." *Confluencia: Revista Hispánica de Cultura y Literatura*, vol. 32, no.1, 2016, pp. 70-85.

Guerra, Lucía. *La mujer fragmentada: Historias de un signo*. Chile: Editorial Cuarto Propio, 1995.

Hardy, Ellen. "Masculinidad y género." Translated by Ana Luisa Jiménez. *Revista Cubana de Salud Pública*, vol. 27, no. 2, 2001, pp. 77-88.

Ortner, Sherry B. *Making Gender. The Politics of Erotics of Culture*. Beacon Press, 1996.

Pacheco, José Emilio. *Las batallas en el desierto*. Ediciones ERA, 1981.

Paz, Octavio. "The Sons of La Malinche." *The Labyrinth of Solitude*. Translated by Lysander Kemp, Yara Milos and Rachel Phillips Belash. Grove Press, 1985.

Pérez Daniel, Iván. "Memorias del derrumbe: Representaciones de la Historia y del nacionalismo mexicano en *Materia dispuesta* de Juan Villoro." *Hispanic Review*, vol. 81, no. 2, 2013, pp. 201-223.

Ruisánchez Serra, José Ramón. "Juan Villoro." *The Contemporary Spanish-American Novel: Bolaño and After*, edited by Will H. Corral, et al. Bloomsbury, 2013, pp. 88-96.

Stevens, Evelyn. "Marianismo: The Other Face of Machismo." *Female and Male in Latin America: Essays*, edited by Ann Pescatello. University of Pittsburgh Press, 1973, pp. 90-101.

Villoro, Juan. *El disparo de argon*. Barcelona, Editorial Anagrama, 1991.

——. *Materia dispuesta*. Alfaguara, 1997.

——. *El vértigo horizontal*. Alfaguara, 2018.

Williams, Tamara. "Toallas ejemplares: masculinidad, sexualidad y nación en *Materia dispuesta*." *Materias dispuestas: Juan Villoro ante la crítica*, edited by José Ramón Ruisánchez and Oswaldo Zavala. Barcelona, Editorial Candaya, 2011, pp. 337-363.

Further Reading

Amar Sánchez, Ana María. "Apuntes para una historia de perdedores: ética y política en la narrativa hispánica contemporánea." *Revista Iberoamericana*, vol. 21, 2006, pp. 151-64.

Novo, Salvador. *Nueva grandeza mexicana*. Buenos Aires, Espasa-Calpe, 1947.

Sassen, Saskia. *Territory, Authority, Rights: From Medieval to Global Assemblages*. Princeton University Press, 2016.

Chapter 4

The Road to Feminist Masculinity and Freedom: Fathers as Patriarchs, Authors as Activists

Kathryn Quinn-Sánchez

Georgian Court University

Hegemonic masculinity limits what is perceived as acceptable behavior by men (and boys) in most societies. Certainly, behavior is taught and modeled by fathers to their children. Amongst Latino (and other) cultures, machismo acts as a detriment as it requires male participants to bully and behave aggressively. Males reinforce each other's masculinity by verbally and physically abusing one another. However, there is a place for a feminist masculinity when men and fathers express love, compassion and support for each other and for their children. Unique is the trajectory of the macho male that chooses the path of the feminist male, yet apart from the typical aggression and anger model, there are examples of men/fathers who represent feminist masculinity. The norm, sadly, continues to reinforce the persistence of hegemonic masculinity making the societal change toward feminist masculinity a challenge.

Although Latina mothers and their relationships with their daughters have been studied at length in Latinx literary criticism, studies of fathers and men in general have received little attention. Alfredo Mirandé writes: "the topic of Chicano/Latino masculinity remains neglected and virtually unexplored both within the so-called new men's studies and feminist scholarship" (118). Furthermore, it must be emphasized that:

> Latino men occupy a contradictory position within a system of privilege, one that offers them advantages but concurrently disadvantages those belonging to devalued social categories, that is, men who come from working-class backgrounds, who are immigrants, who speak Spanish, who often look racially nonwhite, who have a

Latino background, and who may be gay—all statuses that contribute
to experiencing racism, ethnocentrism, classism, and heterosexism.
(Hurtado and Sinha 12)

As members of the patriarchy simply due to their biology, heterosexual Latino
men are likely to feel powerful in certain spaces where gender is the identity
marker at play. However, it is evident that when race, ethnicity or social class
come to the fore, they are not at the top of the hierarchy, that space belongs
exclusively to the white male from the middle or upper class. Consequently,
Latino men are apt to feel inferior due to these identity markers and
internalize these macro and micro aggressions, which may surface later
toward the women in their lives. Indeed, domestic violence occurs as a result
of an unequal society, and most likely to occur when the Latino man is in the
private space of the home as husband and/or father.[1] While power certainly
allows men to exert their physical strength over women, the reason why this is
such a recurring event is due to patriarchy. Men are taught to suppress their
emotions: "Patriarchal mores teach a form of emotional stoicism to men that
says they are more manly if they do not feel, but if by chance they should feel
and the feelings hurt, the manly response is to stuff them down, to forget
about them, to hope they will go away" (hooks 5-6). In other words: "There is
only one emotion that patriarchy values when expressed by men; the emotion
is anger" (hooks 7). Ironically, it is understood that machismo—defined as a
strong or exaggerated sense of power or the right to dominate—is passed on
to the next generation by mothers and their bias for sons over daughters.
Thankfully, fathers do not always fall into the machista paradigm;
nevertheless, it is evident that many behave in such a manner. In this study, I
will portray several types of fathers in order to present a broad range of
treatment that fathers bestow upon their daughters. By focusing attention on
five fathers in Chicana literature, perhaps I can shed some light on how
Chicana authors choose to represent fatherhood and surmise the impact on
the next generation.

Through critical readings of Cherríe Moraga's play *The Hungry Woman* (2001),
Sandra Cisneros' *The House of Mango Street* (1984), and Margarita Tavera
Rivera's play *La condición* (1991) the reader will come to understand how
fatherhood has been represented in Chicanx Literature. Specifically, the texts I
study portray and also defy the traditional definition of what constitutes Latino
masculinity in the United States of America. In the words of bell hooks: "When
culture is based on a dominator model, not only will it be violent but it will
frame all relationships as power struggles" (116). The authors contest the place
that many Latina women are still relegated to, by representing mothers and
daughters who consciously decide that it is time to battle the forces that would
keep them powerless; at times fathers and husbands are supportive, other times

they are the reason why mothers and daughters decide to fight against the gendered norms within the Chicano family.

To destabilize these rigid gender norms, I analyze how Cherríe Moraga portrays the nation and its counterpart, the family, as accomplices that function to categorize and ultimately exile those considered unworthy of citizenship in *The Hungry Woman*.[2] Sandra Cisneros shows in *The House on Mango Street* how machismo seeps into family relationships to reinforce the submissive, silent expectations of Latinas who are taught that their bodies belong to men. Moreover, we see that hooks underscores how men use force—physically or verbally in their relationships: "Men's continued allegiance to a notion of masculinity that could no longer be fully realized on the old terms led them to place greater emphasis on their ability to dominate and control by physical force and abusive psychological terrorism" (127). In particular, Sally and Alicia learn about sexuality from their own fathers. And finally, Margarita Tavera Rivera in *La condición* accentuates the significance of having at least one parent (the father) supportive of his daughter's wish to become a professor. All three works serve as unique portrayals of Chicano fathers, some represent tradition while one shows a progressive slant towards his daughter, even in the face of dire consequences: an angry wife/mother.

La condición

Margarita Tavera Rivera, author of the play *La condición*, presents a family that seems rather predictable in how the parents conform to the expected behaviors that *condition* their children to perform in a society with strict gender norms. Early in the play we hear Juan speak forcefully to his sister Rosario: "Cuándo te vas a dar cuenta que eres mujer y que no puedes ser otra cosa (486).[3] Clearly, one begins to understand that sexist male peers or siblings enforce patriarchal norms. In another exchange between mother and father, we see that Concha expresses distaste of her husband Tomás, due to his imbibing of beer because, by so doing, he has been modeling that behavior for their sons: "Que aprendan a tomar, para eso son hombres" (486).[4] Yet Concha determines that he is not as responsible a father as he could be. Of course, Tomás disagrees and replies: "He tratado de ser justo con todos mis hijos, los hombres y las mujeres" (487).[5] And then we hear the crux of Concha's fear when she replies: "¿Es que me reprochas algo a mí? Tú fuiste el que dejó que Rosario se fuera a la universidad" (487).[6] Concha shows anger towards her husband because he did not follow the norm by insisting that their daughter Rosario marry. Underlying this discussion is the understanding, or lack thereof, that Concha has for her daughter's future. Indeed, patriarchy and the Catholic Church have informed Concha and nurtured her fear that Rosario will lose her virginity or become pregnant if she attends university as a young, unaccompanied woman. Olivia M. Espín has asserted that these thoughts have become normalized: "because women's bodies were presented as sinful, impure, and imperfect by centuries of cultural and religious discourse, [consequently], many women equated sanctity with controlling...their bodies" (103). Furthermore, Brenda Sendejo proclaims: "Church dogma and discourses functioned to suppress women and their sexualities" (82). Due to her own lack of options as a young woman and the internalization of social beliefs, Concha tries to impose the same "*condición*" on her daughter. In a unique twist, Tavera Rivera chooses to subvert the Latina custom of automatic marriage and children for Rosario, and portrays Tomás as a father that supports his daughter's career path, not merely for her undergraduate degree, but through to her doctorate, despite having to deal with his wife and her dissatisfaction. Concha knows that her daughter may never return after her years of study, and if she does, she simply will not be the same. Tavera Rivera privileges Rosario with the personal experience of attaining the highest level of education possible: the Ph.D. Ironically, this achievement is not always perceived in a positive light. The reason is summed up by Concha's fears, and has been articulated by several Latina academics; while reaching for the goal of education, simultaneously they are distancing themselves from those they love the most. Education allows one to think from many points of view with a contextual understanding of the historical moment as well as the prevalent ideology. With this ability, family members begin to see their educated daughters (and sons) as if they were aliens.

The reader of *La condición* soon learns that Concha and Tomás's other daughter Teresa is engaged and the wedding will take place soon. Concha turns their topic of conversation to Teresa's wedding and how disgruntled she is that both their daughters will leave them. Again she is fearful and tells her husband that Teresa is unprepared: "no sabe ni hacer café" (488).[7] Tomás attempts to allay her anxiety by reminding her that she was only seventeen when they were married:

Concha: Pero eso fue diferente. But that was different.

Tomás: ¿Por qué? Why?

Concha: Porque yo no tuve que hacer esa decision, la hizo mi padre. Because I didn't have to make the decision, my father made it.

Tomás: ¿No crees que es mejor que Teresa escoja al hombre con quien compartirá su vida? ¿Es que tú piensas que debí escogerlo yo? Don't you think it's better that Teresa chooses the man with whom she will share her life? (488)

From Tomás's behavior, it is apparent that while he supports his sons' acting as traditional men, he is also open to listening to and permitting his daughters to make their own decisions. Perhaps if his sons were also interested in university, Rosario's life may have turned out differently, but based on the play that Tavera Rivera has written, the father, not the mother, allows for one daughter to break free from the life that her mother, grandmother and great-grandmother have lived, choosing the intellectual life of the university over the traditional norm of marrying and becoming a mother. Moreover, Teresa, the second daughter, is deemed capable by her father to choose her mate and husband, while Concha, her mother, refuses to support Teresa's or Rosario's choice. The author challenges the reader to comprehend how women constantly shape and reinforce our own acceptance/rejection of machismo in our everyday lives. While Tomás does not abuse his family nor reinforce hegemonic masculinity based on aggression, ironically his wife has this tendency to legitimize the social norm of machismo at the cost of "losing" her daughter to a brighter future based on her level of education and rejection of marriage and children.

The House on Mango Street

"Papa Who Wakes Up Tired in the Dark"

"Your *abuelito* is dead, Papa says early one morning in my room. *Está muerto*, and then as if he just heard the news himself, crumples like a coat and cries, my brave Papa cries. I have never seen my Papa cry and don't know what to do" (56). In an uncharacteristic portrayal of masculinity, Sandra Cisneros displays a brief moment of fatherhood when the daughter is the one comforting the parent. It must be pointed out how unique this representation of a man crying is, especially a Latino male. By the sheer act of portraying Papa breaking down in grief due to the loss of his own father, fatherhood becomes much more than an embodiment of patriarchy and power. Rather, it is an emotional relationship based on love, as we can imagine how much Papa loved his own Papa, Esperanza's *abuelito*. And in the act of holding her Papa as he cries, Esperanza showers her own Papa with love, allowing him to express his sadness. Indeed, she takes on the responsibility of explaining to her siblings why they cannot play today, why they must be quiet and respectful of their *abuelito's* passing.

By representing a scene where the father cries, Cisneros opens a window onto the humanity within men that is rarely portrayed. Too many times the emphasis is the stereotypical father that forces his will upon the family, whereas Cisneros paints with broad strokes as she covers the canvas with the entire *barrio*. It is not that we will not see the aspects of a traditional *machismo* (indeed, we will see plenty), but we also see fathers who simply love their families without having to impose their dominance on the rest of the family, which echoes hooks's thoughts: "The truth we do not tell is that men are longing for love" (4). It is unusual to see fathers who express their emotions, even sadness and grief, and show their children their tears. It is the love that Esperanza shows her Papa that helps him through the difficult talk about losing his father. The representation of Esperanza's father displaying his humanity, albeit in the privacy of his own home in front of his daughter, allows Cisneros to counter the dominant images of macho males that bombard us through images, films, and TV shows. For example,

> Still today, popular culture reinforces static, homogenizing, and pathologizing notions of Latino men. Quite often both in popular culture and the social sciences, the diversity within the Latino population or transitions in Latino cultures and societies are not acknowledged. Instead, images continue to proliferate of macho men and passive women embedded in strict patriarchal families, and of conservative religious people with undemocratic tendencies and stagnant cultures. (Torres 462)

The difficulty to enact societal change is continuously challenged by the constant reinforcement of a one-dimensional portrayal of the Latino man and, by extension, the Latino family. Certainly, in the literary examples drawn by Tavera Rivera and Cisneros there exists clear evidence of atypical behavior—loving and emotional fathers that support their daughters' dreams. In contrast, Cisneros and Moraga also display the more typical behaviors of machista fathers and their impact on daughters and sons.

Fathers in Sandra Cisneros's *The House on Mango Street* do not occupy a large amount of text. Their presence appears nuanced, in a few vignettes, yet the underlying message supports, more often than not, their absolute *machismo* within the space of the home. We see this specifically in "Alicia Who Sees Mice," as well as in several vignettes based on Sally and her relationship with her father.

"Alicia Who Sees Mice"

Alicia's mother has passed away and she, as the female, must take on the gendered role of preparing the tortillas for her father early in the morning. At that time of day, it is still dark and Alicia sees mice scuttle across the floor or hide behind the tub. When she tells her father he is dismissive: "Close your eyes and they'll go away, her father says, or You're just imagining" (31). Rather than address the situation and discuss a solution, he tells her to close her eyes, or that the mice are not real. This lack of acknowledgement, underscored here by Cisneros by placing the words in the mouth of the family patriarch, is much more than a mere lack of cleanliness or a symbol of hardship. It underlines the tactic that is the most prevalent way of dealing with challenges: silence. Indeed, women have been taught for millennia that it is not their place to speak, vote, discuss, or even study. Thankfully, times have begun to change for many, and continue to do so, yet we still see evidence of how silence does not serve one in the end. Still, there are instances when: "In contexts of violence where internal self-censorship was seen as protection, silence made sense" (Collins 125). However, when the violence becomes overbearing, women must reject the silence and scream the injustice to whomever will listen. Alicia does not have anyone to whom she can tell about her difficult situation. Indeed, the reader learns a great deal about Alicia from Esperanza, the young narrator, who tells us:

> Alicia, who inherited her mama's rolling pin and sleepiness, is young and smart and studies for the first time at the university. Two trains and a bus, because she doesn't want to spend her whole life in a factory or behind a rolling pin. Is a good girl, my friend, studies all night and sees the mice, the ones her father says do not exist. Is afraid of nothing except four-legged fur. And fathers. (31-32)

The theme of studying appears yet again with Alicia, because she knows, as Rosario did, that her way out of the neighborhood is by attending university. Although her mother has passed (as has Rosario's in *La condición*) Alicia acknowledges she must emphasize her education to avoid being trapped by marriage like so many of the women in the barrio. Presently, while living at home with her father, Alicia must endure the poverty and something much worse. Cisneros very adeptly, *almost silently*, portrays a very real challenge that Alicia suffers. Until she can move out on her own, Alicia is subjected to sexual abuse by her own father.

"Sally"

Cisneros takes the implicit tone of "Alicia Who Sees Mice" and makes it overt in her characterization of Sally in several vignettes. Indeed, Sally's life involves a complicated relationship with her father. We first hear his perspective when Esperanza tells us directly that: "Her father says to be this beautiful is trouble" (81). Sally's father finds his daughter incredibly alluring based on her natural beauty. Sadly, he fears her beauty. Consequently, he tries to control her movements and furthermore, attempts to possess her in as many ways as possible, including sexually. He fears that her beauty will attract other men and eventually she will leave him, which is bound to happen, not simply because that is the typical path of children, but also because she cannot remain bound to him sexually, he is her father. Here Sally's feminine beauty refers to her potentially wild behavior as a sexual being. Implied is the societal attitude that women are innately overly sexual. This underscores why marriage takes place at a young age in many cultures for girls; their sexuality must be controlled. Female sexuality must be restrained as men do not want "their" women to become unruly and sexually interested in another man. Futhermore, the young women who are married off at such a young age historically are married to much older men. The sexual relationship that exists stems entirely from patriarchal power. To illustrate this point, MacKinnon writes: "male power takes the social form of what men as a gender want sexually, which centers on power itself, as socially defined.[...]. Specifically, 'woman' is defined by what male desire requires for arousal and satisfaction and is socially tautologus with 'female sexuality' and 'the female sex'"(415). On a daily basis, Sally faces the truth of living with a father that sees her not as his daughter, as a precious gift to protect and cherish, but rather as a sexual being that exists for him to possess, abuse and rape repeatedly.

As Esperanza's father does not abuse her, Esperanza does not comprehend Sally's life away from school and the limits that her Papa places upon her. She writes: "And why do you always have to go straight home after school? You become different Sally. You pull your skirt straight, you rub the blue paint off your eyelids. You don't laugh Sally. You look at your feet and walk fast to the house you can't come out from" (82). Esperanza doesn't yet realize that Sally's every move is watched by her father. Furthermore, she must be home at a certain time, look a certain way, and act accordingly to avoid her father's wrath. It is an unhealthy, controlling relationship. Not only does he abuse her sexually, but he also abuses her physically, which we see through Esperanza's young eyes as she observes the bruises on Sally's face, to which Sally responds: "He never hits me hard" (92). Here we see how Sally, like many other women in the novel, downplays the significance of the abuse. Of course, Sally does not know any other way, as this is her one and only father, and she does love him: "[W]hen the dark came her father whose eyes were little from crying, knocked on the door and said please come back, this is the last time. And she said Daddy and went home" (93). Sally is fearful of her father, yet at the same time, she wishes that he not suffer nor feel guilt for any reason, including his abuse of her. "Until one day Sally's father catches her talking to a boy and the next day she doesn't come to school. And the next. Until the way Sally tells it, he just went crazy, he just forgot he was her father between the buckle and the belt" (93). There is a limit to how much Sally can take, and finally, when her father hurts her physically to such an extreme, due to his jealousy of other boys and their interest in his beautiful daughter, Sally decides to make a change. She finds a man to marry to escape her machista father and his domination over her. As Ellen McCracken has referred to Sally's case: "her father's attempts to control her sexuality—here a case of child abuse—cause Sally to exchange one repressive patriarchal prison for another" (68). Sally escapes from her abusive father, yet her husband treats her very similarly, as both men see her as an object to be possessed, and fear that she must be controlled or she will have sex with another man.

Cisneros fiercely criticizes all forms of abuse by men toward women in her works. By underscoring these indignities within Chicano culture, Cisneros refuses to be silent, submissive or afraid. Cisneros's resolution is to draw attention to domestic abuse and oblige her readers to an awareness with the hope that abusive behavior ceases once and for all. Manuel Martín-Rodríguez has underlined this cause: "Liberación del ambiente opresivo del "barrio," liberación de los fantasmas personales que afectan al escritor, liberación del silencio que se impone sobre tantas y tantas mujeres del "barrio" (252).[8] Moreover, in the words of Inés Hernández-Avila "When we suffer violence, the wound degrades the spirit, and when the spirit is hurt, a space is opened for shame to enter, and the blame of self can begin to weave a blanket of silence" (299). Chicana authors in recent decades have chosen to write about the taboos that were always silenced, especially those having to do with intimacy. By writing about these taboos, the silence, as well as the shame that accompanies it, no longer hold such power. Rita Sánchez mentions that at the heart of Chicana writing is a significant act of freedom when she asserts:

> Writing, breaking the silence, becomes a monumental and collective act because it signifies overcoming, freeing oneself from the confines and conditions of history. The collective act may not even be expressed in the words themselves, but is manifest in the act of writing down these words. Writing is the tool which allows the Chicana to implement action, critical thought, change. (67)

It is the act of overcoming through freeing oneself that Cisneros draws our attention to with her character Esperanza, a name meaning "hope" in English. While many of the other women suffer at the hands of patriarchy, Esperanza's eyes are repeatedly opened, yet she too experiences the danger of being female in a male dominant society. She is kissed by a man at work who takes advantage of her naiveté. Next, it is an episode wearing high heel shoes that brings the store owner out to the sidewalk to yell at the young girls because their shoes are inappropriate for their age (too sexy). And lastly, and most sadly, Esperanza is raped. While the boy rapes her, he says: "I love you, Spanish girl" (100). The role of gender and ethnicity here come to the forefront as we analyze not only how fathers view their children within Latino culture, but how women of color are viewed by the dominant culture more broadly.

Extremely urgent in Cisneros' portrayals of young women is her call for all of us to comprehend the normalcy of rape in our culture.

Women of color in our society suffer more violence, especially of a sexual nature, than white women. The feminist literary critic, Patricia Collins, has underlined the black woman's experience and the prevalence of violence:

> Rape and other acts of overt violence that Black women have experienced, such as physical assault during slavery, domestic abuse, incest, and sexual extortion, accompany Black women's subordination in intersecting oppressions. These violent acts are the visible dimensions of a more generalized, routinized system of oppression. Violence against Black women tends to be legitimated and therefore condoned while the same acts visited on other groups may remain non-legitimated and non-excusable. (146)

While Collins asserts the historicity of the Black female experience, regrettably, the Latina experience cannot be described to be markedly different. Latina women are sexualized to such an extent that they suffer from domestic abuse and are raped by men of other ethnicities. More often than not, the rapist is known by the victim (as in Sally's case), he can be a member of the family or a friend of the family.[9] Women's agency becomes subsumed to the patriarchal cultures as women are taught by both mothers and fathers to keep secrets about rape as it is perceived to bring shame to the entire family. Moreover, patriarchal, dominant cultures enforce the idea that the woman is to blame; it is her fault she is raped. From beauty, silence, and shame come generations of families who endure hegemonic masculinity and its resulting abuses.

In her essay "A Woman of No Consequence Una Mujer Cualquiera," Cisneros has underlined why she specifically underscores sex: "I want to talk about sex, because not only will it get your attention, but because it is the thing we don't talk about in my culture, especially not as women. There is so much left unsaid in my family, in my community. So much that is left is taboo and not permitted me to say, do, or even think as a woman of Mexican ancestry" (78). However, Cisneros breaks the silence along with many other Chicanx writers, who also write about the secrets of Chicanahood. One such secret is revealed to us when Esperanza realizes that the ideal of beauty is not an asset to the women of Mango Street; rather it points to the potential for one or more abusive relationships with men. Beauty becomes an object that some men wish to possess; however, once attained the men fear losing their precious possession(s). To prevent this loss, the woman must be stripped of any type of freedom, thereby becoming a prisoner in her own house.[10]

The Hungry Woman

The play, *The Hungry Woman* (2001), takes place in the second decade of the twenty-first century. The narrative unfolds in an imaginary future based on the outcome of a revolution fought at the turn of the millennium, which resulted in the division of the United States of America into several ethnically defined countries. Furthermore, each nation has refused citizenship to its homosexuals. The city of Phoenix (the "in between" space where the "unwanted" from Aztlán are abandoned) is where the main character, Medea, once a military leader of the Chicano revolt, has been exiled with her lover Luna, her son Chac-Mool, and her grandmother Mama Sal. The women have been exiled due to their lesbianism, a quality that is unabashedly disavowed by each of the newly formed nations. Purging society of sexual deviants, who are considered morally inferior, is deemed ethically appropriate because of "the threat of contamination and [the] challenge to hegemonic values" (Sibley 39). At issue with the just formed nations is the fact that lesbianism removes men from their habitual social location of power, especially within the domestic sphere (the home). Since the family is a subsection of the nation, the father, also Medea's ex-husband, threatens to take his son and re-educate him to embody the masculinity of heterosexism and thus superiority over women. Medea refuses to allow this to occur.

In the present narrative time, Medea has been placed in a mental institution. The scenes flash between the past and present to provide the background to Medea's decision to take her son's life. During the opening scenes, the spectator learns of Chac-Mool's father Jasón, who plans to claim his son at the age of thirteen and return to Aztlán. Since Medea was once married to Jasón and therefore determined to be heterosexual by society, she has the option for the disgrace of lesbianism to be rescinded if her machista ex-husband so chooses. It is paradoxical that the role of Jasón as father will eventually force Medea's hand, as he will drive her to take a position on gender and nation that, in the end, subverts patriarchy. In this way, Moraga points to the power of women in nation-building while simultaneously rejecting patriarchy's tenets.

Privileging her role as a mother and acknowledging the option to return to Aztlán to live with her son, Medea contemplates separation from Luna, her lesbian lover. We see in the following exchange how Mama Sal (Medea's mother) laments that Medea may not choose to remain with Luna:

M: Good. She's [Luna's] a liability.

M.S.: ¿Por qué hablas así? Why do you say that?

M: I can't bring her into this. It'll make things worse.

M.S.: They can't get worse, Medea. We lost it all already, ¿no recuerdas? Remember?

M: Not my son. I didn't lose my son. (18)

In this discussion, three revelations aid us in our comprehension of the roles of ethnicity and gender in the play. First, Medea comes to grips with the fact that society views her relationship with Luna as a detriment. By staying with Luna, and not returning to Aztlán *as a heterosexual*, she will undoubtedly lose her son. Secondly, Mama Sal's attitude reflects a much larger concern; she comments that the war for social equity for non-heteronormative sexualities has already been lost. The nation (Aztlán) has refused to accept men and women as equals. Moreover, non-heteronormative individuals have been exiled to a physical location (Phoenix) thereby removing their citizenship along with the rights that traditionally pertain to nationals. As she recounts to Chac-Mool, "we were contentos for awhile until the men told the women to put down their guns and pick up their babies. And in the meantime, all the newly liberated colored countries 'threw out their jotería'" (24). Choosing to "pick up their babies" refers directly to the role of women as mothers, which carries over to the requirement, in the eyes of the machista nation-builders, of women choosing a traditional family, over any other prerogative. Yet, the meaning of family differs radically for Medea, as it does for all the exiles of Phoenix. Finally, Medea's statement about not having lost her son *yet* discloses how passionately she will fight for him. The crux of the play comes down to Medea's desire to keep her son free of her ex-husband's influence, and the broader ramifications of who he would become if allowed to learn the cultural tenets of machismo, which are evident in the following exchange between Jasón and Medea:

> J: You will always be my woman because of our son. Whether you rot in this wasteland of counter-revolutionary degenerates or take up residence in my second bed. You decide. I'm not afraid of you, Medea. I used to be afraid of that anger, but not anymore. I have what I want now. Land and a future in the body of that boy. You can't stop me.

> M: My son needs no taste of that weakness you call manhood. He is still a boy, not a man and you will not make him one in your likeness! The man I wish my son to be does not exist, must be invented. He will invent himself if he must, but he will not grow up to learn betrayal from your example. (69)

Irrefutably, Jasón's use of the pronoun "my" reveals the rights of ownership that inherently belong to the male gender. Jasón's sentiments shed light as to how the hierarchical male/female binary dictates the relationship to such a degree that there is no true emotion, merely possession. The possession extends to the child as well, since he is male and of indigenous blood, therefore valuable. Medea's reaction strongly rejects how Jasón (and Aztlán) define masculinity. Medea means to include all types of masculinity known to her, since she adamantly states that the type of man she wishes her son to be does not yet exist.

This condemnation of machismo shows Jasón as merely a pawn in the larger frame of social injustice. Indeed, the hegemonic powers that keep machismo and heterosexuality infused with absolute, rigid authority are the true adversary. As one can readily ascertain, the power struggle between Jasón and Medea purports to be in Jasón's favor. Ironically, the knowledge that Medea was a successful military leader against Gringolandia bears no significance because of her perceived sexual transgression. Although she fought for Aztlán's freedom, the more valuable citizen is perceived to be Jasón solely because he is male. Medea confirms this by saying: "I am a woman. A Mexican woman and there is no protection and no place for me, not even in the arms of another woman because she too is an exile in her own land" (70). Although having fought and won their independence from the dominant Gringolandia, the nation still clearly determines who is considered a worthy citizen. That is to say that the battle between men and women has not progressed significantly. Furthermore, the acceptance of gays and lesbians into society, whether white or of color, is not achieved in the imagined future of *The Hungry Woman*. This failure to achieve social equality is the cause for Medea's exile and the logic behind her refusal to give her son to Aztlán.

Having fought for her nation successfully, Medea now expresses hatred towards her country and its hegemonic masculinity. She has been marginalized for what is perceived as aberrant behavior and she has been stripped of the rights of citizenship. While contemplating the circumstances surrounding her exile, she realizes that the existence of Phoenix as a space where lesbianism is removed from the larger society means that no other married or heterosexual woman will be allowed to experience homosexuality. As the new nation's leaders require strictly heterosexual citizens, there will be no opportunities for intimate relationships of the same gender in Aztlán. Medea highlights this by saying: "I, my kind, am a dying breed of female. I am the last one to make this crossing, the border has closed behind me. There will be no more room for transgressions" (46). In this proclamation, Medea admits the impossibility of returning to Aztlán. She understands that neither she nor Luna could live in a place that inherently denies their love. Without the option to return, Medea sees herself trapped by a hierarchy of oppression that is much larger than a one-on-one relationship. Aztlán continues to hold her in place; she must remain in Phoenix as long as she refuses to define herself as heterosexual.

Like her namesake from the Greek tragedy, Medea is betrayed by a man named Jasón (as well as by her country, Aztlán). Like the Greek Medea she would rather kill her offspring, not merely to exact revenge on Jasón and the Chicanx culture, but to protect Chac-Mool from becoming brainwashed into thinking that males or heterosexuals are superior to females and homosexuals. Medea *cannot* allow her son to identify himself with the Chicano, patriarchal, homophobic society that teaches that masculinity and heterosexuality are superior.

In conclusion, it is evident in Moraga's play that Medea will never climb to the social strata of Rosario in *La condición*, due to her lack of education. Although Rosario has been lucky due to her father's support, the cultural map implied is quite clear: she will never come to terms with her mother who never supported her education or what it means: freedom. This is quite different from Esperanza's options which are left open as she is still an adolescent at the end of the novel. Esperanza, Medea, and Rosario all act out of revenge when they consciously make decisions based on freedom from a lifetime of objectification and submission to patriarchy and machismo. Indeed, Latina authors are asserting their voices against the dominant culture while simultaneously liberating themselves of machismo's and patriarchy's cultural limitations. Rita Sánchez asserts:

> The Chicana writer, by the fact that she is even writing in today's society, is making a revolutionary act. Embodied in the act of writing is her voice against others' definitions of who she is and what she should be. There is, in her open expression and in the very nature of this act of opening up, a refusal to submit to a quality of silence that has been imposed upon her for centuries. In the act of writing, the Chicana is saying "No," and by doing so she becomes the revolutionary, a source of change, and a real force for humanization. (66)

The true revolutionaries, Tavera Rivera, Cisneros and Moraga, reject the labels that the dominant, patriarchal society has historically placed upon all women, with stricter limitations on women of color. By the act of writing, silence no longer gives the patriarchy the power to abuse women without retribution. Through standing up and drawing a line, Latinas take back their power as women and as humans that deserve to be treated with respect and care. It must be emphasized that calling out patriarchy as a source of abuse in our society is no simple accomplishment. Sánchez proclaims that:

> By becoming a writer, the Chicana has to have already rebelled against a socialization process that would have her remain merely the silent helpmate. Everything in her society, the schools, the church, the home has sought this goal for her: she must be sheltered from the evils, noise, confusion, from the realities of the outside world, from sex to politics, even at times from intellectual dialogue, to be considered acceptable. In short, she should make no intrusion into adult or male conversation. Now, the Chicana, by voicing her own brand of expression has rejected the latter in favor of telling anyone who wishes to read her work, hear her voice, exactly what she is not, and who she, in fact, is. (66)

In other words, through rejecting society's norm that women remain in the private space of the home for their "protection," Latina authors create their agency as activists for social change. Moreover, they reject the machista, cultural norm that portrays women as submissive and uneducated. Most importantly, they seize their right to self-define, to speak openly, and to deny patriarchy the power to place women in a limited social location, one that simply exists to serve men. That is to say: "nothing less than healing patriarchal and colonized constructions of female sexuality and spirituality" will allow society to fully feminize (Lara 123). By incorporating a path to heal from the centuries of patriarchal abuses, women and men express their emotions as human beings, rather than as a representative gender, sexuality or social location. The next generation, the children of these authors, and of the Chicana community, whether real or fictional (from their writings) will no longer be subjected to "*La condición*" that Rosario rejected, nor will they suffer from the misogyny that allows for a culture of rape to be acceptable or normal. And finally, they will not be "exiled" in any way as a consequence to their sexual identity. Freedom for all through breaking down barriers is the goal of the Latina feminist movement. While patriarchy slowly moves from hegemonic masculinity to feminist masculinity, where men, like Esperanza's Papa, emote without a backlash, authors like Tavera Rivera, Cisneros and Moraga will continue to model an open society that is based on love, compassion and understanding, not on hate, labels and limitations. The challenge has been issued. Let us reclaim our humanity and allow all human beings to be who they were meant to be—beings of light and love, of compassion and joy.

Notes

[1] Alfredo Mirandé mentions that some academics give credence to patriarchy by maintaining their privilege when pressed to declare their allegiance to feminism: "Although most advocates of men's studies have assumed a profeminist stance, a substantial antifeminist strand exists within the larger so-called men's movement" (121).

[2] The Page Act (1875) and the McCreary Amendment (1893) in the United States gave immense power to the immigration officers to allow or reject certain individuals (at that time, it targeted Asians) from entering the country. "The border…immigration officers constructed policies, tests, and measures that were designed to identify—and, consequently, interpellate—individual bodies as appropriate or undesireable" (Goldman 102).

[3] Beginning here and continuing throughout this essay, I will include my own translations of the original Spanish text: "When are you going to realize that you are a woman, and you cannot be anything else" (486).

[4] "Let them learn to drink [alcohol], this proves they are manly" (486).

[5] "I have tried to be just with all my children, men and women" (487).

[6] "You blame me? You were the one who let Rosario go off to college" (487).

[7] "She doesn't even know how to make coffee" (488).

[8] "Freedom from the oppressive environment of the neighborhood, freedom from the personal ghosts that affect the author, and freedom from the silence that is imposed upon so many women from the neighborhood" (252).

[9] The Latina Feminist Group have several selections in *Telling to Live Latina Feminist Testimonios* that support this claim. For example, from "Night Terrors" the anonymous author recounts: "It turns out that the rapist was an acquaintance of my father's. One night, drunk as usual, Daddy told me this, anger in his voice, as if somehow I had hurt him (*Telling to Live* 281).

[10] Please see Quinn-Sánchez' "Social and Geographical Landscapes: The River as Metaphor for Female Sexuality" in *The Image of The River in Latin/o American Literature* for an in-depth discussion of how patriarchy has controlled women's sexuality for centuries.

Works Cited

Cisneros, Sandra. *The House on Mango Street*. Vintage, 1984.

——. "A Woman of No Consequence Una Mujer Cualquiera." *Living Chicana Theory*, edited by Carla Trujillo, Third Woman Press, 1998, pp. 78-86.

Collins, Patricia Hill. *Black Feminist Thought: Knowledge, Consciousness, and the Politics of Empowerment*. 2nd ed., Routledge, 2000.

Espín, Olivia M. "Saints in the Cuban Heat." *Fleshing the Spirit: Spirituality and Activism in Chicana, Latina, and Indigenous Women's Lives*, edited by Elisa Facio and Irene Lara, University of Arizona Press, 2014, pp. 102-12.

Goldman, Dara E. *Out of Bounds: Islands and the Demarcation of Identity in the Hispanic Caribbean*. Bucknell UP, 2008.

Hernández-Avila, Inés. "Telling to Live: Devoro la Mentira, Resucitando mi Ser." *Telling to Live: Latina Feminist Testimonios*, edited by The Latina Feminist Group, Duke UP, 2001, pp. 298-301.

hooks, bell. *The Will to Change: Men, Masculinity and Love*. Altria Books, 2004.

Hurtado, Aída and Mrinal Sinha. *Beyond Machismo*. University of Texas Press, 2016.

Lara, Irene. *Fleshing the Spirit: Spirituality and Activism in Chicana, Latina, and Indigenous Women's Lives*, edited by Elisa Facio and Irene Lara, University of Arizona Press, 2014, pp. 113-34.

MacKinnon, Catharine A. "Sexuality from *Toward a Feminist Theory of the State.*" *Feminist_Theory.* 3rd ed., edited by Wendy K. Kolmar and Frances Bartkowski, McGrawHill, 2010, pp. 413-25.

Martín Rodríguez, Manuel M. "The Book on Mango Street: Escritura y liberación en la obra de Sandra Cisneros," *Mujer y literatura mexicana y chicana: Culturas en contacto II*, edited by Aralia López González, Amelia Malagumba, and Elena Urrutia, Colegio de la Frontera Norte, 1990, pp, 249-54.

McCracken, Ellen. "Sandra Cisneros' The House on Mango Street: Community Oriented Introspection and Demystification of Patriarchal Violence." *Breaking Boundaries: Latina Writing and Critical Readings*, edited by Asunción Horno-Delgado, Eliana Ortega, Nina M. Scott and Nancy Saporta Sternback, University of Massachusetts Press, 1989, pp. 62-71.

Mirandé, Alfredo. *Hombre y machos: Masculinity and Latino Culture*. Westview Press, 1997.

Moraga, Cherríe. *The Hungry Woman*. West End Press, 2001.

Quinn-Sánchez, Kathryn. "Social and Geographical Landscapes: The River as Metaphor for Female Sexuality." *Written on the Water: The Image of the River in Latino/American Literature*, edited by Elizabeth Rivero and Jeannie Murphy, Lexington Books, 2017, pp. 117-37.

Sánchez, Rita. "Chicana Writer Breaking Out of Silence." *Chicana Feminist Thought.* edited by Alma M. García. Routledge, 1997, pp. 66-68.

Sendejo, Brenda. "Methodologies of the Spirit: Reclaiming our Lady of Guadalupe and Discovering Tonantzin Within and Beyond the *Nepantla* of Academia." *Fleshing the Spirit: Spirituality and Activism in Chicana, Latina, and Indigenous Women's Lives*, edited by Elisa Facio and Irene Lara, University of Arizona Press, 2014, pp. 81-101.

Sibley, David. *Geographies of Exclusion*. Routledge, 1995.

Tavera Rivera, Margarita. *La condición. Panoramas literarios de américa hispana* edited by Teresa Méndez-Faith. Houghton Mifflin Company, 2008, pp. 484-95.

Telling to Live: Latina Feminist Testimonios, edited by The Latina Feminist Group, Duke UP, 2001.

Torres, Lourdes. "Becoming Joaquin and Mind If I Call You Sir?: Exploring Latino Masculinities." *Biography*, vol. 34, no.3, 2011, pp. 447-466.

Chapter 5

¿De tal palo, tal astilla?[1] Chicano Masculinities and the Legacy of the Patriarchal Dividend in Two Chicanx Coming-of-Age Narratives

Bryan Pearce-Gonzales

Shenandoah University

Introduction

Domingo Martinez and Dagoberto Gilb are prolific authors of contemporary Chicanx literature that centers on male characters navigating through worlds defined and controlled by an overbearing patriarchal social order.[2] In his autobiography *The Boy Kings of Texas* (2012), Martinez recounts his difficult childhood and adolescence growing up in the 1970s and 1980s in a barrio established by his step-grandfather in Brownsville, Texas. Gilb textures his writings with an insider knowledge of the lives of blue-collar Chicano male figures that inhabit the fringe spaces of mainstream society, such as construction workers, drifters, or adolescent sons of single mothers. In his novel *The Flowers* (2008), the author traces the everyday actions of Sonny, a Chicano teenager living in a mundane apartment complex owned by Cloyd, his mother's new husband whom Sonny refuses to recognize as his father.

In these works, Martinez and Gilb explore the effects of a patriarchal hegemonic masculinity on the formation of the son's concept of masculinity, of self, and of family. In both of these narratives, the model of masculinity promoted by the father figure, and presumed to be adopted by the son, overwhelms and eventually disrupts the family unit by way of violence, sexual exploitation, and unrestrained bravado so that the sons are left to seek new, transformative ways of conceptualizing their own masculinities. This study analyzes the effects that the dysfunctional relationships between the hyper-masculine patriarchs (el palo) and their sons (la astilla) have on the shaping of

Chicano masculinities. The aim of my analysis is to offer a contemporary reading of Chicano masculinities that is divorced from traditional, patriarchal prescriptions and instead explores new, transformative interpretations of what it means to be a Chicano man. R.W. Connell, perhaps the most widely-read scholar within the field of masculinity studies, and their thoughts on the concept of the "patriarchal dividend" will inform my analysis.

El legado del Rey

Domingo Martinez, a memoirist whom María Venegas compares to Junot Díaz and describes as "irreverent, judgmental and unapologetic," bursts onto the scene of Chicanx letters with the 2012 publication of his autobiography *The Boy Kings of Texas* (Venegas). In this, the first of his major publications, Martinez recounts the major scenes of his childhood, particularly as they relate to his father and his influence on the author's conceptualization of masculinity. As Martinez traces his development from childhood through adolescence and ultimately to adulthood, he invokes conversations he has had with his therapist, Sally.

In the Prologue of *Boy Kings*, Martinez shares with his readers an epiphany he comes to as an adult, perhaps as the result of a therapy session with Sally. He recalls a favorite song of farmworkers along the Texas-Mexico border called "El Rey" performed by "El Rey de la Canción Ranchera" himself, Vicente Fernández. This song, like many of Fernández's songs, follows the *ranchera* formula as the male singer expresses his feelings of social and public alienation, low economic status, deep sadness, solitude and, of course, unreciprocated love – all things that the singer is resolved to overcome by sheer emotional strength and dogged determination. The epiphany comes when Martinez realizes that "El Rey," complete with all its metaphorical and symbolic trappings, is actually a melodic rendering of the psychological composition of Chicano masculinity. In reflecting on this particular song, Martinez identifies and outlines the Chicano male archetype, detailing extensively what it means to be a man in his particular cultural and familial setting. This normative definition of Chicano masculinity, to which his father and outwardly masculine (or, to use the author's word, "butch") grandmother subscribe, outlines what Chicano men ought to be (Martinez 51). However, throughout his memoir, Martinez reframes this definition as an impossible model that causes physical, emotional and psychological suffering for him and his older and much more physically imposing brother, Dan.

Martinez opens his autobiography by recounting two vivid and contrasting memories of his father. The first is a bittersweet recollection of the early days of the Martinez family in Brownsville. Domingo Sr. had just brought home a Chihuahua-mix puppy that the children immediately fell in love with and would eventually name Blackie. Sometime later Blackie mysteriously goes missing, and it is Domingo Sr. and his mother (the author's paternal grandmother) who are the first to find the puppy's mangled corpse. After the initial shock of the discovery, it is concluded that this horrific crime was committed by the dog pack of Domingo Sr.'s step-uncle, the patriarch of the Rubios, a rival family who seeks to usurp Domingo Sr.'s claim to authority in the barrio that was created by his stepfather.[3]

After a ceremonious burial in the family's backyard, Martinez recounts another memory in which he proudly describes his father in terms of the Chicano masculine archetype. In this memory, Domingo Sr. quietly leaves for work and Martinez, instructed by his mother, watches his father drive down the dirt road that leads past the Rubio house where the ferocious dogs lived. Slowly and methodically, Domingo Sr. aims a pistol out of the lowered driver's side window and shoots each one of the dogs that belonged to the Rubio family. Just as calmly as he pulled the trigger, Domingo Sr. drives away and Martinez recalls feeling an extreme level of pride in his father's vengeful actions that day.

While Martinez characterizes the memory of his father's actions in terms of the chapter's title – "Border Justice" – upon closer analysis the reader notes that it embodies much more than an act of righteous retaliation. Martinez feels immensely proud of his father at this moment, particularly so in terms of the way in which Domingo Sr. exemplifies the positive traits of the Chicano male archetype outlined in Fernandez's song "El Rey." Martinez admired his father for his ability to reclaim his position of authority in the barrio after it had been threatened by his step-uncle. *El palo*, in this instance, personifies the normative definition of what Chicano males ought to be and *la astilla* is proud of him for it.

It is telling that the author recalls being about five years old in this first memory detailing Blackie's death and his father's reaction to it. Martinez begins the next chapter, titled "His Favorite Place," by admitting that, at fourteen years of age, a sense of distance began developing between him and his father. Domingo Sr., cognizant of this distance, would sometimes try to relate to his son via awkward small talk that would often venture into questioning Martinez's sexual exploits as a teenager. In one particular conversation, Martinez's father asks him a seemingly innocent question: "Where's your favorite place?" (Martinez 10). After pondering the remote possibility that his father might be attempting to have a profound, perhaps even philosophical, discussion with him, Martinez answers carefully with the trite response that his favorite place is a "water bed at night." To his horror, his father responds by saying, rather proudly: "Mine's inside a nice, warm pussy" (11). This outward, verbal display of heterosexual bravado and sexual prowess reflects R.W. Connell's definition of machismo as: "a masculine ideal stressing domination of women, competition between men, aggressive display, predatory sexuality and a double standard" (31). Domingo Sr.'s efforts to emotionally connect with his son are limited by these demands of machismo.[4]

It is important to note that Martinez's reaction to his father's vulgar display of heterosexual masculinity is one of horrified stupefaction that causes a physiological response of cringing and stomach pain. Martinez, physically repulsed by this memory, signals a desire to break with the machista ideal of heterosexual masculinity that his father represents. In an attempt to be as dissimilar as possible to his machista father, Martinez quietly prays that God turn him gay. Here, an adolescent Martinez reveals that, unlike the pride he felt for his father's embodiment of the Chicano male archetype during the Blackie episode,[5] he now feels a strong sense of revulsion in the face of that machista model as his father now embodies it. *La astilla* is pained upon recognizing the dysfunction that *el palo* seeks to pass on.

As Martinez matures from a toddler to a teenager, he begins to recognize that his patriarchal role model no longer embodies righteousness and justice, but instead represents a Chicano manifestation of what Connell calls hegemonic masculinity: "the configuration of gender practice which embodies the currently accepted answer to the problem of the legitimacy of patriarchy, which guarantees (or is taken to guarantee) the dominant position of men and the subordination of women" (77). Martinez's autobiography is replete with memories of his father's efforts to legitimize his dominant position over everyone else – but especially over his own sons and women.

In one particular memory, painful for Martinez to recount, he is a first grader returning home from school and boasting to Domingo Sr., in hopes of winning his affection, that he was the fastest kid in first grade. However, instead of giving the approval his son wanted, Domingo Sr. reacts by challenging him to a race in order to "establish his authority over his eight-year-old boy" (356). After Domingo Sr. easily wins the race, he childishly mocks his son for challenging his athletic prowess. Remembering this episode and its lasting effects on himself as an adult, heterosexual male who feels compelled to dominate all of his social and romantic relationships, Martinez admits that he was "[d]oomed from the start" (357). In another painful recollection, Martinez recounts the time when Domingo Sr., by this point mostly estranged from the family and from Martinez's mother, hears that his wife might be in a romantic relationship with another man. In an aggressive display of power, Domingo Sr. rips her out of her boyfriend's car and beats her to the ground in the parking lot of a JC Penney, eventually leaving her there crying.

Domingo Sr., in his quest to establish and legitimize patriarchal domination over his wife and children, adheres to the model of hegemonic masculinity that Connell outlines. However, in his quest to validate his patriarchal dominance over the family, Domingo Sr. risks rupturing the very family unit that substantiates his position as patriarch.[6] Through his violent, machista behavior, Domingo Sr. had injured his family, and in adhering to the model of hegemonic masculinity, his actions became too severe for the family to withstand. His wife divorced him, and his children, especially his sons, moved away from the family to Seattle, a city so different from the bordertown he called home that Martinez describes it as "the opposite of Texas" (303).

In light of the destruction of their family tree at the hands of *el palo*, *las astillas* decide to move as far away from Texas as their means and imaginations will take them. From the distance that Seattle provides, Martinez offers a telling description of his relationship to his home state, a relationship that he characterizes as "disturbingly patriarchal" and "abusive" (321). Free from the patriarchal tyranny and abuse that characterized his childhood, Martinez and his brother begin exploring alternative ways to forge a new sense of family, a fraternal effort on their part to (re)produce what their father had destroyed.

In his first quest to establish anew the idea of family with his girlfriend, Martinez seems to understand that the fraternal effort must necessarily oppose the patriarchal effort that his father epitomized. For this reason, after his girlfriend admits to cheating on him and being caught in the act, Martinez reveals that he looked to his father's model not as something to emulate, but rather as, in his own words, a "reverse compass" (385). We will recall that Domingo Sr., embodying the idea of hegemonic masculinity, beat his wife mercilessly for carrying on a relationship with another man. Martinez, looking to avoid being defined in terms of "a dominating, patriarchal machismo Mexican man" (386), instead sought to comfort his cheating girlfriend, even offering to make her a cup of tea. In this episode, Martinez seemingly becomes aware of what Connell calls "the patriarchal dividend, the advantage men in general gain from the overall subordination of women" (79), and he makes a marked effort to avoid complying with it. In the end, however, he fails at this self-imposed mission. Sometime later, Martinez shamefully reveals that, for all his efforts to behave differently in this situation than did his father, he ultimately complies with the patriarchal dividend of hegemonic masculinity when he kicks in the side of his girlfriend's truck while she is sitting inside of it. A concerned passerby witnesses the act of physical aggression and feels compelled to ask Martinez's girlfriend if she is in danger. At this moment, Martinez understands that, according to his behavior toward his partner, *la astilla* has become *el palo*. His quest to build a family with this woman failed, and Martinez seems to learn from this experience that his father's legacy, the patriarchal dividend, is his inheritance.

Ten years after the ugly breakup with his girlfriend, and still struggling to understand his involuntary compliance with the patriarchal dividend during that episode, Martinez again seeks to recreate an idea of family that is not encumbered by the machista archetype of hegemonic masculinity. To this end, Martinez's second attempt focuses not on a heterosexual model within which a patriarchal, hegemonic masculinity operates but instead on a fraternal conceptualization of family that would sidestep the patriarchal dividend entirely. This new endeavor centers on rebuilding the strained relationship he shares with his older brother, Dan, by moving into an apartment together in Seattle.

Reflecting on this new living arrangement, Martinez recognizes that he and his brother seemed to be recreating their shared childhood, albeit this time without the threat of emotional and psychological abuse at the hands of their father. Martinez admits that he is clearly aware of his and Dan's impulse to recreate a semblance of a family that does not adhere to the same model of patriarchal, hegemonic masculinity that worked to destroy the one they knew as children. However, as the two brothers share childhood stories, Martinez becomes aware of how embedded the patriarchal dividend is within their adult lives even with the distance afforded by Seattle and free from the immediate threat of their father.

One particularly traumatic recollection surfaces while he and his brother, both drunk at the end of a long day, are watching television when they see something that triggers a childhood memory of Martinez breaking his arm while playing football in the street. At first the memory rushes back innocently as they both recall how the accident happened. However, the memory quickly turns insufferable as Martinez recounts running home to seek the assistance of his parents when his father, drunk and unemployed at the time, reacts violently to the news of his son's broken arm. Domingo Sr. punches his son so hard that he falls to the ground, an act of such patriarchal violence that it moves Dan to come to his brother's rescue by slamming their father against a wall in order to restrain him. In recalling this incident, Martinez tells how he eventually wakes up in the hospital after having been knocked unconscious by the force of his father's blow. Upon returning home, Martinez's father is gone and he does not see him again for two weeks, when his father suddenly reappears and tries to make light of what happened on that day. Back in Seattle, after the two brothers share this memory, Martinez thanks his older brother for "protecting [him] from [their] father that day," causing Dan to cry to himself (418). This emotional response not only clearly marks the difference between *la astilla* and *el palo*, but it also serves to highlight the extent of the emotional toll of their traumatic childhoods.

Martinez and his brother would go on like this for a year, but eventually the shared recollection of childhood moments, even mundane and seemingly happy ones, would take its toll on the new family they had both worked hard to re-create fraternally. He admits that their attempts to come to grips with their childhood had led to feelings of mutual hatred and alienation, all of which he attributes to the consequences of their father's "twisted exaggeration of machismo" (427). The new, fraternal construction of family was only somewhat sustainable for about a year when both Martinez and his brother begin to realize that their familial re-creation still bears the fissures of a shared, abusive past at the hands of their father.[7]

Martinez, in a lengthy reflection on who he and his brother had become, once again invokes the image of the archetypical Chicano model of masculinity from Fernández's song "El Rey." Martinez and Dan are now adult Chicano men, and as such have inherited the King's legacy of "alienation, narcissism, and self-destruction." *Las astillas*, like *el palo* before them, have succeeded in destroying the family unit they had worked so hard to re-create.

Sonny Boy

Dagoberto Gilb is a well-established Chicano author, having published numerous collections of short stories and several novels. In his novel *The Flowers*, Gilb traces the coming-of-age of Sonny, a fifteen-year-old Chicano who lives with his single mother in Los Angeles during the days and weeks immediately preceding the Rodney King Riots of 1992. Sonny's adolescent life is shaped by his interactions with the various residents that live within his apartment complex, a nine-unit building named Los Flores [sic] that is owned by his new Anglo stepfather, Cloyd Longpre. Interestingly, Sonny never mentions anything of his biological father, leaving the reader to infer that Sonny had been raised by his single mother and therefore had never known a father figure before his mother married Cloyd.[8]

The novel opens with Sonny recalling the moments that lead to his mother hastily deciding to marry Cloyd. In this particular memory, the reader quickly learns of his mother's overcharged social life, which serves to introduce Sonny to various men who take little to no interest in him but rather are attracted to the striking beauty of his mother. In this moment of reflection, Sonny recounts how he had been stabbed by one of his mother's suitors who, in a drunken rage, broke down Sonny's front door in an effort to locate his mother but instead found a fearful Sonny holding a knife as his only defense. This unstable and at times hyper-violent world reflects Connell's model of hegemonic masculinity that seeks to guarantee "the dominant position of men and the subordination of women" by way of socially accepted gendered behavior that allows for violence as a means to lay claim to authority (77).

As a coping strategy, in light of his mother's passive dismissal of this violent and unstable environment, Sonny often retreats into his own mind to escape. Sonny's desire to mentally distance himself from his home life marks his first step in breaking from the destructive effects of a hegemonic masculinity model that would position him as the beneficiary of the patriarchal dividend. At this point, Sonny is still a child, and as such his only option to escape the threat of hegemonic masculinity represented by his mother's suitors is to retreat inside his own thoughts. However, as the story develops and Sonny matures both physically and emotionally, his attempts to retreat from the violence of hegemonic masculinity evolve and eventually he begins to actively explore his own masculinity in transformative ways.

Following the stabbing incident, Sonny's mother introduces him to his would-be stepfather, Cloyd Longpre, a landlord who owns the Los Flores apartment building into which Sonny and his mother are relocating. Sonny, by now astute at gauging the true interests of his mother's suitors, reveals that Cloyd would try to engage superficially with Sonny by asking him questions whose answers were of no legitimate interest to Cloyd. However, Sonny eventually admits that he goes through the motions of small talk with Cloyd in order to appease his mother, whom he does genuinely love. Cloyd, in his efforts to impress Sonny's mother, only succeeds in patronizing her son with small talk of guns and sports. In this way, Gilb has designed Cloyd's character according to a normative definition of patriarchal masculinity that dictates what men ought to be. Within this definition, traditional symbols like guns and sports are given authority to signify what it means to be a man.

While keeping up with Cloyd's condescending attempts at small talk, Sonny recognizes an opportunity to destabilize the authority of a patriarchal masculinity by outwitting his new stepfather, who smugly promises to give Sonny "one big thing" (13). Sonny responds to this promise by requesting to visit Notre Dame, carefully admitting that this request was inauthentic and that he only wanted to patronize Cloyd in the same way that Cloyd was patronizing him. Cloyd, according to the limitations of the patriarchal model of masculinity to which he subscribes, incorrectly assumes that Sonny's wish is to attend a game of a well-known college football team. However, when Sonny explains that his request is really to visit the Notre Dame Cathedral in Paris, he succeeds in subverting Cloyd's assumed position of authority for the first time by casting his stepfather as intellectually inferior. Sonny will repeat this same act of discord several times throughout the novel, each time destabilizing the model of patriarchal masculinity that his new Anglo stepfather promotes.

In another telling scene, Sonny and Cloyd are eyeing the dead animals that hang on Cloyd's wall as hunting trophies. As Cloyd explains to his new stepson the difference between a deer and an elk, he assertively states: "You got a lot to learn, boy" (30). Cloyd uses the deprecatory referent "boy" when speaking with Sonny throughout the novel, thereby casting Sonny as inferior within the patriarchal hierarchy of masculinity (Cloyd = *el palo*, Sonny = *la astilla*). Sonny quickly recognizes this and becomes frustrated by the epistemological limitations embedded within this model, as it affords Cloyd the discursive space and authority to declare that he is a man because he kills animals. Implicit within this model, Sonny understands, is the inability to lay claim to a legitimate masculine identity if one does not engage in the killing of animals for sport. As a result, Sonny voices his unwillingness to adopt the limitations that would be imposed upon him if he were to adhere to the stepfather's restrictive example of what it means to be a man; that is, white, heterosexist, patriarchal, anti-intellectual, and anti-effeminate. This model of masculinity reflects what Mercé Cuenca identifies as a "containment narrative" insofar as it serves to oppress Sonny's potential to explore alternative modes of defining what it means to be a man (Cuenca 135). Sonny, instead of casting Cloyd as a father-figure to emulate, seeks to dis-identify with him, and in this way he comes to resent all that is associated with his stepfather – hunting, belief in the virtuousness of manual labor, objectifying women, and most importantly, only acknowledging as equals other men who subscribe to the same model of hegemonic masculinity.

Once Sonny establishes his desire to dis-identify with Cloyd's containment narrative of masculinity, he begins to spend more time outside of the apartment so as to avoid interacting with his stepfather. It is at this point that Sonny begins to socialize with the various tenants of the Los Flores apartment complex that his stepfather owns and manages. There is Cindy, the lonely and attention-starved nineteen-year-old who got married too young and now feels imprisoned in Unit #3 and to whom Sonny eventually loses his virginity. Ben and Gina are an unmarried couple that resides in Unit #2. Mr. Josep, an older Russian immigrant who stops Sonny to converse from time to time, lives in Unit #5 with his wife. Cloyd's best friend, Bud, is openly racist and misogynistic, and he lives in Unit #7 with his wife Mary. Nica, Sonny's true love interest, lives with her family in Unit #4. She speaks no English and, like Cindy, feels imprisoned in her apartment by her overbearing stepfather who requires her to take care of her little brother and perform all the domestic chores while the parents spend the majority of their days working outside the home. Pink, an albino African-American who Cloyd does not realize is not Anglo, lives in Unit #6 and sells cars to members of the African-American community in front of the apartment building. Finally, a relationship also begins between Sonny and Mr. and Mrs. Zúñiga, the owners of the local bowling alley.

Each relationship serves as an example in Sonny's exploration of an alternative model of masculinity. He meets Cindy first, and in his interactions with her Sonny adheres to a more patriarchal model of masculinity. The two engage in flirtatious interactions that quickly escalate to drinking alcohol and smoking marijuana alone in her apartment while her husband is at work. After several sexual trysts, Sonny seemingly loses interest and, in spite of Cindy's pleas for more attention, he begins to avoid her and instead spends more time with other characters in the novel. Sonny's relationship with Cindy, as short-lived as it was, serves as a first step of sorts in his exploration of what it means to be a man. By first adhering to a patriarchal model of masculinity, Sonny is afforded the opportunity to partake in the hegemonic pattern by benefiting from the overall subordination and/or objectification of women. However, Sonny eventually recognizes his dissatisfaction with the patriarchal dividend and actively rejects it by ending his relationship with Cindy.

At this point, through his interactions with Mr. Josep, Mr. and Mrs. Zúñiga, and especially Pink, Sonny is introduced to alternative masculine identities that differ from the hegemonic model to which he has become accustomed. From his conversations with Mr. Josep Sonny learns to talk and, perhaps more importantly, to listen. Unlike Cloyd, Mr. Josep never raises his voice in anger or disappointment. Interestingly, after learning of the physical relationship between Sonny and Cindy, Mr. Josep never chastises Sonny for sleeping with a married woman as the reader might expect. Instead, Mr. Josep seems to recognize the affair as an inevitable consequence of the situation and perhaps even a "teachable moment" from which Sonny might learn a valuable lesson in manhood.

Mr. and Mrs. Zúñiga, the owners and operators of Alley Cats, the local bowling alley, also play a pivotal role in Sonny's formation of a masculine identity. Like Mr. Josep, Mrs. Zúñiga engages Sonny in familial conversation, asking about his day at school or his life at home. She converses with him over meals that she prepares especially for him, which characterizes her as a traditional maternal figure fulfilling the gendered roles of cooking and nurturing. In this way, the bowling alley becomes a familial space in which Sonny feels comfortable enough to be himself.

In this safe space, Sonny learns to weigh the consequences of his actions after an incident in which Sonny rolls a bowling ball poorly and curses in frustration. Mr. Zúñiga, though a man of few words, publicly scolds Sonny and warns him that his establishment will not tolerate such language and behavior and that another outburst would mean that Sonny would not be permitted to bowl there again. This public chastisement would seem, on the surface, to be another example of a patriarchal model of masculinity in which the child is punished by the father-figure for not correctly acting like a man.

However, Sonny, after a brief moment of angry defiance, is able to take inventory of what the Zúñigas and the bowling alley mean to him. He recalls the specially prepared food and pleasant exchanges with Mrs. Zúñiga and the free games Mr. Zúñiga always gifted him, admitting: "I didn't want to screw up. I didn't want to get mad because I wanted to come there" (146). Because the bowling alley does what his home never did, that is to say it meets Sonny's most basic needs – food, shelter, conversation, structure – it represents a space of stability in his life and Sonny realizes its value as such when he genuinely apologizes for his verbal transgression, thus marking an important moment in Sonny's emotional development.

The most important relationship in the novel, however, is the one that develops between Sonny and Pink. Pink's character is designed as a foil to Cloyd's. Where Cloyd's masculine *modus operandi* dictates manual labor and subordination of others in his claim to authority, Pink is best described as a streetwise hustler who earns a living by illegally selling used cars and depending on the cooperation of those around him to enable him to do so. Sonny and Pink almost immediately form a fraternal bond stemming from their mutual dis-identification with Cloyd and all he represents. Pink understands that Sonny's stepfather is racist and that if he knew that Pink was actually African-American, he would not allow him to rent a unit in his apartment complex and would turn him in for his used car hustle. Pink identifies in Sonny a partner with whom to work on a mutually beneficial project of undermining Cloyd's claim to authority under a patriarchal, hegemonic masculinity. Indeed, the used car salesman consistently refers to Sonny as "little brother," "partner," and "good man," thereby establishing a fraternal relationship between the two and directly contesting the implication perpetuated by Cloyd that Sonny is not his equal and needs to be taught how to be a man.

Pink represents the strongest male role model for Sonny of all of the other characters. He takes it upon himself to share with Sonny knowledge about sex, the importance of moderation when drinking alcohol, and how to drive; he even gives Sonny his first car. When Sonny does Pink a favor, Pink financially reimburses his "little brother." By offering payment to Sonny for doing a job for him, Pink's behavior contrasts with Cloyd's containment narrative of masculinity wherein physically demanding, unpaid manual labor is elemental to the process of learning how to be a man.

These social interactions with members of his immediate community enable Sonny to explore alternate models of what it means to be a man. In his dis-identification with the containment narrative of hegemonic masculinity, he becomes unrestricted by the prescriptions of the patriarchal dividend that would demand that he participate in the overall subordination of women. His

newly fashioned notion of masculinity is characterized more clearly by the
desire to forge a collaborative relationship with a woman instead of a sexual
one. This desire is most clearly displayed toward the end of the novel as he
begins to spend more and more time with his true love interest Nica, the
young woman from Mexico who is unable to leave her apartment and must
care for her little brother day and night.

It is important to note that, although Sonny admits on several occasions
how physically attracted he is to Nica, he never tries to conquer her sexually
as a hegemonic masculinity model would prescribe. Instead, his desire to be
with her focuses on conversing with her in her apartment while watching
television and eating pizza. Through their conversations, Sonny learns of
Nica's unhappiness in her restrictive, gendered role of caregiver to her baby
brother and custodian of the domestic chores. His repeated requests to see
her and hang out with her are frequently rejected because of her domestic
responsibilities and fear of her stepfather's punishment if they are left
unattended. In this way, Sonny emotionally identifies with Nica as he
uniquely understands the restrictions placed on her life by the code of a
patriarchal, hegemonic masculinity.

The somewhat mysterious final scene of the novel takes place on April 29,
1992 – the first day of the Rodney King Riots. In this scene, textured by the
immediate threat of the chaos, violence, and destruction of the Riots, Sonny
picks up Nica at the Los Flores apartment building and narrowly succeeds in
driving her through the upheaval to the bus depot. Here, Sonny gives Nica all
of the money he had amassed over the course of the novel, buys her a bus
ticket back to Mexico, and while passionately kissing her, puzzlingly admits
that: "She wanted me to touch her everywhere and in every way. I didn't want
her like that, as much as I did..." (249). Nica is likewise confused by Sonny's
behavior when she discerns that he has no plans to escape with her and
Sonny offers no satisfactory explanation for his reasoning. I argue, however,
that as a newly-conceived Chicano man, Sonny defies conceptualizations of a
hegemonic, patriarchal masculinity that would dictate a heterosexually
romantic and domestic future in which Nica would likely remain imprisoned
in a familial existence as caregiver and housewife. Sonny succeeds in
eliminating this threat of patriarchy and therefore exemplifies a new Chicano
man as one who is free of the patriarchal dividend and therefore is able to
serve as a feminist ally.[9]

Sonny's response to the model of hegemonic masculinity defies his
privileged destiny within the cycle of the patriarchal dividend. *La astilla*
(Sonny) is keenly aware of, and simultaneously resists, his position as the
masculine successor of *el palo* (Cloyd). Instead, his dis-identification with that
model leads him to explore his own masculinity in transformative ways. As a

new Chicano male, Sonny is unrestricted by the patriarchal dividend and is able to function as a feminist ally who seeks to liberate all from the same social cycle that serves to restrict men and subordinate women.

Conclusions

The old, patriarchal axiom "*de tal palo, tal astilla*" excuses potentially damaging and abusive behavior on the part of boys and men by implying that the son (*la astilla*) has no agency in determining his own masculine identity but instead is a passive recipient of the masculine identity assumed by the father (*el palo*). The impossibility for transformation expressed in this saying becomes further crystallized when one takes into account Connell's assertion that men benefit from the overall subordination of women, what the theorist calls the patriarchal dividend. Both of these paradigmatic designs of masculinity promote the idea of masculinity as a cycle that is always and already perpetuated by the gendered roles that are dictated by society. Recent texts by Domingo Martinez Jr. and Dagoberto Gilb, however, relate stories of Chicano sons who actively seek to break from the self-perpetuating cycle of hegemonic masculinity in their own personal lives.

Martinez and Sonny aim to explore new, transformative interpretations of a Chicano masculinity that are divorced from the traditional, patriarchal prescriptions exemplified by their respective father figures. Martinez, while contrasting the notion of hegemonic masculinity that defines his father, has been complicit in sharing the benefits of the patriarchal dividend that first surface during the breakup episode with his girlfriend. Likewise, his efforts to fraternally re-create the family unit that his father had destroyed go awry when the shared memories of childhood lead to self-destructive impulses and overly defensive postures on the part of him and his brother.

Sonny, on the other hand, exhibits a level of self-awareness not shared by Martinez. Sonny, whose name directly positions him in the space of *la astilla*, comes to understand his role as the inherent beneficiary of the patriarchal dividend. In liberating Nica from her domestic existence as caretaker and homemaker, Sonny takes his first steps in breaking the cycle of patriarchy. When he drives Nica to the bus station and then decides not to run away with her, he renounces his position as heir of the patriarchal dividend and paves the way for Nica to live a life free from the patriarchal impositions that would be imposed upon her as a woman if she and Sonny ran away and started their own family together. Had the two escaped and begun a romantic relationship, Nica would remain in a position of subordination in relation to Sonny, and the cycle of patriarchy would have continued.

Domingo Martinez Jr. more clearly embodies the "*de tal palo, tal astilla*" proverb. However, it is promising to note that, in this case, *la astilla* is keenly aware of, and simultaneously resists, his position as the masculine successor of *el palo*. Perhaps this awareness may one day lead to (an)other fraternal re-creation of the family, one that is more constructive and is able to overcome the legacy of the patriarchal dividend.

In refusing to create anew a patriarchal notion of family with Nica, Sonny is more successful than is Martinez in his attempts to explore a transformative notion of what it signifies to be a man. While it may be precipitous to deem Sonny a feminist ally, as the very un-patriarchal actions that warrant such a consideration directly stem from his empowered subject position as a man, I argue that Gilb purposefully positions him as such at the novel's ending. In disrupting the cycle of a patriarchal, hegemonic masculinity, Sonny has opened a space of agency for Nica, one she can choose to claim or not to claim as she sees fit. Upon ridding himself of the advantageous position afforded to him by the patriarchal dividend, Sonny comes to represent a new Chicano man, one who is truly capable of valuing the equality of all and his role in ensuring that equality.

Notes

[1] This expression is a common way to informally criticize the character of a child (usually a son) by implying that the child's parent (usually the father) is indirectly to blame for the behavior/personality of the child. A literal translation of the phrase would be, "From such a stick, such a splinter," and the implication is that the stick symbolizes the father and the splinter symbolizes the son. In English, the saying "The apple doesn't fall far from the tree" is very close in meaning.

[2] For the purposes of this study, I employ the term *Chicanx* to refer to the Mexican-American community broadly, inviting the inclusivity that is implied with the gender neutral term. Conversely, I employ the term *Chicano* when specifically referencing masculinities present within that community.

[3] As patriarch of the neighboring Rubio family, the step-uncle feels that the Martinez family does not rightfully belong in the barrio and therefore does not deserve to inherit the family trucking business. In this way, the Rubios represent a challenge to the patriarchal authority that Domingo Sr. attempts to claim.

[4] There is an ongoing scholarly debate regarding the concept of machismo and whether it should be regarded as a positive or a negative characteristic. For the purposes of this study, machismo, as it relates to Domingo Sr., is meant to signify what Alfredo Mirandé outlines as the "negative conceptions of 'macho'," namely "synthetic/exaggerated masculinity, male dominance/authoritarianism, violence/aggressiveness, and self-centeredness/egoísmo" (Mirandé 69-71).

[5] Just as Mirandé outlines the negative conceptions of machismo, he also outlines the positive machista traits of "courage, honor, and integrity" (Mirandé 72).

6 This paradoxical occurrence brings to mind Connell's recollection of Michael Messner's example of the athlete who played his sport too violently (read: with too much masculine aggression) and therefore risked undermining the very institution (the sport) that legitimized the athlete's claim to masculine authority (Connell 37).

7 Domingo Martinez went on to write *My Heart is a Drunken Compass* (2014) – another memoir that, in many ways, can be read as a sequel to *The Boy Kings of Texas*. In *My Heart*, his attitude toward his father is much more exculpatory and apologetic than it is in *Boy Kings*. His first memoir, however, is capable of standing alone as a text, and I chose to analyze it as such without the complications of his apologetic stance in *My Heart*.

8 The narrator briefly mentions that Sonny has a sister but that, perhaps as a result of criminal activity on her part, she no longer lives with him and his mother. She is never mentioned again.

9 It is interesting to note that in this scene Nica is not yet capable of understanding a newly conceptualized Chicano masculinity as Sonny embodies it. She remains limited by the patriarchal dividend and therefore expects Sonny to save her by escaping with her, thereby perpetuating the patriarchal model.

Works Cited

Connell, R. W. *Masculinities*. U of California Press, 2005.

Cuenca, Mercé. ""You Do Not Do:" Deconstructing White Masculinity in Cold War American Literature (1945-1965)." *Men In Color: Racialized Masculinities in U.S. Literature and Cinema*. edited by Josep M. Armengol, Cambridge Scholars Publishing, 2011, pp. 121-142.

Gilb, Dagoberto. *The Flowers*. Grove Press, 2008.

Martinez, Domingo. *The Boy Kings of Texas*. Lyons Press, 2012.

Mirandé, Alredo. *Hombres y Machos: Masculintiy and Latino Culture*. Westview Press, 1997.

Venegas, Maria. "He's a Rebel." *The New York Times*, 11 January 2015, p. 12.

Chapter 6

Machismo, Maricones and the Ethnicization of Masculinity in Telenovelas

Jess Brocklesby

Queen Mary University of London

As the most-watched television format in Mexico, telenovelas are the promoters of implicit and explicit messages about the diverse identities represented in these productions. The audience for a telenovela crosses categories of age, sex, race and socio-economic status through which Mexican society becomes cohesive in its viewership. These melodramatic series are prominent, airing five days a week for one hour, for approximately six months of the year. Because telenovelas are the most easily accessible representation of identity within Mexico, the various forms of masculinity as represented through the telenovela redefine the concept of masculinity as it begins to shift in a Mexican culture and move toward post-patriarchy.

Masculinity in Latin America is perceived with a quintessential sense of "maleness," conflating gender and sex with identity. In its Mexican context, it is typically referred to as machismo, a perspective that allows and encourages male domination over women in all spheres: economic, legal, cultural, psychological and many more. Machismo therefore conflates with manhood and performs itself negatively as hyper-masculinity, leading men to take risks, become aggressive toward women and men, build sensitivity to insult and a desire to demonstrate self-worth through sexual conquests. These specific negative traits are not the only indicators of machismo, however, as it can also be used to explain positive traits such as dedication of fathers, sense of honor and pride in the family unit (Frevert and Miranda 16). Men are expected to be authoritative, aggressive and dominant (Durik et al. 429). Machismo idealizes males as providers and protectors, strong, virile, courageous and sexually free in a way which is prohibited for females. It is a contradiction (evidenced by Dowsett 10) consisting of courage, generosity and stoicism as well as arrogance and vainglory, in which the outward appearances contain empty boasts which conceal an inner vulnerability. However, in recent years, criticism has acknowledged machismo in its discussion of masculinity and its place in Mexican society (Murray, Prieur, Balderston and Guy, Buffington). Critics such as these have allowed machismo to develop into a discourse to be accepted or rejected, rather than allowing these beliefs to be enshrined into Mexican society.

Linguistically, this gender binary is reflected in Spanish words that have either a masculine or feminine connotation, for example nouns that are categorized as either masculine (often ending in –o) or feminine (often ending in –a). While words ending in –o can encompass both male and female identification, they prioritize the masculine and exclude those who fall outside of the gender binary altogether. Even in the most basic of linguistic senses, the gender binaries of Mexico are entrenched. Mexican identity is understood through a series of gender and sexuality binaries (masculine versus feminine, straight versus gay, strong versus weak), but through representation via media and television, this thinking has arguably been revitalized. Stereotypically feminine behavior is no longer the exclusive domain of women and homosexual men, and stereotypically masculine behavior is no longer attributed solely to the heterosexual man. The new representation of various forms of masculinity via telenovelas has served to reflect and change society as it paves the way for a post-patriarchal Mexican masculinity. Genealogically, the narration of masculinity in Mexican telenovelas from the beginning of the century began to emphasize the importance of the characterization of homosexual men. This evolving narrative allows for new explorations of various types of masculinity: toxic, homosexual and cross-cultural. The addition of these masculinities creates a space for a new cultural response to previous sacrosanct performances of machismo.

Historically, the marginalization of effeminate males is well-documented. In his well-known and often-cited study of Mexican identity, *The Labyrinth of Solitude*, Octavio Paz posits that the masculine/feminine binary continues as a defining aspect of Mexican character. It is the closed, or impenetrable, nature of men, Paz argues, that protects them from the domination of conquest to which women are subject by nature (30). The male who allows himself to be penetrated, or assumes a womanly position, is considered less than a man, while the man who penetrates another man may actually be seen as more of a man because he conquers both women and men. Thus, in this reading of homosexual encounters, it is only the passive partner who is stigmatized, not the active partner, whose perceived masculinity may actually be amplified by being the active partner in a homosexual encounter (40). Here again, it is effeminacy that is the stigmatizing force rather than a particular sexual activity.

Since their debut, Mexican telenovelas have limited the presence of homosexual characters. The presumed homosexual characters have, for the most part, been limited to the sporadic inclusion of feminized men who inhabit typically feminine occupational spheres (hairstylists and designers) and, often, the "gay best friend" role. These characters have consistently been supporting roles and typically function as the humorous counterpart to the protagonist. These characters are never fully developed and are never allowed to reach the validity of identity assumed by heterosexual male characters within the genre. As a result of their exaggeratedly feminine demeanor, they have functioned more as a caricature of the gay man than representing diversity within the gay community. For Huizar, this concept conflates the idea of homosexual men as fulfilling the role of the female: "No son jamás los protagonistas y tampoco figuran para reivindicar la imagen social que se ha forjado la audiencia de ellos: si no se mueven, manotean amanerdamente ni hablan como histéricos, no pueden representar la imagen que se ha construido de los *gay*" (38). Huizar's use of "hablan como histéricos" conflates biological maleness and femininity within the same, masculine (-o ending) gendered word. While the word 'histérico' is linguistically gendered masculine (and thus somewhat neutral in the plural, in spite of its masculine preference), the root word derives from the Greek 'hystera' meaning uterus. The Greeks used this word to denote a physical ailment in which the uterus travels through a woman's body, eventually rising to the throat to cause asphyxiation and induce somatization. In spite of the physicality of this ailment, its connection to the most feminine of all images renders the masculine character incapable of acting hysterically. Homosexual masculinities are therefore biologically defunct as they are reduced to the assumption that they are afflicted by hyper-feminine ailments. The connection to speaking with hysteria is important as it suggests a social presentation of femininity to which homosexual masculinities are expected to relate. According to Huizar, the inclusion of homosexual characters is merely a way to reinforce problematic stereotypes of the gay man as an effeminate caricature, masquerading as femininity. With their current status as "newcomer" within telenovelas, homosexual masculinities fight against typically Mexican heteronormativity. By including new forms of masculinity in telenovelas, homosexuality serves as the catalyst for a re-examining and reconfiguring of gender narratives within popular fiction, allowing representations of different types of masculinity to humanize characters, ultimately leading to change and acceptance within Mexican society.

The Mexican telenovela, "La Vida en el Espejo" (1999) addressed the topic of homosexuality directly through two of its supporting characters, Mauricio and Jim. The supporting characters negate Huizar's argument as they are not defined by gendered behavior, but instead defined by their object choice which dictates their sexuality. At the start of the telenovela, Mauricio is involved in a romantic relationship with a young woman. While his mannerisms, dress and general being protect him from stereotypical effeminacy and thus conflation with homosexuality, Mauricio begins to admit his attraction to men and crafts his identity around this basis.

During Mauricio's journey to his ultimate acceptance of his sexuality, he attempts to adhere to strict masculine gender binaries as dictated by Mexican society. Set up as the foil to his artistic, naïve sister, Mauricio is a conservative student of finance. Characterized by his place within the center of a traditional family, his dress, occupation and personality demonstrate particular attention to traditional masculinity. When we first meet Mauricio in the first episode, he is in his family home, typified by traditional American trinkets (Mejía 1.1). The height and length of the rooms in which they reside, along with the expensiveness of the items within them, match Mauricio's conservative, black outfits. Camera angles that focus on lengthening and heightening the room allow him to appear taller and more commanding, adding power to his appearance. Mauricio is filmed primarily with low angled shots in the first episode, far more so than any character other than his father. The correlation between the men of the house and low angle shots suggest a masculinization of power as camera angles depict sight and its role in creating perception.

Mauricio's insistence on chastity until after marital vows have been exchanged becomes the viewer's first true insight into his sexuality. For a telenovela that speaks so openly and frankly about sexual relations, Mauricio's vow of chastity reinforces his role as conservative and very traditional. However, his attempts to adhere to the Christian heterosexual institute of marriage with a suitable young woman emphasizes his struggle between self-identification and Mexican identity burden. While Mauricio attempts to assume the role of the masculine as he has understood it, he is unable to consummate a male/female sexual relationship. Owing distinctly to Catholic dominance in Mexico, it is difficult to underestimate the role of religion for the purposes of representation. Viewers are able to see a man who is struggling with his sexuality and who is also a man of the church. This allows the character to become a sympathetic one, as adherence to Catholicism is heavily linked to concepts of goodness.[1] A Mexican audience is able to see, identify with and begin to like Mauricio prior to exploring his sexuality because he is introduced and characterized, through dress, as a Catholic. His traditionalism and Catholicism demonstrate his masculinity ensuring a sympathetic response to the character.

In chapter 57, Mauricio and Jim visit a bar and order drinks when two beautiful young women, dressed in revealing clothes, attempt to gain their attention. The women attempt to make extended eye contact with the two men throughout the scene, presenting an overtly sexual gaze that is rebuffed by the two men. The women leave the bar immediately when they realize the two men are homosexual, verifying that their interests are merely sexual. The language of the scene is also interesting. Jim finished Mauricio's sentence when he seems to struggle to articulate his sexuality:

Mauricio: porque yo quería ser…

Jim: …homosexual." (Mejía 1.57)

For Mauricio, in spite of the issues that hiding his sexuality presents, announcing aloud that he is homosexual is still a step too far. The word itself is still more powerful than his identity. Mauricio's inability to use the word suggests issues of homosexual sociability. As the spoken word is merely a social expression, it serves no purpose for individual reflection, thus Mauricio being unable to say the word aloud demonstrates a fear of expressing his identity within society. This concept is echoed by the two women's responses to Mauricio and Jim's sexuality: "que desperdicio" (Mejía 1.57). The idea that it is a "shame" they are gay is a reversal of the male gaze, as the women are now looking at the men only as sexual objects. Gay men, in this case, are not even worthy of entertaining conversation. Mauricio and Jim take on the role of the feminine in this scene as they are actively pursued by women who are only interested in them for their sexuality. They are thus reduced to the role of the aesthetic. While this scene is key in demonstrating an appropriate understanding of the difficulties homosexual masculinity faces in Mexican society, it represents homosexuality by conflating it with femininity and therefore reduces the impact of Mauricio's growing acceptance of his sexuality. Homosexual men are nothing more than men who adopt the role of the feminine.

If, as Connell attests, gender is created through power conflict, machismo functions in this context precisely because of its activity. For Connell, masculinity is created through the subjugation of women and femininity is defined through the oppression by men. However, what Connell (and other hegemonic masculinity theorists) fails to grasp is the hierarchy of gender within a hegemonic masculinity. Homosexual masculinities are subjugated not only because their practice undermines the accepted strategy for the subordination of women, but also because their sexual desire undermines the primary importance of reproduction. Linguistically, this argument falls on shaky ground, but sex role theory quotes biological differences between the penetrator and the penetrated as the basis for power disparity. In this most basic of senses, Connell serves to reinforce Paz's conception of penetrating being power. Mauricio and Jim's sexual position preference is not mentioned during the telenovela for obvious reasons, however the concept can be applied to Mauricio's relationship with his first girlfriend; he is unable to complete the primary masculine function and penetrate the female. Defining his femininity through object choice and sexual preference negates the concept of any form of homosexual masculinity, instead of arguing the closest that a homosexual man can hope for is to be the penetrator and thus be afforded masculinity in this strict gender binary.

To combat this, Mauricio further attempts to dissuade his homosexuality by engaging in typical masculine actions. When Jim, his eventual lover, suggests that he might also be gay, Mauricio responds with violence. Another hypermasculine, and problematic, aspect of Mauricio's personality comes to light. In order to physically and socially rebuke Jim's assertion of his potential homosexuality, Mauricio attempts to convince Jim, and himself, that he is not gay by relinquishing any hold over potentially presumed feminine characteristics and reacts with force. In episode 15, Jim admits his sexual preference to Mauricio and then questions Mauricio's sexuality: "Hay una visión. Por favor no me digas que no te habías dado cuenta." Mauricio shakes his head to confirm his unawareness, and Jim responds by asking: "Bueno, no se tú también... ¿eres no?" (Mejía 1.15). It is at this moment, when his sexuality is being questioned, that Mauricio takes the role of the hyper masculine and chooses to start a physical fight. He pushes Jim's arms away from him, breaking the previously warm and tender embrace while he begins to yell "¡No me toques!" at the same time as pushing Mauricio twice further and moves his arm back as if to punch him. Mauricio runs away from this intense display of machismo after reinforcing his own masculinity with an intense display of aggression. It is key that until the word "homosexual" is mentioned, Mauricio is perfectly content to be engaged in an embrace with Jim, further suggesting that the socialization of homosexuality is the issue here rather than his emotional bonds. His struggle to see sexuality as merely a sexual preference and not a series of occupationally, conversationally and societally charged feminine acts undermines his sexual identification. As the relationship between the two men slowly evolves, Mauricio's and Jim's stories become stories of love, emotion and self-identification rather than of ridicule and shame. With this evolution, both characters become much more sympathetic through their rebuttal of compulsory heterosexuality. Normalizing masculine homosexuality in "La Vida en el Espejo" reflects and pushes a process of homosexual normality into the lives of everyday Mexicans.

Jim, however, could not be more distanced from Mexico if he tried. Characterized by his otherness, Jim often finds it difficult to remember his Spanish and has a tendency to fall back into English. It is a convenient coincidence that the word he uses to describe Mauricio is the same in both languages – homosexual. The telenovela appears to use Jim's foreignness to its advantage as it seeks to justify new forms of masculinity as imported rather than evolved. This is especially poignant for the Mexican viewers of the show. As Jim is shown to be completely foreign to the country and to the telenovela, he is also foreign to the audience which allows them to dissociate themselves from homosexuality. Jim is the first person to suggest that Mauricio might be gay. He is the first person to show Mauricio what his life might be like. He suggests Mauricio come out to his family and he is also the person who is able to introduce homosexual masculinities into a family unit and allow them to work effectively. Homosexual masculinities are therefore slightly removed from traditional Mexican society and lean closer to the concept of cultural hybridity.

This othering of Jim is important to a colonialist history. Due to the colonial and spiritual nature of Mexico (also including the thirty-three mutually indistinguishable languages spoken in addition to the well-known Spanish), the development of modernity in connection to tradition has further developed the connection of gender and sex binaries to issues of migration, colonialism, spirituality and race. In *Hybrid Cultures*, Canclini explores the boundaries between modernization and democratization. He posits that the combination of tradition with newer, intellectual ideas is the process of creating and maintaining modernity in Latin America. The process of hybridization, as discussed by Canclini, maintains an interest in the biological, colonial and religious differences between Latin Americans and cites their difficulties in modernizing on these precise differences. It is thereby completely impractical, and impossible, to separate notions of gender from their colonial, linguistic and spiritual affiliations. The precise difficulty in this project arises from this very concept. Questioning the plausibility or practicality of creating a consensual definition of Mexican masculinity when faced with the problem of differentiation in such a diverse land questions the typically applied notion of a common history. This is further exacerbated by cultural and colonial invasion. Ignoring these questions only serves to further the violent oppression with which the country is treated. Nonetheless, pragmatically, the basis of a cohesive Mexican identity surely falls somewhere neatly in the "speaks Spanish" category as a basic requirement. By having Jim consistently fall back into speaking English, he is dissociated from a Mexican macho identity and instead falls neatly into the category of a masculine homosexuality. It is also key to consider the multiplicity of meanings created through the consideration of male and female without losing sight of "the relations of power which are produced and enacted in their construction" (Nencel 59), demonstrating an awareness of the mestizaje and hybrid nature of Latin America and Mexico as a whole.

In spite of this, *Changing Men and Masculinities in Latin America* (2003) discusses the starting points for evolving masculinity in telenovelas. For Carillo, "La Vida en el Espejo" is able to catalyze a discourse of homosexual masculinities that provide responsible representation and begin to lift the burden of identity reinforcement for homosexual masculinities. Carillo argues that: "popular discourses about male homosexuality have traditionally emphasized effeminacy and a "loss of manhood." These associations are changing as more men who are sexually attracted to men disclose their homosexuality yet retain masculine identities" (353). This evolution, in recognizing the varied forms of homosexual masculinities, has a significant influence on Mexican masculinities because it begins to redefine identity boundaries. For Carillo, this discussion does not merely provide benefits for the socially downtrodden homosexual masculinities, but also provides relief for other similarly burdened masculinities, as effeminate masculinities are increasingly insufficient proof of homosexuality. Telenovelas, due to their use of multiple perspectives, character and plot familiarity, and the fact that the average number of episodes for a series tends to be one hundred, are deeply entrenched into Mexican life in a way that other media representations cannot be. The sheer familiarity with which telenovelas are received make them a viable option for creating change, reinforcing Carillo's point that "La Vida en el Espejo" is perfectly capable of catalyzing change in Mexican society.

Moreover, the evolution of Mauricio's and Jim's relationship serves a didactic role in the context of the telenovela as Mauricio's family models for viewers an attitude of tolerance through their acceptance of the couple as a part of the family unit. This legitimizes the relationship between the two men and demonstrates a healthy family unit containing two homosexual masculinities. It is important to note here that both parts of the unit behave with masculine coded actions. This further legitimizes homosexual relationships but, at the same time, also undermines them. "La Vida en el Espejo" avoids falling into the trap which Connell and Paz attest to by refusing restrictive gender binaries. It is, however, noted in the telenovela that the relationship is never truly accepted because the telenovela never ceremonially confirms their relationship. At no point throughout the telenovela is there an expression of ceremonial love between the two men. Alternatively, all of the major heterosexual couples within the story are able to celebrate their love through ceremony. Although the relationship is never confirmed in such a way, it is still legitimized through the telenovela and the acceptance provided by Jim's and Mauricio's families. This relationship seems like a step away from traditional Mexican gender binaries and toward a new, more accepting society in which expressions of machismo are varied and accepted, even if they are not perfect representations.

The use of mannerisms, dress and personality to reflect homosexual masculinities is a clear opportunity to showcase the self. Paz defines Mexican manhood as: "measured through his invulnerability in the face of an enemy, and against the impact of the outside world" (30). His essay, "Máscaras mexicanas," concludes that masculinity is a mask used by men to hide their insecurities, a mechanism Mexican masculinities require to survive socially. The very belief in this concept implies a social necessity to control and differentiate which "máscara" Mexican society gets to see. As the telenovela is a visual media, the emotional/intellectual value of characters is reinforced through associations with fashion. For Rovine, "dress is a primary expression both of deeply rooted cultural identities and, often simultaneously, of the creativity by which conventions are constantly transformed" (6). In this case, the ways in which characters within telenovelas choose to dress and respond is a further layer of socially constructed identity. This is particularly key in highlighting differences in homosexual and heterosexual characters. For many years, homosexual characters, from the fashion-obsessed best friend to the protagonist, have been portrayed across all manner of media and genre. The stereotypically effeminate gay man is an overused and under-respected category in which most homosexual masculinities reside.[2] The media use of this as an extended expression of femininity functions mostly to contrast the masculine men within the media. These polarized and satirical gender performances manifest themselves in the limited characterizations of male characters as either "macho" or "locas." Consequently, the majority of media representations of masculinities for the past century have omitted the existence of the masculine homosexual, the effeminate heterosexual and all forms of masculinity which do not conform to the celebrated categories. The intermedial, cross-genre approach to creating the stereotypical "gay best friend" has been intensely dangerous in representations of masculinity. By bringing material culture fully into the discourse that develops gender and sexuality studies, the representation of masculinities suggests that sexuality is easily discernible and quantifiable. Thus all men who like clothing must be gay.

In the Mexican telenovela, "Velo de Novia" (2003), Jaro is a stylist and wardrobe assistant and Vida, a supporting character, works as a dancer. Jaro is a transvestite whose drag blurs gender constructs to such an extent that his gender is not aesthetically recognizable. He has long, flowing hair, dresses in tight feminine clothes, and his demeanor and manners of speaking all conclude as a manifestation of femininity. He is set up as the drag queen counterpart to Vida, with whom a feminine friendship is emphasized. This character of the flamboyant and feminine homosexual man crosses cultural and linguistic boundaries. In the American remake of a fan favorite Mexican telenovela, "La Bella Mas Fea" (2006), the character of Marc is also exemplified in this role. In the first series, many coded jokes are made in reference to

Marc's sexuality. He plays on words such as "flaming" and "out" but his sexuality is still a secret to his family (Gaitán 1.1-1.20). He even goes so far as to employ both Amanda and Betty as his fake girlfriend solely to cover up his sexuality from his mother. However, when his mother refers to Betty's nephew as "swishy" he becomes angry and explains his sexuality to his mother: "Shut your mouth, Mom! ... that little boy? Swishy? Swishy!? You wanna talk about swishy? Open your eyes Mom and look at your own swishy son!" (Gaitán 1.18). Marc learns to access his own sexuality through sheer outrage about the way his mother responds to homosexuality. Marc and Jaro, while both the "gay best friend" character, differ intensely in the presentation of their sexualities and masculinities. Jaro's homosexuality pushes him into the position of the "joto," whereas Marc's homosexuality is explored and not merely satirized. Marc's sexuality and character were perceived so positively in the United States that the character became a series regular instead of appearing in only one episode as originally planned. Moreover, Slate Magazine in 2007 named him as one of the reasons they were excited for the return of "Ugly Betty." Conversely, the character of Jaro seems to have been mostly overlooked in his respective telenovela. No awards, mentions or responses to the character can be found on social media or relevant websites to promote the telenovela. The simple act of ignoring the character speaks volumes about the reception of the effeminate man in Mexican society.

Jaro is not even a secondary character; he is a secondary character to a secondary character and used as nothing more than light comic relief. His sexuality is never explored, but merely criticized by Vida's stage manager who, on occasion, refers to him as a "joto" or "maricon."[3] While all of these terms are derogatory in nature, the repeated use of "joto" is never critiqued or addressed in any way. This is a far cry from the lessons of tolerance and diversity in the gay community as exemplified a few years earlier. Vida's stage manager is a clear example of where masculinity becomes toxic. His insistence on referring to Jaro as "joto" is a way for him to separate himself from the effeminacy Jaro represents. Using an offensive slur to remind Jaro of his femininity is a form of toxic masculinity because he creates difference by adhering strictly to his perceived macho ideals and by labelling Jaro as feminine. This is not merely a way to differentiate the two characters, but also a way for Vida to actively reject Jaro's lifestyle, essentially delegitimizing Jaro's sexual and social identity.

Buffington explored the use of "joto" and Mexican homosexual machismo in his article "Los Jotos: Contested Visions of Homosexuality in Modern Mexico," in which he critiques Roumaganac's perception of imprisoned homosexualities. Buffington posits the Mexican belief that machismo was viewed with biological roots when he mentions that sexual deviance and especially homosexuality threatened to contaminate "normal" society if left unchecked and the prisoners were to interact with the outside world (120). Roumaganac's sincere belief in the biological processes of homosexuality, when combined with the overwhelming citing of his research, conflated the use of homosexual specific language (such as joto) with the concept of imprisonment or illegality. With the spread of Roumaganac's ideology, the already deeply offensive slur became intrinsically linked with a lack of morality. These so-called "jotos" were then treated as though they had a disease which could turn them into an immoral person. By leaving this slur unchecked and uncritiqued, "Velo de Novia" reverts back to stereotypes developed before the production of "La Vida en el Espejo" and provides evidence that the changing of Mexican attitudes was indeed slower than originally presumed.

While telenovelas are clearly able to reflect and respond to the cultural and social, the concept of media representation catalyzing change in society has been heavily debated. Although this debate seems to have not yet reached audiences in Mexico, the concept of representation politics is a well-recognized academic sphere.[4] The impact of the telenovelas, specifically when applied to gender roles (marianismo and machismo), can be evidenced by the Kjeldgaard and Nielsen study. Their analysis of responses to a Mexican telenovela by young consumers demonstrates that young Mexican females negotiate between the traditional roles that are valued by parents, religious organizations, and a new, more liberal conception of marianismo[5]. This does not necessarily prove beyond a doubt that telenovelas have had a positive impact on the perception of marianismo by young women. According to the authors, the consumers of the telenovela, while willing to bend the stereotype to suit their own needs, still reference their personalities to provide an acceptable identity by adhering to a male response. Their worries about balancing an expression of sexuality that would not be perceived as promiscuous combined with creating a new sense of self-worth that does not emanate from their interactions with the macho man (and his perceived values) are still as clear as ever. This suggests that while telenovelas are not able to provide a revolutionary interpretation of Mexican gender binaries, there is an evolutionary nature to the role of telenovelas and their ability to kick start social change.

It is not only telenovelas and their portrayal of machismo that is able to influence viewers and demonstrate a change of opinion in Mexico. The advertisements played during breaks in the telenovela also have the power to influence the audience. It is precisely because of the intense power relations that characterize the telenovela genre that their advertisements can also have a massive influence. In fact, commercials can be used to reinforce the concept of telenovelic representation to reflect and inform cultural beliefs and attitudes.

While there is a scarcity of information and research surrounding sex roles in Latin American media representation,[6] there is a relatively well-received review by Gilly in 1998 in which she explains how she only found one published study on the topic, but found three hundred and seventy-eight magazine advertisements inside eight magazines published in 1976 where women were portrayed as homemakers. Only one percent of the print advertisements pictured women in professional work. An overwhelming seventy percent of coded messages within the advertisements were used to show women as sexual objects. For Gilly, these results prove Mexico's traditionalism.

In addition, Mexican television commercials continue to portray women in a subordinate role, as product users, recipients of help, or dependent upon others (mother, wife). Fullerton and Kendrick's study continues to support this analysis through the advertisements shown during the breaks in Spanish-language television. Resulting from the lack of research into Mexican responses to television and print advertisements, these findings have been used as proxy since more than half of the Hispanic population of the United States is of Mexican heritage.

In a commercial played on Telemundo in Mexico in 1990, ford escorts are shown as the ultimate family car. The advertisement was shown during breaks in "La Virgen de Guadalupe," "Una Pura Y Dos Con Sal" and "The Johnny Canales Show" in order to increase sales in Latin America. The commercial presents a father and child who actively mimics his father. Dressed in typical formal, conservative work clothes, the boy examines the car by looking inside it and into the mirror while speaking about the quality of the build of the car and how they both look forward to driving to work in the mornings. When the father appears, he performs the same movements as the boy originally did, dressed in a similar fashion wearing only an extra tie, presumably to demonstrate that he will be attending work. The father slaps the car on the bumper and then joins in the child's monologue that the car makes him look forward to the morning, and thus to going to work. This commercial seems innocuous enough in its portrayal of a child spending time with his father and demonstrating a family unit that bonds via a car. The idea of entering the workforce and ownership of a car are also demonstrated in a positive light. Within the commercial, a macho identity is exemplified as being the ideal father, one who is able to simultaneously provide for his family and excel at work. However, this serves to reinforce family gender roles by showing only the boy being able to transition into the role of provider and protector. While the advertisement enforces gender binaries, it also demonstrates a positive form of masculinity as spending time with family members is not usually considered to be a problematic activity.

Interestingly, the commercial portrays the father as both product user and product owner. This shift of representation between roles is demonstrative of a rejection of typically feminine modes of power (or lack thereof), which represents the time when women were unable to own things. The boy is obviously masculinized. However, he assumes the role of product user rather than product owner thus ensuring that he is currently powerless. Indeed, the mimicry of dress and actions suggest that the boy will eventually fulfill the role of his father, adhering to gender binaries and thereby maintaining power. The lack of female representation in the advertisement is worrying in its own right, but this lack also allows for a masculinity to arise from a place other than the traditional power relations between men and women.

However, the advertisement also demonstrates a certain vanity within machismo. When he first appears in the frame, the father immediately checks his reflection in the mirror of the car, even before checking on his child. He does this to straighten his tie and confirm that he looks professional for work. By doing so, he connects male "peacocking" with the workplace and confirms a masculine sense of identity and its inherent connection with boasting via outward appearance. The commercial is incredibly machista in this sense.

The background of the commercial does not appear to be particularly Latin American. The characters are light-skinned, dressed in typically American office wear and are shown outside a typically American home. The color, presentation and decoration of the house is reminiscent of the "white picket fence" American ideal. The ad therefore encourages Mexicans to aspire to an Americanized life by appealing to the machista ideal of being the ultimate father while also benefitting from the gender binary. This indoctrination into Western gender ideals is problematic given the viewership of telenovelas because it demonstrates a wish fulfilment quality to materialism as it is expressed through machismo as a concept, rather than a discourse. Essentially, showing machismo as something to aspire to is problematic.

As a representation of the family, the feminization of the car in the commercial further promotes an unhealthy machismo. Via the sexualization of the car, marianismo is reduced to the aesthetic. Both the boy's and man's consistent reinforcement of the aesthetic value of the car, "Que bien te siento a comenzar la manana" (1.32), demark the pure sexual, aesthetic value of femininity, albeit in vehicle form. Here, the two masculine characters talking about how the car will make them feel in the morning is a reference to the way that other drivers will respond to it. The car's usefulness, much like a woman's, is that other men will be jealous of their ownership. It is interesting here how the car so clearly represents femininity as it supports the husband and son in their roles, thereby suggesting that the role of the woman is limited to looking attractive and serving her family. The way the father interacts with the car is key to understanding the gendered roles within Mexican society, as his actions serve to demonstrate his vanity and the oppression of women as he slaps the car on its proverbial bottom while checking his reflection in the mirror. The car, then, becomes a reflection for macho vanity and family pride.

Not all commercials that play during Mexican telenovelas portray machismo negatively, however. On TV Azteca in Mexico, where there is a plethora of videos of men dancing with women in various state of undress, some of the advertisements seem to depict a healthy masculinity. The commercial for Dual Gran Turismo subverts expectations by showing a man who, at first glance, appears to be taking part in a pole-vault race but, upon closer inspection, actually shows a man competing to be the best decorator in his family home. The ad juxtaposes athletes and stay-at-home husbands and fuses the two as housework becomes a form of competition. In this way, the commercial conflates masculinist identities with housework and thereby breaks conventional gender roles. This demonstration of pride in the home creates a space for a healthy masculinity – combining the wish to be the ideal husband/father with aspects of competition and pride. Using pride of the family home (as opposed to pride of outward appearance and aggression) allows the advertisement to depict a truly respectable form of machismo in which the family home (and thus the family) becomes a source of pride without reinforcing stereotypical masculinities. This ad is particularly interesting when it is seen in the context of a Mexican identity, in which the roles of nationalism and patriarchy are complicated. Policies of globalization and militarization have lent a "muscular" discourse to gender and sexuality as represented in media, which provides continuity to the principle of patriarchy and privilege. The structural impact of this enforces traditional gender roles and places people in binary categories, such as "us" and "them." This discourse marginalizes opposition, difference, and diversity. Each local culture has its own distinct relationship with gender, sexuality and nationalism, making it much more difficult to access the advertisements' various portrayals of machismo. However, as marginalized groups fight for increased agency, they often do so by assuming the power that the oppressor yields. In this commercial, instead of attempting to yield power by adopting masculine characteristics, the gender lines are blurred and the fight for increased agency includes femininity by providing a form of equality.

While this is but one example of a healthy masculine representation alongside many problematic advertisements, it still demonstrates the steps being taken to move toward a post-patriarchal society. Ads like this one show a true devotion on the part of Mexican writers to actively include more positive forms of machismo. While the majority of commercials that play during telenovela breaks follow the same formula the Ford Escort advertisement, more and more ads are challenging the notions of stereotypical masculinities like the one by Dual Gran Turismo. When television commercials cease to promote gender roles altogether, post patriarchy will be in full effect.

Haraway's notion of "situated knowledge" (1991) allows us to explore the concept of multiplicity, in the modern sense, as separate from personal identities. As Nencel notes, it is our current challenge to consider the multiplicity of meanings surrounding concepts of male and female, as unequivocally conflated with: "the relations of power which are produced and enacted in their construction" (59). A further challenge is to understand the ways in which diverse cultural references come to have situated local meanings. This is particularly key in Latin America due to its aforementioned diversity. Even within the same country, Mexican telenovelas can come to have different meanings in different areas of Mexico depending on location and cultural experience. The meanings garnered from the viewership of Mexican telenovelas in the United States and the United Kingdom may be vastly different from the ways they are understood in Mexico (or in any particular area of Mexico). One must further account for the diversity of cultural identities of the audience of one country. For example, Latinx viewers in the United States will likely have a different interaction with the material than an Anglo audience will.

This brings us back to the genre of telenovelas. A popular American telenovela, "Jane the Virgin" (2014) allows us to track American and Latinx perceptions of machismo by including the use of hashtags and thus encouraging social media feedback. While most popular television programs use official hashtags to advertise and encourage viewership, "Jane the Virgin" is unique in its use of hashtags that appear as typed across the screen during certain scenes. The use of official hashtags allows viewers to comment on the series as a whole, but commenting on particular moments within the telenovela allows the audience to document changes in opinion. Twitter and the hashtags typed across the screen during episodes of "Jane the Virgin" can be used to measure audience reaction to key plot points. Hashtags such as "#immigrationreform" (Urman 1.10) and "#votevotevote" (2.5) have a political aspect which demonstrates that the show is not merely escapism but also provides a powerful opening into discussions of political issues. After the episode in which medical repatriation is mentioned in 2015, viewers used Twitter to express their stories of medical repatriation, opening a space for further discussion of key issues facing the Latinx community, with some Twitter users even going so far as to publicize their previous ignorance and how "Jane the Virgin" has helped them to learn more about the concept. The socio-political possibilities of this new type of television are endless, and programs are also able to clearly demonstrate changing opinions as tweets and hashtags can be analyzed from the start of the show to the very end to see how opinions of characters have changed. Rogelio's use of social media and hashtags within the telenovela is both a form of comic relief and a genuine way to facilitate change. Hashtags such as "#GoRo" (1.9) "#RogelioMyBrogelio" (2.7) and "#VivaDeLaVega" (1.9) can be used to analyze changing and developing responses to masculinity.

The process of socializing television blurs the lines between fictional representation and informed political responses and further reinforces television's ability to form a process of social and academic engagement. Therefore, as television viewership can encourage audiences to change, television and social media are inherently politicized, as they highlight the need for change on the screen. A quick search of the hashtag "#RogelioMyBrogelio" on Twitter shows an overwhelming outpouring of support and recognition for the character. It links to ridiculous quotes he has said throughout the show; jokes about the role of the father in literature and politically charged opinions.

Twitter hashtags like these prove the power of telenovelas. They allow for the show to connect its fictional reality with real-world issues by increasing awareness and facilitating discussion. The problematic issues of machismo that are raised during "Jane the Virgin" are subsequently answered during the socialization of the telenovela. Questions about how machismo can function both within a family unit and as part of a larger section of society are being explored on social media, ultimately pointing to a meta-thinking evolution.

Mexican gender binaries are clearly beginning to shift, as can be evidenced through telenovela representations of machismo, homosexual masculinities and masculinity in advertisements during prime-time television. Now more than ever, there seems to be a greater representation of the various forms of masculinity in Mexico. This greater representation reflects a growing acceptance of masculinities in Mexican society. Evidence suggests that telenovelas not only reflect current changing attitudes towards masculinities, but they also promote social discussion as demonstrated through media representation. Although little research has been developed on this particular area, an additional space for academic inquiry could trace attitudes toward machismo and homosexual masculinities after being presented with some of the ideas which "La Vida en el Espejo" presents and then tracking those same ideas through subsequent telenovelas.

Evidencing the change in public opinion about Mexican masculinities after viewership of series such as these would open up masculinity studies to a wide range of topics, including international relations and sociology. A post-patriarchy reality is possible within Mexico, and Mexico is showing signs of adopting a healthier notion of masculinity, even though those outside of Mexico often complicate this through their representation of Mexican masculinities.

Notes

[1] See Nietzche's *Zur Gennealogie der Moral* for further reading on this subject.

[2] The gay best friend or gay sidekick is a further of the concept of The Sissy, as defined by Vito Russo in *The Celluloid Closet* where homosexual masculinities are reduced to comic relief who: "make[s] everyone feel more manly or womanly by occupying the space between." (6)

[3] These are terms for men who deviate from the prescribed norms of masculine behavior and therefore are synonymous with unmanly, feminized behavior.

[4] For further examples of this in European culture, note the BBC's commitment to casting sexual, ethnic and gender minorities in their current projects. For example, the recent adaptation of Dracula finds the casting of ethnic minorities into roles of doctors and other well respected careers in spite of the historical assumptions that due to the period of the original text, this would be historically inaccurate.

[5] Marianismo is considered to be the binary opposite of machismo. It is an aspect of feminine gender roles that promotes the virginity, purity, chastity and moral strength.

[6] For more on the lack of this specific research, see Fullerton and Kendrick, Furnham and Mak, Gilly, and Milner.

Works Cited

Balderston, Daniel and Donna J. Guy, editors. *Sex and Sexuality in Latin America*. NYU Press, 1997.

Buffington, Rob. *Criminal and Citizen in Modern Mexico*. U of Nebraska Press, 2000.

——. "*Los Jotos*: Contested visions of homosexuality in modern Mexico." *Sex and Sexuality in Latin American*, edited by Daniel Balderston and Donna J. Guy, NYU Press, 1997, pp. 118-132.

Canclini, Néstor García. *Hybrid Cultures: Strategies for Entering and Leaving Modernity*. U of Minnesota Press, 1995.

Carrillo, Héctor. "Neither *Machos* nor *Maricones*: Masculinity and Emerging Male Homosexual Identities in Mexico." Changing Men and Masculinities in Latin America, edited by Matthew C. Gutmann, Duke U Press, 2003.

Connell, R.W. "Understanding Men: Gender Sociology and the New International Research on Masculinities." *Social Thought & Research*, vol. 24, no. 1/2, 2001, pp. 13-31.

Connell, R.W. and James W. Messerschmidt. "Hegemonic Masculinity: Rethinking the Concept." *Gender and Society*, vol 19, no. 6, 2005, pp. 829-859.

Dowsett, Gary W. "I'll Show You Mine, if You'll Show Me Yours: Gay Men, Masculinity Research, Men's Studies, and Sex." *Theory and Society*, vol. 22, no. 5, 1993, pp. 697-709.

Durik, Amanda M., Janet Shibley Hyde, Amanda C. Marks, Amanda L. Roy, Debra Anaya and Gretchen Schultz. "Ethnicity and Gender Stereotypes of Emotion." *Sex Roles*, vol. 54, 2006, pp. 429-445.

Frevert, Vada S. and Alexis O. Miranda. "A Conceptual Formulation of Latin Culture and the Treatment of Latinos from an Adlerian Psychology Perspective." *Individual Psychology*, vol. 54, no. 3, 1998, pp. 291-309.

Fullerton, Jami and Kendrick, Alice. "Portrayal of Men and Women in U.S. Spanish-Language Television Commercials." *Journalism and Mass Communication Quarterly*, vol. 77, no. 1, 2000, pp. 128-142.

Furnham, Adrian, Twiggy Mak and Liza Tanidjojo. "An Asian Perspective on the Portrayal of Men and Women in Television Advertisements: Studies from Hong Kong and Indonesian Television." *Journal of Applied Social Psychology*. vol. 30, no. 11, 2000, pp. 2341-2364.

Gaitán, Fernando, creator. *Ugly Betty*. Canal de las Estrellas, 2006.

Gilly, Mary. "Sex Roles in Advertising: A Comparison of Television Advertisements in Australia, Mexico and the United States." *Journal of Marketing*, vol. 52, no. 2, 1988, pp. 75-85.

Guitérrez, Maria Antonieta, creator. *Velo de Novia*. Televisa, 2003.

Haraway, Donna. *Simions, Cyborgs and Women: The Reinvention of Nature*. Routledge, 1991.

——. "Situated Knowledges: The Science Question in Feminism and the Privilege of Partial Perspective." *Feminist Studies*, vol. 14, no. 3, 1988, Pp. 575-599.

Huizar, Alejandro. "La ficción televisiva sale del clóset." *Zócalo: Sabotaje a reforma integral*, May 2010, pp. 38-40.

Kjeldgaard, Dannie and Kaj Storgaard Nielsen. "Glocal Gender Identities in Market Places of Transition: MARIANISMO and the Consumption of the Telenovela Rebelde." *Marketing Theory*, vol. 10, no. 1, 2010, pp.29-44.

Mejía, Marcela, creator. *La Vida en el Espejo*. Azteca Novelas and Argos Comunicación, 1999.

Murray, Steven. *Latin American Male Homosexualities*. U of New Mexico Press, 1995.

Nencel, Lorraine. "Pacharacas, Putas and Chicas de Su Casa: Labelling, Femininity, and Men's Sexual Selves in Lima, Peru." *Machos, Mistresses and Madonnas: Contesting the Power of Latin American Gender Identity*, edited by Marit Melhuus and Kristi Anne Stolen, Verso, 1996, pp. 3-80.

Paz, Octavio. *El laberinto de soledad*, edited by Enrico Mario Santí, Cátedra, 2011.

Prieur, Annick. "Domination and Desire: Male homosexuality and the construction of masculinity in Mexico." *Machos, mistresses and Madonnas: Contesting the power of Latin American gender imagery*, edited by Marit Melhuus and Kristi Anne Stolen, Verso, 1996, pp. 4-104.

Rovine, Victoria L. *African Fashion, Global Style: Histories, innovations, and ideas you can wear*. Indiana University Press, 2015.

Russo, Vito. *The Celluloid Closet: Homosexuality in the Movies*. Harper & Row, 1987.

Urman, Jennie Snyder, creator. *Jane the Virgin*. The CW, 2014.

Chapter 7

On the Border, In the Bar: Approaching Feminist Masculinities through Border Thinking in *Everything Begins and Ends at the Kentucky Club* by Benjamin Alire Sáenz

Joshua D. Martin

University of North Georgia

Introduction

U.S.-Mexico borderland masculinities and their literary representations have long attracted scholars' attention, and interest in the subject continues to grow. Past scholarship has tended to analyze the representation of hegemonic masculinities and *machismo*, highlighting the effects of these cultural staples on both border communities and their male and female characters.[1] As celebrated borderlands scholar Gloria Anzaldúa lamented in her seminal study of borderlands culture and *mestiza* identity, "We need a new masculinity and the new man needs a movement" (106). In recent years, literature of the U.S.-Mexico borderlands has forced scholars to analyze the negotiation of masculinities in response to a number of complex phenomena that challenge patriarchal structures. *Everything Begins and Ends at the Kentucky Club* (2012) by Chicano author Benjamin Alire Sáenz is but one example.

Having written prodigiously across genres, the author has focused several of his texts on Latinx adolescents, masculinized nationalism, and Chicano identity. In *Kentucky Club*, named after the bar of the same name in Ciudad Juárez and recipient of the 2013 PEN/Faulkner Award for Fiction, the author grapples with the changing landscape of borderlands masculinities: homosocial and homosexual desire, racialized antagonisms, generational change among Chicanos, drug trafficking, and the Ciudad Juárez femicides all receive attention throughout the collection. Through an intersectional lens that combines scholarship on masculinities and postcolonial studies, the present chapter argues that the stories studied here ("Sometimes the Rain" and "He Has Gone to be With the Women") challenge patriarchy by privileging what literary and postcolonial scholar Walter Mignolo terms "border thinking." Understood alternately as a type of "epistemic disobedience" (Mignolo, "Introduction" 2) and as a place of "epistemic and political confrontation" (Mignolo and Schiwy 25), border thinking privileges knowledges and subjectivities that challenge patriarchy and its corresponding manifestations of political and cultural hegemony.[2] Emphasizing characters' affective lives, the stories studied here illuminate how the male protagonists cultivate counter-hegemonic (that is, feminist) masculinities that resist the narrow contours of patriarchal power.[3]

Argument

Though its scope aimed for a more emancipatory politics, the Chicano movement has since received criticism for its male-focused and heteronormative preoccupations regarding family and community. Of both the movement and its early literary production, scholar Richard T. Rodríguez argues that "gay, lesbian, and feminist struggles were often seen as antithetical to Chicano liberation ... [since they] presented a challenge to prescriptive kinship formations, the normativity of heterocoupling, conventional gender roles, and heterosexual male privileges and desires" (113-114). In sharp contrast to this underlying preoccupation with brotherhood and posterity, the short stories studied here showcase male protagonists who, as first-person narrators, challenge longstanding notions of acceptable masculinity as overpowering, heterosexual, and standing in binary opposition to an often abjected femininity. In their place, the texts create a space of negotiation and affect, whereby feminist masculinities take center stage and contest the "epistemic and ontological borders," to use Mignolo's phrasing ("Geopolitics" 137), that authorize patriarchy in the first place.

Through an epistemological about-face rooted firmly on the border and in the bar, the Chicano male characters contest and attempt to rectify unequal distributions of power and masculine capital.[4] Both stories wrestle with the appeal of patriarchy along the El Paso-Ciudad Juárez border in the context of larger border culture and the characters' respective family units. Striving for individual and collective healing, the male protagonists combat gender expectations by cultivating masculinities that extend beyond the patriarchal constraints that have long condoned aggression, compulsory heterosexuality, and vast asymmetries in power between men and women.[5] Just as the characters cross the geopolitical border, so too do they transgress the sexual and cultural borders that have long impeded the visibility and validation of their full personhood. Ultimately, the stories here locate the titular Kentucky

Club as a source of healing and hope. Through border thinking and their ensuing actions, characters make their presence known and create an alternative male script that places a long overdue premium on affect and the interrogation of patriarchal dividends. In the end, both stories suggest a necessary and belated shift toward feminist masculinities that, while facing numerous obstacles, might suture enduring wounds that have imperiled both female and male characters alike.

"Sometimes the Rain": Envisioning Futures and Feminist Masculinities

In "Sometimes the Rain," the author considers the appeal of patriarchy and wartime zeal in masculinity construction during the late 1960s and early 1970s among both Anglos and Chicanos in El Paso. Specifically, the story challenges the masculine script that arises from the intersection of nationalism and heteronormative desire, underscoring patriarchy as a longstanding cultural force that pigeonholes characters into repressive gender roles. Readers encounter the two teenage male protagonists early: Ernesto Zaragoza, a Chicano, and Brian Stillman, the son of a successful Anglo rancher.[6] From there, a pronounced racial and cultural chasm renders itself apparent between the two, as Ernesto himself explains early in the story: He hangs out with his fellow "Mexicans who went to school because they had to," while Brian finds camaraderie among gringos like himself who share the same privileges and social capital (129-130). The tensions that advance the story's plot stem from both characters' problematic relationships with cultural prescriptions dictating what men should do and how men should feel. In spite of the different racial backgrounds of both young men, their home environments share structural similarities insofar as patriarchy foregrounds a map for masculine behavior—expectations, readers notice, that yield toxic effects for both characters.

Early on, Ernesto reveals several preoccupations concerning his masculine standing in high school: "I hated myself because I looked like a little boy and wanted to look like a man" (127). Less than a page later readers suspect that much of his anxiety stems from a series of disparate traumas that nonetheless intersect with his own father's indignation, as several unfortunate circumstances that have imperiled the cohesion of the Zaragoza family unit render themselves apparent: Ernesto's older brother is arrested for armed robbery, his sixteen-year-old sister is pregnant and living with her grandmother, and his younger brother dies of meningitis. As the stability of the Zaragoza family receives continued threats, Ernesto, heir apparent to the patriarchal mantle, suffers the ire of his emotionally fraught father. As Ernesto explains, "My father's grief and disappointment turned to rage. The rage was pointed in my direction" (128). Such indignation shouldn't necessarily surprise us, though. Just as the continuity of the Zaragoza namesake remains tied to the perpetuation of patriarchy, so too does its cultural bedrock. Accordingly, threats to patriarchy and any ensuing cultural panic find their logical endpoint in Ernesto, who is expected to face such challenges with unabashed resiliency and to exert time-honored brawn in order to preserve a cultural status quo.

A parallel trajectory of pernicious father-son relationships emerges between the Stillman and Zaragoza families, where the patriarchs deride, threaten, and mock their sons whenever the latter fail to meet either cultural or personal expectations that would otherwise demonstrate a sufficient degree of masculine capital. Of his own father, Ernesto confesses, "He didn't actually want me to be a good boy. He wanted me to be a man" (133).[7] To this point, Ernesto remains ever conscious of the micro-interactions that, to use Judith Butler's timeless insight into gender performativity, "congeal over time to produce the appearance of substance, of a natural sort of being" (43-44): the rituals, handshakes, casual hugs, indeed all the actions (discursive and tactile) that, according to Ernesto, "we learned from watching our fathers" (134).

The story's turning point emerges as Ernesto frets over his untested sexual prowess with women and the compulsion to act "man enough" among his peers. As he walks home from a party, he overhears a couple engaged in sexual activity. The situation soon becomes more complicated, as do Ernesto's emotions. He explains that he hears only the voices of two young men and that one of those voices belongs to Brian Stillman, whom he then overhears lamenting his relationship with his father.

Patriarchal norms operate through arbitrary scripts of inherited behaviors, or a "masquerade of naturalness" to use the term of literary and gender studies scholar Judith Kegan Gardiner (8), that function as a "common sense" way of performing gender roles vis-à-vis male prerogatives, often finding legitimacy and reinforcement both in socio-political systems and in the home.[8] "Sometimes the Rain" explores how patriarchal masculinities pathologize alleged sexual and gender aberrations through a discourse of time-honored tradition and heteronormative masculine compulsions. Rather than present a milieu of simple binaries, though, the story highlights how patriarchy functions, as bell hooks contends in The Will to Change, as "a life-threatening social disease" (17), one that ultimately imperils all characters, since the playing field is always already unequal and deleterious.

The reaches of patriarchy go further than mere symbolic terrain. Of the psychosexual and immediately lived experiences, it presents numerous obstacles. For one, Ernesto can't stop thinking of Brian and his partner, later revealing, "I had them both in my head when I masturbated that night ... Just when I'd started liking myself, I hated myself again" (138). Readers immediately encounter a tension between heteronormative expectations and sexual desires that the larger patriarchal culture deems illicit. Literary scholar Eve Sedgwick, for one, argues that "obligatory heterosexuality is built into male-dominated kinship systems" and that as a result, "patriarchy structurally requires homophobia" (3-4). Ernesto's professed heterosexual libido alongside his private homosexual fantasy, in turn, highlights an important incongruence: once the former faces instability or threats, the latter (a more complex labyrinth of masculine identity and desire) entails shame, dread, and a perceived emasculation.

From here, readers witness Ernesto retreat into a cultural heteronormativity, thereby experiencing a problematic confrontation with his own sexual desires and possible sexual fluidity. This development, in turn, corresponds to the story's perennial meditation on the anxieties that ensue of compulsory heterosexuality at both the personal level and, more broadly, in the characters' deeply patriarchal family units. In particular, readers encounter what Eric Anderson has termed "homohysteria," which arises in part through widespread disdain toward both homosexuality and any deviations from a socially acceptable gender script ("Inclusive Masculinities" 180). As Anderson explains, "[i]n this homohysteric culture boys and young men ... establish and re-establish themselves as heterosexual by aligning their gendered behaviors with idealized notions of masculinity" (183). Rather than simply explore how homosocial desire can act as a harbinger for homosexual desire, the author gives primacy to how the characters confront (and in the case of Ernesto, ultimately disavow) cultural norms in contest with their own sexual and professional prerogatives.

In the end, the story deconstructs this false binary by prioritizing the bar as a place of validation. Ernesto and Brian form a friendship, bonding over their frustrations with the status quo and their exacting fathers. Ernesto hopes to attend college and pursue art. Brian aspires to move to Denver and leave his family's business. Their fathers respond derisively, as their sons' decisions would jeopardize the continuity of their own masculine brands and, by extension, patriarchal home life.

Shortly after Brian reveals that his father is abusive, he and Ernesto go to the Kentucky Club, an experience that cultivates border thinking insofar as they begin to understand patriarchal expectations as obstacles limiting the full expression of their individual subjectivities. "So this is what it's like," Ernesto observes sarcastically, "[t]o feel like a man" (146-147). As Ernesto begins to understand nascent ambiguities (his sexual desire and professional future among them) as positives, Brian ultimately views them as uncomfortable burdens rooted in his own masculine anxiety. The ensuing conversation between the two brings to light these tensions, as Ernesto offers Brian five hundred dollars for a bus ticket to Denver. Brian insists that he can simply enlist in the Army, to which Ernesto responds critically. As both characters interrogate the impact of paternalistic constraints on their respective masculinities, they must choose between a potentially emancipatory future, albeit one fraught with uncertainty, and a trajectory that honors the status quo and its narrow scope of acceptable manhood.

Ernesto eventually forces Brian to accept the aforementioned money, later admitting to himself, "Becoming a man didn't feel anything like I thought it was going to feel" (153). Readers find both characters embarking on distinct paths, espousing markedly different masculinities than those of their fathers. A year later, however, Ernesto receives a letter from Vietnam, enclosed with five hundred dollars, in which Brian admits to having joined the Army after all: "Maybe I wanted to feel like a real man. Maybe that's why I joined up, to prove something to myself" (154). Ernesto writes back, but his ensuing revelation shocks readers. He is unsure if Brian ever received the message, as the latter was killed trying to save a fellow soldier. The melancholic overtones of the story's concluding pages compel readers to assess the far-reaching effects of patriarchy in the lives of the two characters. Ernesto cannot bring himself to attend the funeral, conscious of the irony that only in death has Brian achieved (an allegedly) proper manhood (155). Questions of place and belonging permeate both stories studied here. In his letter, for example, Brian asks if Ernesto will be there when he too returns home (154). As Ernesto prepares to study art at Columbia University, his own father's health declines, compelling him to return to El Paso where he confesses, "It didn't feel like home anymore. It never had" (155). In questions of place, readers understand Ernesto's emotional distance from El Paso as an important marker, as it reflects the degree to which the Kentucky Club (a place of healing and validation) fostered emancipatory potential from patriarchal strictures.

Accordingly, Ernesto's consciousness and ensuing resistance arise from the interstices of sexual, gender, and cultural borders that have long relegated the LGBTQ community to the periphery of the national community, and LGBTQ Chicanos in particular to the periphery of *la raza*. The bar, meanwhile, fosters temporary relief by offering a space for the cultivation of feminist masculinities that counter patriarchy, questioning the legitimacy of the latter and resisting its narrow cultural contours. The Chicano character's "epistemic disobedience," thus, fosters a new masculine brand, opposing the compulsions that have long imperiled his counterparts. While the Kentucky Club renders new masculine scripts tangible, troubling longstanding expectations of desire, duty, and masculine identity, readers understand that such developments would be considered anathema elsewhere. As with the other stories in *Kentucky Club*, "Sometimes the Rain" resists facile conclusions, offering ambiguous but ultimately hopeful imagery in its conclusion. Now much older, Ernesto, the artist, returns to the Southwest. When it rains, he remembers Brian after years of not having done so. Ernesto shouts his name, leaving readers with restrained optimism as he reflects on the sound: "It was almost like a song" (157).

"Sometimes the Rain" casts its father figures as inheritors of a damning system. That is, their insufferable behaviors stem from and ultimately corroborate patriarchy, as much an ideology as it is a cultural continuum. Accordingly, the author's representation of patriarchy as antagonistic underscores the system as a social pollutant, detrimental to both female and male characters who suffer its toxic effects. Just as patriarchy buttresses institutionalized forms of oppression against women, it also erodes men's emotional welfare and denies them any expression of vulnerability.

"He Has Gone to be With the Women": Resisting Patriarchy and Prioritizing Affect

The previous story, as we have seen, highlights the damning effects of patriarchy in families and characters' attempts to combat masculine and cultural norms in the late 1960s and early 1970s. "He Has Gone to be With the Women," meanwhile, charts the burgeoning romance between two gay male characters against the backdrop of the recent Ciudad Juárez femicides—the disappearances and gruesome murders of women and girls that are "rooted in a system of patriarchy," as Latin American studies scholar Rosa-Linda Fregoso contends, and that underscore "the degree to which violence against women has been naturalized as a method of social control" (2).[9] Here, the male characters confront a more virulent version of patriarchy due to the drug cartels' social and political hegemony in Ciudad Juárez. Imbedded in secrecy and male-enacted violence, this power calculus creates structural obstacles for both characters as they seek legitimacy and belonging through feminist masculinities that prioritize affect over aggression.

In El Paso, readers first encounter the accomplished writer protagonist, Juan Carlos de la Tierra, as he enters a coffee shop and admires a man who will become his lover, having already long served as his muse: Javier, a runner, an enthusiast of classic literature, and a chauffeur for the U.S. Consulate in Ciudad Juárez. Most importantly, he loves serious literature and tragedy, and as Juan Carlos himself explains, "[O]n the border you could be in love with tragedy without being tragic" (11). The playful conversation that ensues about their respective heritages forestalls readers' attempts to insert either into neatly defined identity categories, and it parodies too the assumed necessity of violence as a marker of masculinity.

Javier asserts that Juan Carlos "isn't really Mexican," while the latter retorts that while he is neither Mexican nor American, he is certainly something else: "Fucked. That's the disease I suffer from" (13). Javier claims that his father, an Israeli native who grew up in Mexico, loved to fight, and was killed in a bar—a fitting marker, in his view, of one's Mexican identity, and one that contrasts with the personality of Juan Carlos, who admits that he himself refrains from conflict. "Certainly," Javier then responds comically, "you're not a Mexican" (16). The story progresses largely through succinct reflections and dialogues both humorous and somber, all while forcing readers to glean characters' turmoil through both their own revelations and the inferences made by the first-person narrator. More importantly, though, by highlighting the discourses and affective lives of its gay male protagonists, the story privileges how both characters grapple with an insidious variant of patriarchy and the threats it creates both for Ciudad Juárez and themselves.

Scholars Francisco A. Lomelí, Teresa Márquez, and María Herrera-Sobek contend that Chicano writers in the postmodern era tend to focus less on overt political struggles as their literary forbearers, emphasizing instead a "microcosm of life" told from the perspective of their characters:

> Chicanos no longer perceive of themselves as purely victims of a one-way socialization process but rather as human beings who are socially constructed via a confluence of interfacing societal processes. In the process, Chicanos have come to properly value theircultural heritage while continuing to insist on their rights as citizens in American society. (286)

Sáenz understands this dynamic well, never losing sight of the inherently political nature of Chicano existence while also crafting his texts to showcase the precarity and vulnerabilities that underpin his characters' trajectories, both as social actors and as haunted private citizens.[10] Questions of masculinity serve as a focal point in this process, informing characters' private and public selves, just as they loom over their access to power and place.

As Javier and Juan Carlos meet more frequently, the initial dark humor gives way to more solemn ruminations about both men's lives and the perils that they face as non-Anglo gay men living on opposite sides of the border. Javier reveals that he attended school in El Paso and lived with his aunt and uncle while his mother worked in Mexico as a social worker, dedicating much of her time to the trans community. "And then one day," Javier reveals, "she didn't come home. She just disappeared ... The police did nothing. No one did anything" (28). Patriarchy manifests itself here through the veiled machinations of the cartels' institutionalized violence. Like patriarchy, the cartels remain largely invisible, in spite of their impressive grip on the social and political fabric of Ciudad Juárez.[11] In fact, readers initially learn of their existence only by virtue of their reputation for gruesome violence. What's more, characters' reticence to mention the cartels creates a vacuum that further occludes the group's tactics, let alone an interrogation into the androcentric nature of their power. And as in the case of patriarchy, both silence and concealment invest such operations with a nearly impermeable authority to the detriment of women and also men (where the latter typify subordinate masculinities).[12]

The gendered power dimensions of the Juárez femicides, committed at the discretion and by the hands of men, are obvious and immediately palpable. At the interpersonal level, such widespread violence creates ripple effects that alter characters' psychological welfare. Of his aging uncle, Javier comments that he refuses to leave his residence: "*Nos matan*, he says" (20).[13] The story reaches its height of introspection near its two-thirds mark, revealing wounds that force a reckoning of consciousness in both characters: Juan Carlos laments the incessant violence besieging Juárez, Javier understands his dubious chances of remaining in the U.S. long-term, and a broader contextualization of their cross-border situation takes shape, all of which is compounded by Javier's affinity for Juárez: "Your country doesn't want me to stay," he reasons, later adding, "I can't leave Juárez ... What would happen if everybody left?" (34-35). "Then the city would die," Juan Carlos responds, after which he asks his partner a daunting question, "But what if you die?" (35). The threat of violence looms large. As scholar Daniel Enrique Pérez contends, "In any patriarchal society and every one of its concomitant institutions women *and* queers are often the target of ridicule, humiliation, acts of violence, and all the other acts that stem from misogyny and homophobia. But unlike women, gay men must also contend with being placed into the "failed men" or "not real men" ... categories" (145-146). In the Kentucky Club, both characters bemoan the cartels' effects on Ciudad Juárez, understanding the imminent threats they pose to their own safety.

Indeed, for both its geographic location along the border and its status as a place of healing and validation, the bar operates as a figurative and literal midpoint for the numerous crossings of characters in both stories: geographically, from El Paso to Ciudad Juárez, but also in the context of their deepest vulnerabilities—from periphery to center, shame to pride, confusion to clarity. In this regard, Sáenz falls into the literary tradition of other Chicano writers who, according to anthropologist Carlos G. Vélez-Ibáñez, aim to construct "substantive and endearing space and place and cultural solutions in the most unequal of circumstances" (214). Accordingly, the bar allows both characters to create a sense of normalcy against the backdrop of a border milieu where patriarchy finds its modus operandi through acts of gendered violence. The narrator further laments the cartels' effects on Juárez culture, in particular the emptiness of its public spaces and the despondence of its residents, and compelling Juan Carlos to reflect on what the city once was: vibrant, spirited, full of life. He admits to himself that "those days were gone now" and continues on toward the Kentucky Club (36).

Reunited, Juan Carlos and Javier engage in day-to-day activities that would suggest the absence of deeply rooted consternation: they have drinks, they talk, they relive the past. Safe here, they find comfort in each other. Later, they leave, they hold each other, and they make love. They eat breakfast the next morning, and they make plans that never formalize. Now in El Paso, Juan Carlos learns of Javier's own disappearance (38-39).

Only near the conclusion do readers understand the title's irony. That is, while we may initially assume that it refers to hyper-masculine norms—a proclivity for sexual escapades, for example, or unabashed promiscuity—we learn that the title instead insinuates Javier's fate, one embroiled within male-enacted violence against women on the one hand, and on the other, men who embody subordinate masculinities or who pose threats to existing power structures.[14] As Javier's neighbors explain, "He has gone to be with the women. With all the nameless women who have been buried in the desert," although Juan Carlos privately surmises that "*[h]e has gone to be with his mother*" (43). They leave Juan Carlos with Javier's watch, the one given to him by his father. Juan Carlos then returns to the Kentucky Club, and his ensuing meditation on his deceased lover's watch reinforces the perceived timelessness of competing forces: male-enacted violence (its role as both a marker of masculine capital and a tool for societal control) and also reciprocal love (something that traverses generations and bypasses borders, offering hope when all else appears menacing).

Whereas the previous story prioritizes characters' struggles with domestic patriarchy, this narrative charts characters' affective lives in the absence of any discernible stigma in their interpersonal surroundings—a rare moment of hope against the backdrop of pervasive violence. While the conclusion here is more somber and patriarchy more sinister, readers find Juan Carlos at a threshold: on the border, in the bar, and wanting to heal: "I don't know how long I sat there at the bar, drinking, trying not to think. Trying not to hate. Trying not to feel anything. And then I just wanted to go home. But where was home?" (44). As the main characters of both stories engage in border thinking, the narratives prioritize their affective lives, representing them through a prism of normalcy and cautious optimism despite the tacit recognition of possible hazards. And while neither story ends with a celebratory affirmation tying characters' affective lives to a definitive shift in their communities' collective consciousness, the protagonists represent, and anticipate, a future turn toward new masculine paradigms. Indeed, both main characters arrive at a state of sorrow at once contemplative and hopeful, creating a tension that, however painful, nonetheless indicates fissures in the status quo, and reflecting what masculinity scholar Raewyn Connell identifies as "a tendency towards crisis in the legitimation of patriarchy" (73). Thus, the story brings us full circle. To again quote Juan Carlos: "on the border you could be in love with tragedy without being tragic" (11). Just as masculinities arise through historically contingent and culturally sensitive performances (bodily, discursive, or otherwise), so too do the acts of resistance that make any meaningful change at all possible. As with his characters, the author leaves his readers here at this threshold.

Conclusion

Patriarchy and its myriad cultural prescriptions have long operated as metrics for gender performance and as cornerstones in social organization. Throughout *Everything Begins and Ends at the Kentucky Club*, readers situate patriarchy as an enduring force that informs characters' lives, from the societal expectations to which they are held to the anxieties that ensue from its static cultural enclosures. As the stories make evident, the appeal to patriarchy and its attendant cultural expressions hold considerable appeal across time. Though patriarchy gives shape to dominant masculinities, the male protagonists create a new praxis, one that undercuts heteronormativity and interrogates the discourses and cultural assumptions that have given patriarchy such longevity.

While we might expect the main characters to resist uncomfortable ambiguities (sexual or otherwise), they instead find validation in those tensions and interstitial spaces through counterhegemonic (feminist) masculinities—ones that disavow patriarchal strongholds (stoicism, violence, hypermasculinity, heterosexuality) and the discourses that normalize masculine conventions. The closure we encounter is partial at best given patriarchy's enduring appeal, but the author's narrative vision does not foreclose the possibility of meaningful change. His characters are wounded, yes, but ultimately resilient and steadfast in their determination to imagine and work toward futures that reject the status quo. In fact, taken together, the stories suggest that any meaningful confrontation with patriarchy—from its toxic compulsions to its authorization of violence—must first begin with an epistemological reckoning that confronts patriarchy's entrenchment within local culture, as well as its narrow confines governing both sexuality and gender expression. The task is an arduous one, as the characters' experiences attest, but the possibilities for change remain within reach, provided that the characters—and by extension we the readers—resist the arbitrary borders and cultural assumptions that fetter what is normal to what is patriarchal.

Notes

[1] In his article "The United States, Mexico and Machismo," folklorist Américo Paredes provides a cursory overview of the origins of machismo and their connections to U.S. expansion. In her book *Borderlands / La frontera: The New Mestiza*, Gloria Anzaldúa examines identity and gender in the borderlands. For a broader overview of machismo, consult Matthew C. Gutmann's *The Meanings of Macho: Being a Man in Mexico City*.

[2] In his co-authored study with Latin American cultural studies scholar Catherine E. Walsh, Mignolo contends that a "patriarchal/masculine conception of the world and society" has catalyzed "[p]olitical and economic imperial designs" (126). At a more immediate level, Mignolo argues that patriarchy "is where racism and sexism originate and are maintained" while structuring the terms of the modern/colonial order (127, 143).

[3] In her book *Feminism is for Everybody: Passionate Politics*, feminist scholar bell hooks argues that whereas patriarchal masculinity glorifies "male domination of the planet, of less powerful men, of women and children," a feminist masculinity prioritizes "self-esteem and self-love of one's unique being" as a basis of identity (70).

[4] In his book *Inclusive Masculinity: The Changing Nature of Masculinity*, sociologist Eric Anderson, borrowing from Pierre Bourdieu's concept of social capital, identifies masculine capital as "attitudes and behaviors" that, once achieved, allow men to emulate manliness (42). For those who believe that homosexuality connotes weakness or effeminacy, Anderson contends, "Maintaining a high degree of masculine capital helps men refute suspicions of homosexuality" (42).

[5] I borrow the term "compulsory heterosexuality" from feminist poet Adrienne Rich. In her essay "Compulsory Heterosexuality and Lesbian Existence," Rich contends that heterosexuality, as an institutionalized social force, has worked to subjugate women and buttress male power through numerous imperatives (domestic, economic, cultural, or otherwise).

[6] Though much of the story takes place in El Paso, the author's use of the last name "Stillman" is likely a recognition of the Stillman family, whose patriarch Charles Stillman, according to historian Marilyn McAdams Sibley, was "past master in the intricacies of trade and politics" in the Lower Rio Grande Valley given his vast accumulation of land and resources (228-229).

[7] According to sociologist James W. Messerschmidt, several characteristics (among them shyness, passivity, physical weakness, a lack of adventurousness, and homosexual desire) "are seen as polluting 'normal' and 'natural' hegemonic gender and sexual relations" (126).

[8] See hooks (*The Will to Change* 17-24), Vélez-Ibáñez (139), and Gilligan and Snider (135-136).

[9] Scholars have also used the term "feminicide" to describe the systemic murder of girls and women. See Fregoso's *MeXicana Encounters*, Driver's *More or Less Dead*, and Fregoso and Bejarano's edited volume *Terrorizing Women: Feminicide in the Americas*.

[10] In his essay "In the Borderlands of Chicano Identity, There Are Only Fragments," the author asserts that "Chicano identity is ultimately about politics" (79) while insisting that all identities emerge through different and often conflicting discourses (70-71).

[11] Though overall violence in recent years has subsided, hundreds of women in Ciudad Juárez were disappeared and murdered throughout the 1990s and into the first decade of the 2000s, starkly contrasting the 37 documented female homicides in Ciudad Juárez between 1985 and 2002 (Fregoso 2). Political science scholar Kathleen Staudt identifies "institutional flaws in political and criminal justice institutions" as well as "changing gender power relations" within an increasingly globalized neoliberal border economy as key factors that have contributed to femicides in Ciudad Juárez (4).

[12] Sociologist Harry Brod argues that silence surrounding patriarchy bolsters its power: "Any form of oppression maintains itself in power in part by masking how it operates, making its structure as invisible as possible. To shed light on masculinity is therefore at least to potentially threaten patriarchy" (162).

[13] All italicizations that appear in quoted materials are original to their respective authors.

[14] With regards to subordinate masculinities, Messerschmidt writes that "such subordination can be conceptualized in terms of, for example, race, class, age, sexualities, or nationality" (126). He adds that "gayness continues to be socially defined in many contexts as the embodiment of whatever is expelled from hegemonic masculinity, and lesbianism is the embodiment of whatever is expelled from emphasized femininity" (126).

Works Cited

Anderson, Eric. "Inclusive Masculinities." *Exploring Masculinities: Identity, Inequality, Continuity, and Change*, edited by C.J. Pascoe and Tristan Bridges, Oxford UP, 2016, pp. 178-187.

——. *Inclusive Masculinity: The Changing Nature of Masculinities*. Routledge, 2009.

Anzaldúa, Gloria. *Borderlands / La frontera: The New Mestiza*. Aunt Lute, 2007.

Brod, Harry. "Studying Masculinities as Superordinate Studies." *Masculinity Studies & Feminist Theory: New Directions*, edited by Judith Kegan Gardiner, Columbia UP, 2002, pp. 161-175.

Butler, Judith. *Gender Trouble: Feminism and the Subversion of Identity*. Routledge, 1999.

Connell, Raewyn. *Gender*. Polity, 2002.

Fregoso, Rosa-Linda. *MeXicana Encounters: The Making of Social Identities on the Borderlands*. U of California Press, 2003.

Gardiner, Judith Kegan. "Introduction." *Masculinity Studies and Feminist Theory: New Directions*, edited by Judith Kegan Gardiner, Columbia UP, 2002, pp. 1-29.

Gilligan, Carol and Naomi Snider. *Why Does Patriarchy Persist?* Polity, 2018.

Gutmann, Matthew C. *The Meanings of Macho: Being a Man in Mexico City*. U of California Press, 1996.

hooks, bell. *Feminism is for Everybody: Passionate Politics*. South End Press, 2000.

——. *The Will to Change: Men, Masculinity, and Love*. Atria Books, 2004.

Lomelí, Francisco A., Teresa Márquez, and María Herrera-Sobek. "Trends and Themes in Chicana/o Writings in Postmodern Times." *Chicano Renaissance:*

Contemporary Cultural Trends, edited by David R. Maciel, Isidro D. Ortiz, and María Herrera-Sobek, U of Arizona Press, 2000, pp. 285-312.

Messerschmidt, James W. *Hegemonic Masculinity: Formulation, Reformulation, and Amplification*. Rowman & Littlefield, 2018.

Mignolo, Walter D. "Geopolitics of sensing and knowing: On (de)coloniality, border thinking, and epistemic disobedience." *Confero*, vol. 1, no. 1, 2013, pp. 129-150.

——. "Introduction: Coloniality of Power and De-Colonial Thinking." *Globalization and the Decolonial Option*, edited by Walter D. Mignolo and Arturo Escobar, Routledge, 2010, pp. 1-21.

Mignolo, Walter D. and Catherine E. Walsh. *On Decoloniality: Concepts, Analytics, Praxis*. Duke UP, 2018.

Mignolo, Walter D. and Freya Schiwy. "Transculturation and the Colonial Difference. Double Translation." *Translation and Ethnography: The Anthropological Challenge of Intercultural Understanding*, edited by Tullio Maranhão and Bernhard Streck, U of Arizona Press, 2003, pp. 12-34.

Paredes, Américo. "The United States, Mexico and Machismo." *Journal of the Folklore Institute*, vol. 8, no. 1, 1971, pp. 17-37.

Pérez, Daniel Enrique. "Entre Machos y Maricones: (Re)Covering Chicano Gay Male (Hi)Stories." *Gay Latino Studies: A Critical Reader*, edited by Michael Hames-García and Ernesto Javier Martínez, Duke UP, 2011, pp. 141-146.

Rich, Adrienne. "Compulsory Heterosexuality and Lesbian Existence." *Signs: Journal of Women in Culture and Society*, vol. 15, no. 4, 1980, pp. 631-660.

Rodríguez, Richard T. "Carnal Knowledge: Chicano Gay Men and the Dialectics of Being." *Gay Latino Studies: A Critical Reader*, edited by Michael Hames-García and Ernesto Javier Martínez, Duke UP, 2011, pp. 113-140.

Sáenz, Benjamin Alire. "He Has Gone to Be with the Women." *Everything Begins and Ends at the Kentucky Club*. Cinco Puntos Press, 2012, pp. 11-44.

——. "In the Borderlands of Chicano Identity, There are Only Fragments." *Border Theory: The Limits of Cultural Politics*, edited by Scott Michaelsen and David E. Johnson, U of Minnesota Press, 1997, pp. 68-96.

——. "Sometimes the Rain." *Everything Begins and Ends at the Kentucky Club*. Cinco Puntos Press, 2012, pp. 126-157.

Sedgwick, Eve Kosofsky. *Between Men: English Literature and Male Homosocial Desire*. Columbia UP, 1985.

Sibley, Marilyn McAdams. "Charles Stillman: A Case Study of Entrepreneurship on the Rio Grande, 1861-1865." *The Southwestern Historical Quarterly*, vol. 77, no. 2, 1973/74, pp. 227-240.

Staudt, Kathleen. *Violence and Activism at the Border: Gender, Fear, and Everyday life in Ciudad Juárez*. U of Texas Press, 2008.

Vélez-Ibáñez, Carlos G. *Border Visions: Mexican Cultures of the Southwest United States*. U of Arizona Press, 1997.

Chapter 8

Conclusions

Bryan Pearce-Gonzales

Shenandoah University

Kathryn Quinn-Sánchez

Georgian Court University

If masculinity, in its broadest conceptualization, is an answer to the question "What does it mean to be a man?," one might be able to consider a concise, even definitive, reply. However, if one were to take into account, as do the authors included in this collection, the intersections of race, gender, ethnicity, socioeconomic class and sexuality when pondering this question, the aim for a definitive response diminishes significantly as a myriad of different (as well as differing) conceptualizations of masculinity becomes evident.

Indeed, we see within this volume the all-encompassing role of patriarchy that is reflected in many men's lack of willingness to follow the prescriptive norms that hegemonic masculinity force upon them from childhood throughout their entire adult lives. In *The Will to Change: Men, Masculinity and Love,* bell hooks writes: "Patriarchal mores teach a form of emotional stoicism to men that says they are more manly if they do not feel, but if by chance they should feel and the feelings hurt, the manly response is to stuff them down, to forget about them, to hope they will go away" (5-6). Expressing masculinity through emotions is not one of these prescriptive norms, unless that emotion is rage, and there is a reason that rage is allowed, and even fomented. As we see in the analyses within this collection, "[b]oys are encouraged by patriarchal thinking to claim rage as the easiest path to manliness" (hooks 44). In other words:

> Patriarchy both creates the rage in boys and then contains it for later use, making it a resource to exploit later on as they become men. As a national product, this rage can be garnered to further imperialism, hatred, and the oppression of women and men globally. This rage is

needed if boys are to become men willing to travel around the world to fight wars without ever demanding that other ways of solving conflict be found. (hooks 51)

Unbeknownst to most men, they are being manipulated by patriarchy to further the expansion of imperialism—as well as white supremacy—within the constraints of a capitalist system that egregiously separates the haves from the have-nots. While men are at the apex of this paradigm, they are not without anguish. To survive in many instances they must give up their emotional wellbeing and it is likely they will partake in the promotion of the next generation's continued violence upon themselves and upon others. War, as it results from rage, does not allow humanity to move toward social justice using humane methods. Men that consider themselves to be patriarchal cannot deviate from rage as an emotional outlet, as this would imply a *feminist* masculinity. The path forward, then, must be an exploration of masculinity beyond patriarchy, which would make it possible to solve conflicts in ways that are free of violence, rage and oppression.

We have entered a time when men have begun to openly challenge this one-size-fits-all notion of masculinity embedded within patriarchy. Indeed, there has been opposition to this machista ideal for more than a century as evidenced by Víctor M. Macías-González's and Anne Rubenstein's edited collection *Masculinity and Sexuality in Modern Mexico* (2012) which portrays masculinity from the 1880s to present-day in Mexican literature, film, and song lyrics.

The fallacy that a unilateral masculinity exists or has ever existed has contributed to the somewhat imprecise understanding of the uniquely Mexican and Chicano concept of machismo. While some leading scholars in the field of Masculinity Studies have highlighted the more negative connotations of the term, others prefer to focus on its more positive attributes. The inherent tension that this label embodies is a theme repeatedly noted throughout this collection of essays, and the authors who have contributed to this project confront this tension directly in order to continue the unmasking of masculinity in hopes of offering a more complete understanding of what it means to be a Mexican or Chicano man.

Societal Constructions of Masculinity in Chicanx and Mexican Literature: From Machismo to Feminist Masculinity has outlined the array of masculinities present in Chicanx and Mexican literature from their patriarchal beginnings, which heavily restricted the idea of what men ought to be, to a post-patriarchal reality that allows for more inclusive and liberating conceptualizations of machismo. While a majority of the analyses have focused on fictional writings, this collection has embraced analyses of other texts like telenovelas and autobiographies. Interestingly, though not surprising, several overlapping themes have emerged within this compilation of essays. For further study in the field of film and television, the editors suggest the recent work by Nohemy Solórzano-Thompson.

Hegemonic masculinity, and its implications of dominance over and subordination of women, figures prominently in the chapters written by Fernando Hernández Jáuregui, Joshua D. Martin, and Jess Brocklesby. These authors have outlined the ways in which several Chicanx and Mexican literary texts serve to destabilize the legitimacy of a hegemonic masculinity. Hernández Jáuregui offers a profound consideration of the poetic voice present within the works of Ricardo Castillo. In his analysis, he theorizes a new term – "poetic masculinity" – as a loci of enunciation that Castillo creates in order to voice a counterhegemonic masculinity that affords him the claim to (an)other authentic masculinity. In this way, Castillo succeeds in subverting the authoritative masculine discourse of the alpha-male (or cabrón) and identifies new discursive possibilities within the idea of "poetic masculinity" for those men who identify as non-macho. The newly conceived masculine discursive possibilities offered by "poetic masculinity" are echoed in Joshua D. Martin's analysis of Benjamin Alire Sáenz's *Everything Begins and Ends at the Kentucky Club*, in which the Kentucky Club becomes the loci of enunciation of new, counterhegemonic masculine expressions. Martin posits that the interrogation of patriarchy necessarily invokes Mignolo's concept of "border thinking," which allows for the Kentucky Club to become a third space wherein feminist masculinities can be imagined – the first step toward dismantling patriarchy. Jess Brocklesby offers an analysis of various Mexican telenovelas in order to chart the ways in which Mexican gender binaries are beginning to shift, thereby legitimizing other masculinity identities that do not adhere to the hegemonic model. Brocklesby concludes that the various masculine identities present in current telenovelas represent a shift toward post-patriarchy, where homosexual desire and effeminacy are not compulsory identifiers of femininity and heterosexual desire and stoicism are not automatically accepted signs of a hegemonic masculinity.

Alejandro Puga and Patricia Tovar, along with Leigh Johnson, further focus their analyses on a Post-War conceptualization of masculinity, changing gender roles and the effects on heterosexual domestic relationships. Puga and Tovar theorize their own version of a post-revolutionary masculinity that evolves during the period of Mexico's transition from a revolutionary state to a neoliberal one. During these moments of sociocultural change, the "awkward macho" emerges as one who recognizes the limiting effects of an institutionalized notion of a national patriarchy, and yet is not fully equipped to dismantle it completely. Johnson revisits several canonical Chicanx literary texts that have gained a critical reputation for adhering to a hegemonic masculinity model that encourages patriarchal norms. She, however, examines how particular scenes of domestic violence in the works actually lay the groundwork for an empowering of Chicana subjects who are able to prevail in the face of patriarchy's oppression of them. As such, Johnson shows how these particular texts demonstrate a nascent form of Chicana feminism, that is to say, these works take the first step on the path towards a feminist masculinity.

Kathryn Quinn-Sánchez and Bryan Pearce-Gonzales offer unique perspectives on fatherhood, the family, and the idea of a feminist masculinity. Pearce-Gonzales grapples with the concept of the patriarchal dividend, in which all men are inherent beneficiaries of the overall subordination of women, and how newly conceived Chicano masculinities seek to break free from its social and psychological constraints. His conclusions offer an optimistic take on the future of Chicano masculinities that allow for, and even encourage, Chicano men to actively seek ways in which to become feminist allies. Quinn-Sánchez offers a similar analysis of machismo and patriarchy and how they serve to objectify and suppress women. She concludes that Chicanx and Mexican authors, through the very act of writing, are participating in a revolutionary act that seeks to destabilize the accepted position of authority held by patriarchy and fatherhood. In this way, Chicanx and Mexican authors are paving the way for a newly imagined open society based on acceptance and edification instead of limitations and destruction.

The findings of this collection point to the fact that masculinity, as a social construct, has evolved dramatically within Chicanx and Mexican communities and that it will continue to do so. Perhaps controversial at one time, the idea of a feminist masculinity is gaining ground, especially in literary texts being created and consumed during the 21st century. It would be meaningful for scholars to continue to examine other texts within these same theoretical frames in an effort to identify other authors and texts that grapple with newly conceived expressions of masculinity, thereby answering bell hooks' call to "envision alternatives to patriarchal masculinity," and that "[t]o end patriarchy we must challenge both its psychological and its concrete manifestations in daily life" (33).

Canonical writers like Sandra Cisneros, Denise Chávez, Arturo Islas, Cherríe Moraga, Ana Castillo, Rudolfo Anaya and Guillermo Gómez-Peña, as well as more contemporary writers like Maceo Montoya, Matt de la Peña, Diana López, Reyna Grande, Luis Alberto Urrea and John Phillip Santos have produced texts in which Chicanx or Mexican masculinity figures prominently, and we believe that new analyses via theoretical frameworks presented in this collection may prove enlightening. Likewise, films like *Real Women Have Curves* (2002) *Lowriders* (2016), *La Mission* (2009), and *The Book of Life* (2014) each figure a Chicano male character that invites an analytical approach to their masculine identity constructions. In the subject matter of YA (young adult) literature, work has just begun to highlight recent narratives that delve into how Latinx adolescents negotiate being "other" in the US while also dealing with the challenges of coming of age.[1] We hope that deep analyses of Chicanx and Mexican works will offer further considerations of newly constructed masculinities that seek to break free from the restrictions of patriarchy. We believe that this work is necessary because patriarchy, which hooks defines as a "social disease," is hostile to society in that it does not allow men to express themselves emotionally unless those emotions are anger and/or rage. Consequently, all who are in a relationship with men (parents, children, spouses, lovers, siblings, colleagues and friends) are likely to suffer from the manifestations of hegemonic masculine behavior, including the men themselves who must constantly repress their feelings. Mexicans and Chicanxs struggle against these patriarchal prescriptions to which society dictates they must conform.

Culturally, there is a shift happening. While some stereotypes are being enforced enthusiastically, others are voicing their support for a feminist masculinity. This project has traced the ways in which being masculine in a patriarchal society has started this shift, albeit slowly, toward a post-patriarchal reality that is liberated from gendered constraints. The editors believe this collection of essays contributes to this cultural shift toward wholeness, where all individuals, as well as all relationships, are successfully able to overcome the unhealthy aspects of what culture has taught and reinforced for centuries in relation to gender norms.

Notes

[1] See *Nerds, Goths, Geeks, and Freaks: Outsiders in Chicanx and Latinx Young Adult Literature* edited by Trevor Boffone and Cristina Herrera (2020).

Works Cited

hooks, bell. *The Will to Change: Men, Masculinity and Love.* Altria Books, 2004.

Macías-González, Víctor M. and Anne Rubenstein, editors. *Masculinity and Sexuality in Modern Mexico.* U of New Mexico Press, 2012.

Contributors

JESS BROCKLESBY is a PhD student at Queen Mary University of London. Her doctoral research investigates masculinity in its various iterations across English, French and Spanish literature as perceived through sex tourist fiction. She takes a multidisciplinary approach which combines the fields of art, culture, ethnography, literature, media, and sociology.

FERNANDO HERNÁNDEZ JÁUREGUI has a PhD in Latin American Literature from Cal State University. His research focuses on contemporary Latin American and Latinx poetry, in particular, the processes of knowledge and subject formation, in what he terms counterhegemonic forms of the lyrical subject. Translation is an important component of his research interests and his poetry translations have appeared in several publications. He is a Lecturer within the California State University system.

LEIGH JOHNSON is an Associate Professor of English at Marymount University (Arlington, VA) where she teaches Latinx literature, literary theory, and composition. She directs the small but enthusiastic Gender Studies program on campus. Her research interests are Chicana motherwork, recovering early Latinx writers, and literary activism. Her most recent work "Imagined Alternatives to Conquest: Linguistic Resistance in Aurora Lucero-White Lea's 'Kearney Takes Las Vegas''" appears in the 25th-anniversary volume of *Recovering the US Hispanic Literary Heritage.*

JOSHUA D. MARTIN completed his Ph.D. in Hispanic Studies at the University of Kentucky. His research interests include the representation of masculinity construction and space (particularly borders) in literature and political discourse, and his publications have appeared in the *Arizona Journal of Hispanic Cultural Studies* and *Nasty Women and Bad Hombres: Gender and Race in the 2016 US Presidential Election*, among others. He is Assistant Professor of Spanish at the University of North Georgia where he teaches all levels of Spanish courses.

BRYAN PEARCE-GONZALES is a Professor of Hispanic Studies at Shenandoah University in Winchester, Virginia. He comes from a large Chicano family that has resided in Corpus Christi, Texas for many generations. He is the author of several articles focusing on Chicana/o literature and Cultural Studies.

ALEJANDRO PUGA is an Associate Professor of Hispanic Studies and the Laurel H. Turk Professor of Modern Languages at DePauw University. In his course offerings and research, he specializes in Mexican narrative, and particularly literary representations of Mexico City, which he has explored in various publications, and as co-director of a Mellon-funded collaborative grant of the Great Lakes Colleges Association (GLCA). He is the author of *La ciudad novelada* (2012). His co-edited volumes include *Mapping the Megalopolis* (2018), and, with Carmen Patrica Tovar, *María Luisa Puga y el espacio de la reconstrucción* (2018).

KATHRYN QUINN-SÁNCHEZ is Professor of World Languages and Cultures at Georgian Court University in Lakewood, New Jersey, USA. She serves as coeditor of the online, peer-reviewed scholarly and creative journal *Label Me Latina*. In addition to several articles of literary criticism, she has authored *A Literary and Political History of Post-Revolutionary Mexico: Redefining "The Ideal"* (2006), as well as *Identity in Latin American and Latina Literature: The Struggle to Self-Define in a Global Era where Space, Capitalism, and Power Rule* (2014). She is editor or coeditor of *Negotiating Latinidades, Understanding Identities within Space* (2015), *Not White/Straight/Male/Healthy Enough: Being "Other" in the Academy* (2018), *Contemporary U. S. Latinx Literature in Spanish: Straddling Identities* (2018), *Teatro Latino Nuevas Obras de Los Estados Unidos* (2019), and *Whiteness at Work* (2020).

CARMEN PATRICIA TOVAR is a Visiting Assistant Professor of Hispanic Studies at Oberlin College. Her area of specialization is Latin American narrative of the 20th century with an emphasis on contemporary Mexican literature. Her scholarly interests center on the portrayal of metropolitan spaces and their symbolism in contemporary Mexican urban novels, and more specifically, on historical spaces as symbolic places of intersection of collective memory and subjectivity. She has published articles on Carlos Fuentes, Luis González de Alba, Hugo Hiriart, María Luisa Puga, Ana Clavel and Gonzalo Celorio in various national and international academic journals. Her collaboration with Alejandro Puga includes a co-edited volume, *María Luisa Puga y el espacio de la reconstrucción* (2018), published by the Autonomous Metropolitan University in Mexico City (UAM), and a co-written chapter in a collection of essays on Mexico City titled *Mapping the Megalopolis: Order and Disorder in Mexico City* (2018). She is a graduate of UC Irvine and a member of UC-Mexicanistas, Intercampus Research Program.

Index